DELAWARE
Eyewitness

Behind the Scenes in the First State

To Tom & Jet
Tom, from golf to business
you have been a big part of
my life. Thanks and I
hope you enjoy the book
John

JOHN RILEY

Cover design and interior layout by Michael Fontecchio, Faith & Family Publications.

For more information: delawareeyewitness.com

ISBN: 978-0-578-56822-5

Printed in the United States of America

Dedication

This book is dedicated all Vietnam veterans, especially three American heroes who, for at least a portion of their lives, called Delaware home: Lt. Commander James J. Connell, Colonel Murphy Neal Jones, and Brigadier General Jon Reynolds. These men endured starvation, torture, and solitary confinement for a combined eighteen years as prisoners of war in North Vietnam.

Jimmy Connell, who grew up in Wilmington and graduated from Salesianum, died at the hands of his captors, never giving in to their demands. While I did not know Jimmy Connell, I was honored to speak and write about his heroic service. Neal Jones and Jon Reynolds both returned to their families and beloved country and went forward to successful careers in the military and beyond. They carried the scars of their maltreatment with dignity and without complaint, inspiring all who have known them.

Contents

PART IV

Delaware
Economic Development

Part V

The *Decline* and *Fall* of *Hercules*

Foreword
by Michael Fleming

The exact circumstances of how John Riley first came to write for our website Town Square Delaware are not entirely clear in my mind, but to paraphrase the immortal words of Rick Blaine in *Casablanca*, it was the beginning of a beautiful friendship … as well as this book.

John's first piece, "Hell Above and Hell Below, a Delaware Story of War," presaged the winsome storytelling that was to flow from his talented pen over the following eight years. It was a compelling tale of bravery, patriotism and—importantly—included a special Delaware connection to the action.

The dozens of articles that sprung from John's uncanny memory and his wry watcher's eye have captivated readers who couldn't help but feel moved by his graceful knack for storytelling and the extraordinary breadth of his life experience. Through John, we have strolled the fairways of Augusta National and shot craps in the old caddy shack at Wilmington Country Club. We encountered unscrupulous fight promoters and raffish rascals in gritty urban boxing gyms. We read about the influential, inspiring history of once great institutions like Christ Our King parish. And we met true American heroes such as Jon Reynolds, Murphy Neal Jones, and James J. Connell, while coming face-to-face with the supreme sacrifice of local boys who went off to war and never returned.

As it turns out, those stories were just a small appetizer to the entree served up in this enjoyable, bustling book. Following a year that included teaming up with best friend Kevin Reilly on his autobiography, *Tackling Life,* and leading the launch of the Delaware Prosperity Partnership, John devoted himself to recalling, researching, and writing about the people, events, and crazy coincidences that have made his life story pretty darn remarkable. The final product is a gift to all of us who love history, humor, and Delaware.

The title promises to bring us "behind the scenes," and this book certainly does that, offering a candid, firsthand account about major business and political events that have grabbed headlines and indelibly shaped our state. John has never been one to toot his own horn, and his modesty and discretion have made him a trusted advisor to governors and CEOs. To be fair, though, he spent plenty of time in the public spotlight himself. Moments recaptured in this book will be a delightful surprise to both old friends and those who have never met John alike.

In 2017, when John was being honored for his longstanding service to Easterseals and those with disabilities, I wrote about him as a kind of "First State Zelig:"

> *We've all crossed paths with some truly memorable individuals. You know the type: upbeat friends you look forward to grabbing a coffee with, people always ready with a crazy story or big idea. Characters with character. Natural leaders who effortlessly make friends and exude integrity—impressive folks who don't take themselves too seriously and are good listeners.*
>
> *But anyone who knows John is aware that his Easterseals service, impactful and noteworthy as it is, is only a small part of his extraordinary—and uniquely Delaware—story.*
>
> *John Steven Riley is a product of Wilmington's 9th Ward, grandson of the Chief of Police, one of nine children and a proud "Kinger" who earned tips as a double-bagging caddy at Wilmington Country Club then went on to become a championship golfer himself. Riley's tale is part Horatio Alger, part First State-Zelig: over the last forty years this Renaissance Man has repeatedly shown up at noteworthy moments.*

I have never heard John use the term, but fate put him on Earth at the front end of the fabled post-war Baby Boomer generation in the second half of the "American Century." So his story provides a riveting tour of the halcyon Eisenhower and Kennedy years, when the country's ambitions knew no limits, the unrest of the Vietnam era (including John's experience with the draft and Army life), the awkward '70s, the go-go '80s and so on into the '90s and the Internet age.

John's default setting is optimism, but like any autobiography worth reading, his includes disappointments, failures, and a dose or two of pain. *Delaware Eyewitness* takes us back to the often-challenging circumstances in the Riley household, acknowledges personal fears and insecurities, and shows how opportunities once thought lost forever can reappear in the most unusual ways. That makes for inspiring, delightful reading.

If you are like me, when you are devouring this book, your thoughts will inevitably drift to your own story ... your roots, family, faith, and the extraordinary people you have crossed paths with along the way. Everyone has their story, and thank goodness John has taken on the herculean task of sharing his with all of us in such an elegant, entertaining way. Enjoy!

Introduction

While working with my friend, former Philadelphia Eagle Kevin Reilly on his memoir *Tackling Life,* I began to think about writing my own story. While the events of my life bear little resemblance to the high drama of Kevin's athletic rise or life and death struggle, they have overlapped with one of the most dynamic periods of social upheaval, economic growth and transformation in Delaware's history. I was fortunate to not just observe this up close but to be deep in the middle of it, which brought me into contact with some of the most interesting Delawareans of the era. Through leadership positions in government, business, sports, and the non-profit world, I have worked with and for an assortment of prominent Delawareans, including Republican and Democratic governors and multiple CEOs, often during critical events. While at times these episodes—political campaigns, corporate takeovers, major economic development deals and more— played out in public, most of the real action unfolded behind the scenes.

My experience collaborating with Kevin on his book convinced me that if someone did not write all this down, it will fade into time, just like the Huber bread factory or Chrysler plant where I worked during college have disappeared—as has my former employer, Hercules Incorporated.

Before I share stories from my diverse professional career, I will retrace the unlikely path that led me to be "in the room" where the decisions were made. This journey begins in Wilmington and involves people, institutions, and landmarks familiar to many. A central part of my early story was linked to a war being fought half a world away. Although I trained as an infantry officer when two hundred men were dying every week, I never made it to Vietnam. But the draft and the war reached deep into the lives of everyone of my generation, and I hope to capture some of the mood that swept through Delaware and the country during that tumultuous period.

In 2005, the *Newark Post* published an article on the occasion of my daughter Carie's graduation from the University of Delaware entitled "True Blue Family Goes Five for Five." I often joke that I am as Delaware as they come. My grandfather was the chief of police of Wilmington; my father and father-in-law both spent their careers with DuPont; I met my wife at the University of Delaware (UD), where she was a cheerleader; and all three of our children also graduated from UD.

How did I end up in the board rooms and cabinet rooms—and "ringside" during so many key Delaware moments? I believe part of the answer has to be growing up in the frequently challenging conditions of Wilmington's east side with my eight brothers and sisters, a strong mother and difficult father. We had to learn to adapt in the often stressful environment and recognize and respond to opportunities when we saw them. Two of those opportunities for me would result from my fascination with golf and politics. These passions would lead to relationships with people who would have a great impact on my life. Some of these connections not only improved my life, on at least one occasion they may have actually saved it.

While I witnessed and participated in the events in this book, this is as much the story of hundreds of Delawareans I encountered along the way. Many are prominent men and women who accomplished important things for our state. Others are not well known but often surprising and colorful—and their stories deserve to be told as well. This being Delaware, if you do not know them personally, you surely know someone who does.

The Day Had Arrived: May 1969

"Do you know anyone in politics?"

"John ... John, it's time to get up." I cleared my eyes and looked up to see tears on my mother's cheeks. She quickly turned away and headed downstairs to cook my last breakfast at home for a while. Today was my day of days. Soon, I would be catching the local train from Wilmington to Philadelphia, where I would raise my right hand to be sworn into the U.S. Army. Like nearly every red-blooded American male facing the draft in 1969, I had dreamed of ways to avoid my date with destiny. I had watched dozens of friends secure a spot in the National Guard, a military reserve unit, or a coveted "1Y" draft status for a mysterious ailment or injury I never heard them mention before. Hearing one day about openings in a Dover reserve unit, I drove down to discover a line around the block. When I finally spoke to the recruiter, he asked me if I "knew anyone in politics." People with connections were burning up the phone lines to get their sons out of harm's way. It was easy to get caught up in the unfairness of it all and to feel sorry for oneself.

Facing such a long and strenuous day, you would think I might have had the good sense to get to bed early, but like so many soldiers to be, I could not pull myself away from my fiancée, Sharon. For our last night together, we went to our favorite restaurant, the Lenape Inn in Chadds Ford. Afterwards, as we often did, we sat in the car in front of her family home in Woodland Park holding each other and talking until the early morning hours. Sharon would soon be moving with her parents to Clinton, Iowa, where she would be planning our April 5th, 1970 wedding. This would be a week after I was scheduled to complete Officer Candidate School (OCS).

My motivation to avoid the day of reckoning was twofold: I had come to recognize the futility of the war in Vietnam, and I was needed at home. My father, Curt Riley, had been emotionally unstable for years, and I was the buffer between him, my mother, and my younger siblings.

Three of my siblings had moved out soon after high school. Patricia, the eldest had married and brother Tom joined the Navy. No doubt several were motivated by a desire to get out of my father's way. At that point in his life, he experienced dramatic mood swings. One day he would be overly animated, talking incessantly; the next, he would be sullen and his anger would have us diving for cover in our crowded home. Our mother took the brunt of it—often stepping in between Dad and my older brother Curt. By his senior year in high school, Curt was not backing down. Following an ugly confrontation after Curt came in late, punches started flying. This led to Curt packing his bag and heading out the door.

My father grew up as the oldest son of a tough cop, James Curtis Riley, who went on to become the police chief of Wilmington. Dad, like his father before him, prided himself on his talent as a fighter, having won twenty amateur fights as a young man. Never able to make enough in his day job at the DuPont Experimental Station to care for a family of eleven (which included my mother, nine kids, and my grandmother in a tiny house with one bathroom at 36th & Pine Street on the east side of Wilmington), he took a series of night jobs, driving everything from a taxi to a dry-cleaner's truck, to a library bookmobile. He also found a job as a golf teaching pro at the Valleybrook driving range just over the Pennsylvania line.

To stay awake at night, Dad popped what he called "circulation pills," often swallowing them with a beer or two. Years later, when he was hopelessly addicted, my mother learned the truth about the pills. They were amphetamines, prescribed by Dr. Joseph Russo, a family physician. As each of my siblings and I gained our driver's license, we were sent on "emergency" trips to Russo's office to pick up my father's pills. (Russo would later be indicted on drug charges in May 1974.)

While life with father was a major challenge, our mother, Bernadette, somehow managed to hold everything together. In many ways, life had dealt this daughter of South Philadelphia a cruel hand, but her love seemed to know no bounds. All nine Riley kids and an assortment of family and friends gravitated to her for comfort and advice. Through it all, she would maintain a troubled but constant loyalty to the man who made her life so difficult.

In an effort to multiply his meager monthly salary, Dad would often gamble with his cash and with money he borrowed. He gambled both at poker and on the golf course. On more than one occasion, I remember when my uncle would show up on payday to collect money my father had borrowed that Mom didn't know about. It was the first time I ever saw my mother cry.

All of the kids in my family worked almost from the time we could walk: paper routes, shoe shining, snow shoveling, grocery carriers, caddying, local dry-cleaning clerks, and other various odd jobs. The great challenge was keeping some of what we earned. Much of it was willingly handed over to Mom to help with the groceries, but we all resented Dad demanding what we had worked hard for; we suspected he was going to blow it in a card game. Occasionally, he would win some cash and arrive home with a bundle of hard-shell crabs. At those rare moments it seemed like all would be well from now on.

Over my final year in college and just before my induction into the Army, I had been earning decent money working the night shift at the Huber Baking Company (a union job on the bread line) and substitute teaching the third grade at Forwood Elementary School north of town. I, along with added financial assistance from some of my older siblings provided back-up support when cash was short, and my adult presence in the house forced my father to work hard to control his excesses. But on that May morning in 1969, this arrangement was coming to an end.

I was able to stretch my military induction day from June 1968 all the way to May 1969 due to a reprieve from the draft board, allowing me to complete another semester to gain my undergraduate degree. When I had first contacted the draft board in 1967, the war was still escalating and there was a high demand for infantry 2nd lieutenants. To be eligible for what was known as the "college op" program, I needed to complete a degree followed by two years of service after my commission, which was expected to take about a year. It would be my good fortune to have completed four years, nine credits short of graduation.

Before the military would agree to assign me to one of the Officer Candidate Schools (OCS), I had to go to the Philadelphia induction center on North Broad Street and be interviewed by a panel of three officers. I remember being a nervous wreck that day, wondering if I would be immediately inducted if I failed the interview. The initial questions were fairly simple, but one of the officers was clearly unimpressed with my resume, which included "three year-member of the golf team"— not exactly one of the martial arts. He began to describe the physical and mental stress I would be subjected to during six months of OCS. He explained that the program, which had been developed by General Omar Bradley to prepare officers for World War II, was the Army's most demanding training and that only half completed the course. He wanted to know why I thought I could survive the test.

I was not prepared for this question, so I blurted out the first thing that crossed my mind. I said, "Sir, I have eight brothers and sisters, have survived twelve years of Catholic education, and have been living with my father for over twenty years. I can endure anything they throw at me." Fortunately, smiles broke out across all the three officers' faces, and one of them said, "good answer, you're approved." It also bought me a ninety-day extension, pushing my reporting date out to May 7, 1969.

That morning, after breakfast, I hugged Mom goodbye and jumped into Dad's 1962 Chevy for the short drive to the Wilmington train station. I had decided to confront him on his condition one last time and urge him to seek the help he needed. As we drove, however, I could see the tears streaming down his face, and I lost my nerve.

Like most twenty-somethings who think they will live forever, I did not believe I would die in this war. With the news from Vietnam being so grim, though, it was understandable that my parents feared the worst. Affection with my father had always been awkward, and today was no exception. The scene on the train platform that morning became increasingly emotional, and I began to pray that the 6:05 train would soon pull up. With the words stuck in my throat, I decided I would write what I had to say.

PART I

Wilmington

Chapter 1

Pine Street, 1950s

"John Rollins please call the office … John Rollins, please call the office."

I was in my forties before I met and spoke to Delaware's most famous business leader since Pierre S. du Pont. When I told John Rollins how I would wake up most mornings of my childhood to the sound of his name being blared into the bedroom I shared with four brothers, he roared with laughter. Such was life, living basically in the middle of a car lot on Wilmington's east side. A half block away at the corner of 36th and Market was Nealis Motors (promoted as "Dodge City"), then came Rollins Ford stretching to 37th, followed by Colonial Chevrolet, where my uncle, the father of fifteen Quinn kids, worked.

On the opposite side of Market stood a Nash Rambler dealer and The Tire Center, a business run by Mr. Ed Lower. His son Teddy was one of my friends. They lived in an apartment above the tire business. We thought they were rich because they had a TV and lots of food in their refrigerator— and they didn't even have to tape the refrigerator door shut. We Riley kids would eat anything that was not nailed down, though we somehow managed to be fussy eaters. Just another challenge for my mother.

Wilmington in the '50s had a population of more than 100,000,

Pine Street days with the Vietnam generation: (left to right) Big brother Curt, Delaware National Guard, 1965-71; cousin Joe Butler, captain, 101st Airborne, Vietnam 1967-69; the author, captain, U.S. Army Armor, 1969-71.

compared to approximately 70,000 today. The exodus to the suburbs was just beginning, and buses were the primary way family and neighbors travelled around the city. On stretches of several streets, including Market, trolley tracks remained visible.

One of my favorite pastimes was to meet my Uncle Tom's "Delaware Coach Company, 4-1 Union Park Gardens" bus and ride for free all over town with him. Sometimes we would stop at the "bus barn," which today is known as Trolley Square. Diagonally across the street from the bus barn and opposite the "Logan House" was the old B & O Train Station. A clipping in the family scrapbook from a 1952 column by *Wilmington News Journal* sports editor, Marty Levin noted that in 1909, my grandfather fought in what was labeled the "last local private fight" (bare knuckles). He described how the event kicked off at the B & O station. Levin wrote:

A crowd of over a hundred met at the B.&O. Railroad Station on DuPont Street and took the 11 o'clock train to the old station up near Carrcroft. And that's where they fought, right in the railroad station. The bout ended in a six-round draw. There was no train returning, so the whole gang walked to Shellpot Park to get a trolley back to town.[1]

Every day, my mother somehow insured we were fed, dressed, and sent out the door to Christ Our King School, approximately a one-mile walk from our one-bathroom home. (Governor John Carney and I sometimes exchange stories about the challenge of growing up in a house with nine kids and only one bathroom. I like to remind him that our situation was even more challenging since our bathroom was on the first floor next to the dining room—and there was no shower!)

My older sisters, Patricia and Bernadette, would look out for the younger siblings as we made our way to and then home from school. Lunches could be challenging. Most days Mom packed us a sandwich, usually a slice of something called "spiced ham," smothered in mustard on puffy white Huber's Sunbeam Bread. Brother Tom, two grades behind me, would eat almost nothing. His daily lunch was a "mustard sandwich" and it had to be French's mustard. His Thanksgiving dinner consisted of a bowl of Shredded Wheat.

Since my father was paid monthly, cupboards were bare well before the end of the month, and Mom would have to become creative to get us fed.

---

[1] In those days, Shellpot Park was an amusement park at the base of Penny Hill, behind where the Department of Labor sits today.

One method was to have us walk over to our Aunt Babe's house, a couple blocks from school. Aunt Babe would always come up with something. Some mornings Mom would rifle through my father's pockets, turn her purse upside down, and reach down under cushions hoping to come up with enough change to send Curt or me to the Orange Meat Market at 38th & Market for a half pound of cheap baloney or spiced ham, sliced very thin.

Market Days at 4th & King
courtesy of Larry Anderson

When Curt and I picked up paper routes, the strategy changed. Mom or dad would send us out to collect from several customers. We would buy a few groceries, and then figure out how to pay the route manager by the end of the month. It was sort of a 1950s-style credit card arrangement. When I would knock on the neighbor's door to collect, they would look at me and say something like, "Aren't you collecting early this month?" I'm sure some knew why we were doing it but didn't say anything. I always felt guilty (a permanent condition if you attended Catholic school) and embarrassed when someone would refuse.

Another indicator of how complicated it could be to make ends meet in the Riley household was our shoe situation—we only had one pair each. And we were hard on shoes due to the nearly two-mile round trip to school. The pattern during those years was that we would wear the soles through completely and find cardboard or other material to slip into the shoe until the day all of us had holes through to the socks. Then we would head by bus or in my father's old Studebaker to Mr. Battaglia's shoe repair shop at 4th and King. There we would sit in a stall for a couple hours while Mr. Battaglia and son would put new soles on every pair. We were a little embarrassed about this arrangement but would never forget the smell of the glue and leather that filled our heads while we sat there.

On days Mom couldn't come up with something to put in our lunch box and Aunt Babe was unavailable, our favorite alternate plan was a little delicatessen called Bole's on 29th Street off Washington, three blocks from school. At Bole's, a half dozen Rileys or more would purchase two hoagies for thirty-five cents each and have them cut into twos or threes. This was not a restaurant, so there was no place to eat except on top of the ice cream chest. When customers came in, Mr. Bole would have to clear things away, so he could reach inside. Looking back, I don't know how the man tolerated these Riley invasions.

Aunt Babe welcomed our visits because we were family, but also because we were great entertainment for her physically and intellectually disabled son, Tommy, who loved all of his cousins. We would spend much of our lunch visit taking naps. Aunt Babe would pay us a nickel to lay on their couch with our eyes closed while Tommy would adjust our arms and head to the exact position he desired while we pretended we were asleep. Younger brother Chris was the best at this and would sometimes actually fall asleep. Tommy also enjoyed pushing us off a chair onto the floor with his good arm. The entire time, Elvis hits would be playing on his 45-rpm record player.

"Elvis is still king" – Brothers Tom and Chris join me to wish Tommy a Happy Birthday

Doctors had told my aunt and uncle that Tommy would not survive past his teens. As it turned out, the doctors missed this forecast somewhat; Tom lived to be seventy-six. When Tom lost his parents in the mid-'70s, he was placed in the Stockley Hospital for the Mentally Retarded in Millsboro. It was a long haul to visit him, but thanks to Chuck and Charm Welch, founders of the Mary Campbell Center for people with disabilities, I was eventually able to work out respite stays for Tommy at their beautiful facility in North Wilmington. Eventually, Tom was placed in a group home in New Castle County, and I later became his legal guardian in partnership with another cousin, Veronica Eid.

Due to my interest in Tom, I became involved with Easterseals, serving several board roles, including chairman. Every year on Tommy's birthday I would hire Ted Tharp, an Elvis impersonator, to entertain Tom and the other day program participants at Easterseals. Due to Ted's Elvis charisma, and his embrace of these people with special needs, everyone loved that day. When Tom died in 2017, Ted sang at Tommy's funeral which was a new experience for St. Joseph's on the Brandywine Catholic Church in Greenville.

Chapter 2

Life on the East Side, 1950s

"They need every penny they can get."

In May 2016, I authored an article run by Town Square Delaware about the closure of Christ Our King Church (COK) in Wilmington. The article received a record number of comments as former "Kingers" reminisced and expressed sadness over the end of an era.

To me, COK had become more about my mother and our family's legacy than anything else. Mom remained loyal to the institution until her death in 1998, and my wife, Sharon, and I were determined to keep the candle burning. Our family history had been embedded in COK's church and school for more than seventy years. Not only were Sharon and I married there, as was our daughter Amy, but the very year of the church's closing our new grandson, Patrick, joined granddaughters Hailey and Ava as the third grandchild baptized at COK.

During the years our children attended St. Mary Magdalen School in suburban Wilmington, we still drove into the city most Sundays to pick up my mother to take her to COK. As meager as her Sunday donation might be, she felt it was important because they "needed every penny they could get." After Mom died, we kept up the practice and worked with Father Brennan, the pastor, and other "die hard Kingers" to try to keep things going.

In addition to carrying on for my mother, I felt a need to pay-back the parish for support through my high school years. While tuition to Salesianum was not very high in the early "60s," there was no way my family could afford to have Curt and me in the school (in addition to Bernadette at Padua Academy and Patricia at St. Peter's in New Castle). I was told at the time that the parish helped us. As a result, I would devote one or two nights a week answering the phone in the parish rectory.

While much has been written about the stern discipline meted out by nuns of that era, there is little doubt in my mind there were benefits to this approach. Most importantly, there was order in the classroom, which at least created an atmosphere for learning in rooms jammed with eighty or more Baby Boomers. For years we were drilled in arithmetic, English, religion, and penmanship, with plenty of singing and church time thrown in for good measure. And boys and girls alike were encouraged to participate in sports. The one unnerving element for all of us were the periodic drills to protect ourselves in the event of a nuclear attack.

Christ Our King Church was in the part of Wilmington known as the Ninth Ward. Unlike many other blue collar parishes that sat in district ethnic enclaves, such as St. Hedwig's (Hedgeville/Polish), St. Anthony's (Little Italy), and St. Anne's (Forty Acres/Irish)—COK was part of a more diverse community, with the northern sector being primarily Jewish. Next to the school was an asphalt covered schoolyard with a couple basketball courts, simply referred to by the kids as "the Yard." The neighborhood kids would hang out there playing pick-up basketball games or at Ashenbach's, the nearby corner soda shop. While there was talk about "the Yard" being a tough neighborhood or even the stomping grounds of a notorious gang, it was mostly tranquil.

The neighborhood produced its share of individuals of the highest courage and character. One example is Naval Academy graduate and former commander of the U.S. Navy SEALs, Vice Admiral Tim Szymanski. I once heard the former wrestling and jujitsu champion say in a speech that he learned most of what he would need in later life, growing up in his COK neighborhood.

I n September 2018, Kevin Reilly and I were invited by Rear Admiral Szymanski to attend the "Change of Command" ceremony for the SEALs at the Naval Special Warfare Center in Coronado, California. Szymanski had been nominated to the rank of Vice Admiral and promoted to become deputy chief of all US Special Operations. This quiet leader is not well known in Wilmington, but he has maintained a relationship with the Salesianum, where he was named to the school's Hall of Fame in 2015. He returned to speak at the senior sports banquet in 2017. Szymanski's leadership exploits include serving as deputy commander of the famed and secretive SEAL Team Six.

Change of Command
Rear Admiral Tim Szymanski
United States Navy

Unfortunately, speaking commitments kept Kevin Reilly from attending the ceremony that was rich in Navy and SEAL Team tradition. Had he been there, he would have been as stunned as I was to learn the background of Rear Admiral Collin Green, who was taking over for Szymanski. It turned out that Green's family roots were also in Wilmington. His father had graduated from Salesianum and like Szymanski's father, had been a Wilmington city fireman.

During the ceremonies, Tim Szymanski was lauded by Vice Chief of Naval Operations Bill Moran and commander of US Special Operations General Raymond Thomas—and Tim's wife, Marci, was honored for her service to the families of fallen SEALs.

I couldn't help but smile when Rear Admiral Green mentioned that his lone regret that day was that his father could not make the trip to San Diego. He said the reason for the regret was that he wanted "to introduce his father to another Sallies graduate." As I looked around at the hundreds in attendance, I said to myself, "I must be one of the few here today that has a clue what this man is talking about."

Like most of my friends, I lived for sports. That meant playing football, basketball, and baseball on the COK teams. By seventh grade I was beginning to realize that my body type was not built to excel at the sports I loved. As an eighty-pound defensive end, I was run over on a sweep by the entire St. Anthony's backfield and relegated to the bench for most of the rest of the season. Our quarterback, James "Jimbo" Ford would one day become chief of the Wilmington Fire Department.

In the seventh grade I was the last kid selected for the school basketball team. My love for the game was crushed when I got a call one day from the coach informing me that I was being kicked off the team for missing a practice I did not even know about. I was immediately replaced by an eighth grader who had just transferred into the school, Stan Mosiej, who would start for the team and later become one of the top football players in the state as well. I continued to make it in baseball, but I had a growing concern that playing at the high school level might be beyond my reach.

My brothers, friends, and I spent summer days walking the ten blocks from East 36th Street down to Prices Run Park and pool. We roamed all over the east side of Wilmington looking for things to do, often getting chased out of the Riverview Cemetery when we found the gate open and cut through. We liked to stop-off at the Nehi bottling plant off Market Street and be mesmerized by the thousands of orange sodas rushing by on the line. We would beg for a soda, but rarely met with success. Sometimes, when we would walk all the way to the Brandywine to fish, we would try the same routine at the Borden's Ice Cream plant at 26th & Market—and typically struck out there as well. Other stops along North Market Street included the Food Fair supermarket, where we tried to earn some change helping carry groceries home, and the DelSteel plant to watch the metal products being forged by the workers.

In the fall, we would all gather for a pick-up game of no equipment tackle football on the field next to the Pepsi plant at 35th Street and Governor Printz Boulevard. I think I still bear some scars from being hit by big Bert DiClemente. In later life, Bert would become state director for Senator Joe Biden. And of course, we spent hours on the car dealer lots stretching north on Market, gawking at the new cars and yearning for the day we might own one. No day was complete without being chased out of the Sears store at Market Street and Lea Boulevard.

My younger brothers, Tom, Chris, and Denis, were obsessed with all living creatures and spent entire days wondering through Shellpot Creek and Bringhurst Woods just north of the city line, turning over rocks and collecting turtles, salamanders, frogs and the grand prize of all, snakes. I don't know how my mother tolerated it, but they would fill the house and yard with the various crawly creatures. I awoke one morning and was staring straight into the eyes of a black snake that had escaped from one of the containers. When a local family put out an all-points bulletin for help to rid them of snakes near their house, the only responder was Tom (with Chris and Denis tagging along) and the Wilmington media. The next day, *The News Journal* ran a headline, "Snakes Duck Out on Reptiler, 15."

Chapter 3

Caddying at the Rock and a Little League Champion, 1957–1963

"What the hell did you lose for? I was telling everyone back on the corner, that was me in the paper."

At age ten, Dad introduced us to caddying at the Rock Manor Golf Club, the city-owned and operated course on the northwest end of town. "The Rock," as it was commonly referred to, was the center of competitive golf or at least the gambling side of golf in Delaware. The caddy fee was $2.75 a round, usually rounded up to $3.00. Some players would spring for $4.00, so we would scramble to grab those bags.

Although today's Rock Manor is an excellent course, benefiting from land acquired during the AstraZeneca expansion, it was disappointing to some that the designers did not preserve any of the original holes. The first time "The Rock" underwent a major facelift was in the '60s when Interstate 95 was extended north out of the city. While those changes had a significant impact, about half the existing holes were retained. Under the original layout, the tenth green, the entire eleventh hole, and the twelfth tee were positioned where we find the I-95 southbound lane today.

On most summer days, Curt and I walked to Rock Manor. Our route was up 36th Street to P.S du Pont High School, past Haynes Park, across Miller Road and up a stone covered road behind the Harper-Theil metal plating plant. The gap from Miller Road to the golf course was a sort of "no-man's land" of thick undergrowth and trees that, unbeknownst to us, would one day become I-95. As detailed in Celia Cohen's book *Only in Delaware*, the final decision on the I-95 corridor was made by a Republican-controlled lame duck Wilmington city council in 1957. One of those fighting the "Adams-Jackson Street Freeway" was my friend Kevin Reilly's grandfather, State Senator John E. Reilly. Looking back from the present day, there seems to be only regrets over the I-95 decision. In the name of progress, it seemed they had cut out the soul of the city.

Sometimes, Curt and I would try hitch-hiking up to the official golf course entrance near the crest of "McKee's Hill" on Concord Pike. From there you could look out over the small cluster of buildings in central Wilmington, the Delaware Memorial Bridge and New Jersey in the distance. I sometimes wondered what was going on in those buildings. From listening to my father and others, I knew this was where the important people were, and important decisions were made. But our lives alternated between survival or fun, so the thoughts didn't linger for long.

In those days, Route 202 was still a two-lane country road all the way to the Brandywine Raceway, the site of today's Town Center. Although the Charcoal Pit had recently opened, today's shopping centers, including the Concord Mall, were all farms and fields. The great post-war suburban expansion was underway, however, and the paychecks used to pay the mortgages for those "Brandywine Hundred" homes were mostly being generated by Wilmington's chemical companies—DuPont, Hercules, and Atlas.

From the 1930s through the '50s, my father was one of the top golfers in the state, wining the DuPont Country Club Championship five times. He played at "The Rock" for one purpose—for the chance to bet and win some much-needed cash. He teed off many times with no way to pay up if he lost, so he played under a lot of pressure. Due to the stress he had put himself under, Curt and I dreaded caddying for him; we knew we were not going get paid, and we were almost certain to become the target of his infamous Irish temper.

In those days, the caddying culture was interesting to say the least. Topping out at about eighty

Son of a tough cop, champion golfer and boxer

pounds, I was at the bottom of the sociocultural ladder. Ironically, the "alpha male" at the top of the food chain then was a guy also named John Riley. From a tough area of Wilmington known as Becker's Corner, John was tall and good looking, with hair reminiscent of "Kookie Burns" on the popular TV show *77 Sunset Strip*. John was respected by the other caddies, many of whom also hailed from Becker's Corner. They included John's tough younger brother, Norwood, Anthony Dorazio, and a big guy named Larry Dorsey.

Upon my introduction to the caddyshack, John recognized there was a problem with having a namesake around. He immediately declared that from then on, he would be known as "John R from the City" and I would be "John R from the suburbs," which was technically correct since our house on the east side was exactly twelve feet outside the northern city line. Later in my teenage years, when I was in the news after losing in the state championship golf finals, John approached me with a complaint. "What the hell did you lose for? I was telling everyone back at the corner it was me in the paper!"

Of course, there were many characters with colorful nicknames among the gambling golfers, referred to as the "cutthroats" by the caddies. Most of these men hailed from Wilmington's Little Italy and included brothers Vince, "Chipper," and "Crackers" DiCampli, Phil and Adam Freccia, "Blackie" DiBattista, "Coochie" Del Grosso, Vic and John Catalina, Pete Keough, Paul "Bailey" DiEleuterio (the golfing cop), "Neek" Bove, Joe "The Cat" Sylvester, "Chick" Ghione, "Chick" DeFiore, "Tut" Talley, Saul Savitch, John D. Kelly, golf pros Carmen and Tony Steppo, and "Pro" Clint Kennedy. While many of the cutthroats were fine golfers, a case could be made that the best player at "The Rock" was a woman, Betty Richeson. The quiet, pleasant Richeson won three state women's championships by 1960 and would go on to win several more.

With the possible exception of perennial state champion Ellis Taylor, whose family owned the Artesian Water Company, most of the Rock regulars learned the game as caddies at Wilmington Country Club and other courses during the Great Depression. That was the case with my father as well. They all idolized a kid from their ranks named Ed "Porky" Oliver (whom they referred to as "Snowball" from an incident in his youth) who had gone on to win many times on the PGA Tour and play with Ben Hogan, Sam Snead, and Byron Nelson on three Ryder Cup Teams. (My father won the Philadelphia caddy championship in 1930 in a field that included the great Oliver.)

John D. Kelly was one of the most colorful of the Rock Manor characters. Stand-up comic and proprietor of Wilmington's famous Logan House, who the first time I met him, introduced himself by saying, "Hi, Johnny Riley, my name is John D. Kelly and I'm Jewish." Always believing whatever I was told, that pronouncement had me scratching my head for the next several years.

Speaking of ethnicity, Jews and blacks were excluded from many country clubs. As a public course, "The Rock" took all comers. Nine-time Brandywine Country Club club champion Saul Savitch was a regular, as was a black gentleman named Willie Stokes, a favorite of many of the kids. I still recall the day in August of 1963 when Willie told us he was going to Washington to the March for Civil Rights, where Martin Luther King delivered his famous "I Have a Dream" speech.

Saul Savitch, like many of the golfers at the course, was a veteran of World War II. Every so often someone might whisper that a certain individual had been a "hero" or had been severely injured in the War, but I guess it was so common that it tended to be downplayed. For example, the recent obituary of Rock regular, Dominick "Neek" Bove, appeared in the local press and noted that he had fought with the 3rd Marine Division and was awarded both the Bronze Star and Silver Star for heroism. The 3rd Marines fought at Bougainville, Guam, and Iwo Jima. Obviously a tough guy, Neek Bove would live to be ninety-five. (Nathan Field, author of the website "A Tribute to Wilmington's Greatest Generation" reports that over 10,000 Wilmingtonians served in the military during WWII and more than 400 lost their lives. This total includes some fifty-eight from in and around the city's Ninth Ward, the section of town closest to Rock Manor.)

Although I don't recall him joining in with the cutthroats, another regular at the Rock was a gentleman by the name of Fritz Marston. My North Wilmington neighbor, Dick Lewis, would some thirty years later reveal that Marston was the courageous captain of a B-17 during the war that had been shot down over France. Lewis' own plane, "Mr. Five by Five," was shot down after Marston's, and they met while being protected by the French Underground. Unfortunately, a spy inside the Underground would betray them, and they were later captured during their escape attempt. Lewis wrote in his memoir *Hell Above and Hell Below* how he watched in horror as Marston refused to provide any information to their Gestapo interrogators while being beaten and threatened with being shot.

My brother Curt was immediately captivated by golf and has remained so through the subsequent six decades. He would go on to win the 1970 Rock Manor club championship and lead a reformation of the Delaware State Golf Association after the long-time executive director was charged with embezzlement. As a kid, he would come up with any scheme to get to and on a golf course. His favorite mode of transportation was hitchhiking. Expecting cars were unlikely to pick him up carrying a set of golf clubs, he would hide them on the side of the road and when a driver pulled over, he would pull them out of hiding and present himself to the driver. It usually worked, and I was often along as a witness.

In 1957, we played in our first golf tournament, the Delaware State Junior Amateur Championship. I was eleven, shot 135, and lost my first match to my cousin Ernie Riley. Completely humiliated, I decided I would stick to baseball.

Baseball was my first love, and my Little League career was progressing nicely. In 1958, I was chosen to play on the Wilmington Optimist All-Star Team. We would go on to win the state

Little League All Star Team: I'm standing in center back row with Ken Westerside on my right; manager Gene Harkins stands on the far right with Mike Reed kneeling below in the first row. Dave Missimer holds the State Championship trophy

championship that year and advance to the regional competition of the Little League World Series in Frederick, Maryland—the farthest I had ever traveled from home at that point. Three standouts on that team, Ken Westerside, Mike Reed and Dave Missimer, who all went on to outstanding athletic careers, have died in recent years. Westerside attended the University of Arkansas on a baseball scholarship, while Missimer went to Oklahoma State on a football scholarship. Mike Reed was an all-state basketball star at Salesianum. Both Westerside's and Reed's obituaries listed our Little League World Series team as one of their career highlights. Missimer's obituary told of his two-year service in Vietnam as an Army operating room specialist. Another interesting connection to my later life was the All-Star team manager, Gene Harkins. Eighteen years later I would meet his son Michael in the political world—more about that later.

Chapter 4

High School and Junior Golf, 1960–1963

"You are not country club kids, you have to work if you want to play golf."

A ttending Christ Our King School, it seemed almost mandatory that we would all move to Salesianum (Sallies) for high school. Curt was already at Sallies, and while I do not remember having a choice, I would have probably chosen the school regardless to be with friends. Sallies was nearly two miles from our house, and due to the bus routes of the time, transportation options were limited. Most mornings during my freshman and sophomore years, Dad would drop us off on the way to work. After school, I would make the hour-long trek through the west side neighborhoods, often accompanied by my friend Bill Ritchie. While conditions were generally safe, there were a few run-ins with other kids along the way, particularly in the area of Warner School and P.S du Pont. You learned quickly who to walk with and what routes worked best.

It took me a while before I figured out how to fit in at Sallies. Famous for its football success and competitive basketball teams, you were lost in the middle unless you excelled at the big three sports or academically. I was one of those plugging up the middle, so I guess I just went with the flow. To help work off some of the tuition costs, both Curt and I sold football programs at the Sallies games in addition to answering the phone in the Christ Our King parish office.

By the end of the decade, Fidel Castro had overthrown the Cuban government of Fulgencio Batista. As Castro installed a communist, atheistic state, he shut down Catholic churches and sent priests and nuns into exile. Large numbers of Cubans who were exiled or who escaped the regime came to the U.S., with children often separated from their parents. This would have implications for Salesianum.

A small colony of Cuban boys were taken in by the Oblates of St. Francis de Sales, the religious order that staffed Salesianum. The boys lived in a home run by the Oblates and attended school with us. While the big picture relating to Cuba, such as the Bay of Pigs invasion and the Cuban Missile Crisis dominated the news in the early '60s, we saw the impact of the Cuban revolution firsthand as these boys suddenly appeared in our classrooms one day. One of these new students, Miguel Bezos, would go on to have a significant impact on the future of American business. As the stepfather of Amazon founder Jeff Bezos, he became one of the company's first investors.

The summer before my freshman year I started caddying at the Wilmington Country Club and began to become competitive in the junior golf ranks. I have written about some of my caddying experiences at Wilmington in Town Square Delaware. The biggest boost to my golf development, though, was a junior golf membership to the DuPont Country Club. I did not realize it at the time, but my father had given me the gift of a lifetime. In addition, he taught me the fundamentals of the game and more. Sometimes it was delivered in an unconventional fashion to the way others learned the game, but I survived. Golf would become for me a way to compete, meet people (including making some lifelong friends), open doors, and provide a much-needed boost to my confidence and self-esteem.

The DuPont Country Club environment in the late '50s and early '60s was nothing short of idyllic for a kid from Pine Street. It also made me begin to realize that our family was on the bottom rung of the country club social ladder. Curt and I wore mostly "hand-me-down" clothes, played with mismatched, used clubs and never played with a purchased golf ball. In fact, "ball hawking" was both how we equipped ourselves for the game and another means to make cash.

I do not think any of this even phased Curt. He didn't have a social climbing bone in his body, and everyone loved him for it. On the other hand, I began to compare my lowly state to the country club kids, before I had even seen Wilmington Country Club. There, instead of hanging out with the son of a DuPont section manager, I was caddying for the chairman of the board and members of "the Family."

Most summer days, my father would drop Curt and me off on Kirk Road, about a half mile from the Wilmington Country Club caddyshack. We would hike across the golf course and then sit for hours soaking in the unique caddy culture and hoping for the chance to earn a few bucks that day. Aside from the Murphy and Riley brothers and cousins, most of the caddies were from Little Italy. In addition to the more common Italian nicknames like Gigi, Rocky, Angie, and Sonny, there were others with more colorful monikers like Lurky, Frog, Moose, and Hey-man. After completing our day at Wilmington, we would either walk or hitchhike the three miles back to DuPont with hopes of getting some golf in before my father picked us up at five o'clock. Some days we would ask to be allowed to go to DuPont to play with our friends, which would result in another life and social standing lecture from my father—"Goddammit, you are not country club kids, you have to work if you want to play golf."

By sixteen, my game had progressed. I was expected to be one of the contenders for the Delaware State Golf Association junior title at the Cavaliers Country Club, but after qualifying for the championship flight (top 16), I lost to an emerging top player, Daryl Nieliwocki in the first round. Fortunately, my golfing results improved during the summer of 1962 as both Curt and I qualified to represent the state in the International Jaycee Jr. Golf Championship. This was the other "major" of junior golf. (I had missed on two attempts to qualify for the United States Golf Association national junior championship.) Also qualifying that year were Gibby Young of Newark and Steve Smith of Wilmington (Steve later became a golf professional). We traveled to Huntington, West Virginia for the tournament to compete against the top players in the country.

One of the favorites that year was my future friend Charlie McDowell from Virginia Beach. Charlie had won the national junior championship in 1961 and nearly became the first junior to successfully defend his title (a distinction that would ultimately be captured by Tiger Woods). While I did not meet him at the Jaycee tournament that year, I did the following year at Wilmington Country Club. One day, Chris Coulson, a member of the club and a fine junior golfer, approached me in the caddyshack and asked if I would be interested in caddying for him and his prep school roommate the next day. Chris and Charlie attended the elite Exeter Academy in New Hampshire. A little turned off by the idea of caddying for a couple of preppies, I responded skeptically. "Caddy for you?" I said. He then explained that his guest was the former national junior champion.

Charlie and Chris were both perfect gentleman in addition to being fine golfers, so the round was enjoyable and less laborious than most of my rounds chasing members errant shots all over the golf course. (Plus, their golf bags were far lighter than the adults.) I was totally focused on Charlie and his game, but it was not as dominant as I expected. While he shot a respectable round on the difficult Wilmington South Course, he did not seem to hit the ball farther than me. When he hit a poor second shot on the twelfth hole, the thought crossed my mind that I could be as good as this guy.

Years later, Charlie moved to Wilmington to practice law, and we became close golfing friends and have worked together on many community endeavors, including service on the East Side Charter school board and the Mike Purzycki mayoral campaign. On the course, I have had many opportunities to compete against Charlie since the day I caddied for him, but my wins are few and far between—Charlie is not just a good golfer, he is a very tough competitor.

Unfortunately, there is a tragic element to this story, as Chris Coulson would be killed in an auto accident not long after caddying for him that day. The Junior Golf trophy at Wilmington Country Club is named in his honor.

As they say, all things are "relative," and that was certainly the case for me and traveling to the International Jaycee Championship that year. Having only journeyed from Delaware as far as Frederick, Maryland, you may as well have said I was going to Paris. I was in awe of the mountains and rivers as well as the big tournament atmosphere at a national event, with talent on display by future stars of the game, such as three-time U.S. Open champion Hale Irwin.

During tournament week in Huntington we stayed in dormitories at Marshall University. Adjacent to our rooms were members of the Tennessee team, including future All-American football star Steve Sloan of Alabama. One night after golf, Sloan and some others put together a touch football game that had overtones of the Civil War—North vs. South. Most would have put their money on Sloan and the South, except the bespectacled golfer from Colorado dominated the game. Hale Irwin not only won the NCAA golf championship, he also became a two time All-Big Eight defensive back in football.

The summer following my junior year at Sallies would be my last chance to win the junior state golf championship. It was a goal I never stopped thinking about since losing early in '62. The tournament was to be played at Rock Manor, a course I knew very well. In addition to being the course where I had learned to caddy, it was our home course for high school matches. On qualifying day, though, I received some very unwelcome news—my father said he would be caddying for me. In golf, tension is not a good thing, and being around my father was often a cause for tension. In as tactful a manner as I could think of, I tried to persuade him otherwise. He would not listen, as usual.

In spite of the tension, I was at even par as we reached the very tricky ninth hole at the Rock. After bending a perfect tee shot around the trees, my nine iron second shot stopped short of the green, but only about twenty feet from the cup. Rock Manor was a course in less than perfect condition with fairways populated by crab grass and bare patches. When I selected my wedge to pop it over the grass, my father stopped me. He said, "I want you to putt it."

My adrenaline immediately shot up as I responded that I wanted to chip it. "Goddammit, you do exactly as I tell you," he muttered between his teeth as my playing partners stood by. Alarms were now going off in my head, and just like the famous line of the movie, I thought to myself, *I'm mad as hell and I'm not going to take it anymore.*

I looked at him and said, "OK, I'll putt it, but give me my damn clubs. I'm playing from here without you."

I really thought he was going to tag me right there, but he just steamed off.

Shaken, but determined, I settled down and had made it through the difficult stretch of back nine holes and stood at only two over par as I played the seventeenth. Friends were letting me know that only a single shot separated me from the leader, my buddy Fred Dingle. Suddenly, as I looked at the seventeenth green, I saw him—my father was back! I managed a par on the hole and as I went to pick up my bag after putting out, I saw it hanging from his shoulder. With my head spinning, I finished off with a two-over 74 on the difficult course, one behind Fred. Somehow, Dad had calmed down and was clearly pleased by my finish, perhaps relieved that I had not gone completely into the tank on the second nine. He seemed to understand he had crossed the line, and he never insisted on caddying for me again.

In the quest for the title I won several close matches before facing the red-hot Fred Dingle in the finals. In both the junior and adult ranks, Fred had become the best putter in the state, and he would roll in five birdies against me in the finals. I congratulated Fred after we finished; I was simply outplayed. After college and the Navy, Fred became a CPA. He remains not only my tax preparer but one of my closest friends and advisors.

1962 International Jaycee Golf Championship, Huntington, WV. Gibby
Young is ready to hit with Steve Smith to my right and Curt to the left.

Chapter 5

The Ring Mass Fiasco, 1963–1964

"John, did you hear they shot President Kennedy!"

Due to my name appearing numerous times on the *News Journal* sports page that summer, I seemed to enjoy a little more status amongst all the Sallies jocks. As "one of the boys," so to speak, I joined other seniors to plan a beer party after the Ring Mass that fall. The Ring Mass was an evening ritual with families in attendance where the senior rings were distributed. One of my classmates, Bill Downey, had rather inappropriately invited the entire class to his family's uncompleted home off Marsh Road, north of Wilmington. One of my best friends, fellow golf team member Bobby Oliver, the son of the late great Delaware golfer, had his inside methods for getting things done, and he easily secured most of the beer for the evening.

Of course, any idiot over the age of twelve would have recognized that the Ring Mass party on a new housing construction site was certain to end badly. Sure enough, just an hour into the partying, the shout rang out—"Cops!" Dozens of kids ran in every direction. Downey would soon be taken into custody, along with another classmate Bob Kraft, but Bobby Oliver and I escaped into the nearby woods along Marsh Road. As we hid in the woods, state troopers roamed up and down Marsh Road looking for us. I was content to stay put after they passed, but Bob insisted we were in the clear and that anyway, he was a master of talking himself out of these jams. He had learned early in life that his famous father's name was a sort of "get out of jail free card." So we crept out onto the road right in front of Officer Clark Jester's car and a bullhorn sounded – "Freeze!" The next thing I heard from Bobby was, "Damn it's Clark Jester, he hates Sallies' guys!"

We were hauled into Troop 1 at the Penny Hill police station, and there sat Downing and Kraft. Everyone agreed not to reveal where we got the beer. They asked Downey first and he responded, "I can't tell you. I'm not a rat." We all followed suit.

We were released to our parents and told that Salesianum would be notified. Sallies was infamous for its strict discipline, so all of us were understandably concerned about the reaction from school administration. Bobby's famous father, Porky, had died of lung cancer just two years before, and his mother Claire was not a disciplinarian. So Bobby had little to fear on the home front. I, on the other hand, was certain all hell would break lose at 3603 Pine Street. Under my father's pressure, I gave in quickly on who got the beer. I was immediately ordered to never be in Bobby's company again.

Back at school I feared I might either be kicked out of school or off the golf team, but after being strongly reprimanded by the school disciplinarian, Father Thomas J. Hopkins, we were sentenced to a month of after school detention, aka "JUG" ("Justice Under God") and banned from extra-curricular activities including our senior prom. Fortunately, I was told I could rejoin the golf team in the spring if I stayed out of trouble.

While Bill Downey and I became "partners-in-crime" our senior year, we never became close friends. I can only recall one time in my life when I talked to him following graduation. Over my Christmas leave from Ft. Benning OCS in 1969, I ran into Bill in a bar in Wilmington. He had fought as an infantry officer in Vietnam, made it back in one piece, and had just mustered out of the Army the week before. We were both somewhat amazed to realize that we had just spent the previous four months only yards apart; he had been the company commander of the OCS company immediately adjacent to mine at Ft. Benning. Bill was the classic "happy-go-lucky" kid in high school, and I have never been able to truly get my head around the idea that he was leading an Infantry OCS company at Benning, let alone leading men in combat in Vietnam. Sadly, Bill recently passed away, and his Vietnam service was prominent in his obituary.

Following my stumble with the Ring Mass episode, the athletic director, Father Robert Kenney, reached out to offer his support. I did not have him for a class or as a coach, but he understood that I needed some direction and stepped in. In later life, I heard a quote from championship Notre Dame football coach Lou Holtz: "When people need love and understanding and support the most is when they deserve it the least."

Those words reminded me of my experience with Father Kenney—I did not deserve his kindness. He said he wanted me to attend college, but I resisted. Though I dreamed of college and had received letters of interest from the golf coaches at West Point and Ohio State, I never followed up. Those institutions seemed beyond my reach and I thought it best to find a full-time job. With the oldest kids out of the house, my paycheck would be needed at home and besides, I thought I wanted to become a golf pro and felt college would only slow down that path.

Reverend Robert
Kenney, O.S.F.S.

One day in November of '63, I was making a turn in the hall to head to our last period history class with Mr. Nardozzi. As I passed my classmate Jack Holloway (an All-American in football that year who would go on to be a teacher and one of the greatest wrestling coaches in state history), he stopped me and said, "John, did you hear they shot President Kennedy?!"

As we entered the classroom, Mr. Nardozzi told us to shut up and take our seats. He turned on the TV and we all watched as Walter Cronkite took off his glasses and declared to the country that the president was dead. We were stunned, as was the entire country and the world. It would be thirty-eight years later—September 11, 2001—before we would experience anything as shocking and horrifying as that moment again. Kennedy's violent death, and the subsequent assassination of Robert Kennedy in 1968, had a profound impact on me. It fueled my interest in politics and affirmed my sense that, like my mother and father, I was a Democrat. That commitment would begin to change exactly ten years into the future.

As the spring of 1964 approached, I was named captain of the golf team. We would finish the season with a perfect record and I had the added satisfaction of scoring a win over my archrival from Brandywine High School, Fred Dingle, and Jim Monkman from A.I. du Pont, a rising star in state golf. There was no formal state high school championship at the time, but years later Salesianum hoisted a banner in their gymnasium on Broom Street declaring our team state champions. Coached by Father William Campbell, my fellow team members included Tom Ciconte,

Bob Murphy, John Prettyman, Jack Shepard, Bob Oliver, Sonny Resini and Mike Robinson.

Mike Robinson was one of my closest friends. Tragically, he would be killed the summer following our freshman year at UD in a car driven by another DuPont Country Club junior golfer, Paul Storm. Paul was a sophomore at Cornell. I was supposed to meet them that evening at the club with prospects of attending a party in Greenville, but I arrived late. I was at work the next morning at Hanby Office Furniture in town when my brother, Curt, told me that Mike had been killed.

That afternoon, July 29, 1965, Mike's photo would appear on the front page of the *Evening Journal* under the headline, "U. of D. Student Killed in Crash." I still have that edition of the paper after all these years. The lead headline that day reported that the 101st Airborne had landed in Vietnam; it was the start of Johnson's build-up of American forces in Southeast Asia. Also, on the front page was something else of historical significance: The U.S. Senate had just passed Medicare by a vote of 70–24, with Delaware senator Caleb Boggs voting for the measure and fellow Republican John Williams voting against.

Sallies Golfers Are Good – Mighty Good

It pays to practice, if you are interested in perfection. Father William Campbell's golf team is interested in perfection, so they practice plenty. The result: near perfection — a 14-0 record. And what's even more impressive they set down the reputed king, Brandywine, the current Blue Hen Conference Champs and also the always strong team from the Philadelphia Suburban League Malvern Prep.

The Sallies linksmen have literally devoured all the local and nearby competition available. Only three of their opponents managed to score any points against them and two of the three got the sum total of one point apiece.

The team is captained by John Riley, a senior. Other team members are Mike Robinson, Tom Ciconte and Joe Sheppard, all seniors. They are supported by sophomores Bob Murphy and John Prettyman.

What's the secret of their success? According to Father Campbell it's "balance and plenty of practice added to a fine supply of talent."

Within the next few weeks the State finals will begin. Father Campbell is confident his boys will do very well in this competition. Since the States matches are based on individuals entries, and not team play, it is quite possible that the Sallies sextet will tee off against one another for the title in the finals.

Our undefeated fairwaymen — Mike Robinson, John Riley, Tom Ciconte, Prettyman, and Bob Murphy, pose with the pro, Fr. Wm. Campbell.

Chapter 6

Almost a Champion, 1964

"You're leading the tournament, you're leading the tournament!"

With only days left of school in my senior year, Father Kenney stopped me in the hallway and asked me to meet him in his office. While he had previously urged me to consider college, this time he would not take no for an answer. Together, we completed an application to the University of Delaware and then filled out paperwork for a National Defense College Loan. The loan was for $700 per semester, which covered full room and board to UD. I was to pay it off after completing military service. No doubt that Father Kenney's involvement was life-changing for me; I attended college because he cared.

Before I heard back from UD, I would compete in the 1964 Delaware State Golf Association's (DSGA) Men's State Amateur Championship at Brandywine Country Club. The night before the tournament, my father and I went out to play a practice round at the DuPont course. He was highly critical of how I was drawing the ball (i.e., hitting the ball with a right to left shape) into greens with my irons and insisted I change to what was known as a fade (i.e., moving the ball left to right was the favored shot trajectory of the famous Ben Hogan). Feeling tense and doubting his golf wisdom, I just couldn't hit the shot he wanted. His famous temper flared and following a heated exchange, I angrily walked off the course with my mind a mess heading into the first qualifying round of the championship.

While my father had taught me the fundamentals of the golf swing, stanch and grip, I continued to refine my game by watching others and attempting to mimic what they were doing. At first, I copied the swings of the best players that I caddied for, but later began to simulate the top pros I followed on television. My favorite was Tony Lema, who tragically died in a plane crash two years after winning the 1964 Open Championship at St. Andrews. I also made a rather feeble attempt to reproduce the swings of Jack Nicklaus, Arnold Palmer, and Ben Hogan. When out on the course alone, I would play three balls assuming three different swings and personalities. If an adult happened along, I quickly reverted to being just John Riley.

Although I reacted with anger at my father's last-minute swing advice, I suspect that some of it might have sunk in because my play the next day was the best of my young golf career. I had never previously been under par in state competition but found myself on the 17th hole on the Brandywine Country Club that day twenty feet away from an eagle that would put me five under par for the round. About five feet off the green with another fifteen feet to the hole, I started to line up my shot when another former Sallies golfer and past state junior champion Fred Philipsen yelled over to me from the next fairway to see how I was doing. I yelled back, "I'm three under."

That kind of golf in Delaware was fairly rare, so Fred erupted. He dropped his bag, threw his hands in the air and yelled, "You're leading the tournament, you're leading the tournament!"

Of all my friends from my teen years, Fred Philipsen was the biggest risk taker. When we traveled to golf tournaments, he sometimes carried hunting rifles in his car. He had the eyes of a hawk and could spot a groundhog at a hundred yards while driving fifty m.p.h. He would pull over, fire, and then jump out of the car to retrieve his latest victim. It came as no surprise to any of us that Fred would end up as a fighter pilot in the Navy, flying F-4's off carriers attacking targets in North Vietnam. After he left the service, he moved to the West Coast and became a pilot for Alaska Airlines.

With Fred's major overreaction, my body began to go into a semi-state of shock. My hands began to shake, and I lost my focus and composure. Struggling to gather myself I chose the wrong club and "chunked" my chip, then followed it with a three putt. I went from easy birdie or better to bogey. Still rattled, I snap-hooked my tee shot off the 18th tee into the pine trees on the left. I finished with a double-bogey six for an even par round of 71, dropping me to third place in the first day of the 36-hole "medalist" rounds.

Full of regrets about what might have been, the next morning I opened the sports page to see a headline that read, ***JOHN, 18, TOPS GOLFING RILEYS.*** Dad had shot a 76 and Curt a 79. Whatever was

working kept on working for me
the next day, while first round
leader and frequent state champion
Roy Marquette ballooned to a 78.
I hovered around par all day and
word came out to me that I would
need a birdie on the last hole to
catch medalist leader Ed Richetelli.

I had never met the prominent,
barrel chested Richetelli, but there
he was with a hundred of his best friends behind the eighteenth green
waiting for me to finish. Unfortunately, a birdie was not in the cards, so
my 71–73 finished second. Richetelli came over to me after I putted out
and gave me a big hug. That was the beginning of a long relationship
with the golf champion, a former WWII fighter pilot, and his family.

At this point, I was brimming with confidence, believing that I could
beat anyone in the field. I easily won my first match play round over Walt
Kehnast. My next match would be against Bill "Doc" Ferguson, a former
DuPont club champion. As I stood on the first tee the next morning ready
to go, there was no Bill Ferguson in sight. As time expired, tournament
official Tony Dominelli, executive director of the DSGA, approached me
to request that I wait for Ferguson. I knew the rules: Ferguson should
have immediately been disqualified, but he was a family friend. Plus, I had
been well trained to obey my adult superiors, so I just meekly submitted
to the request.

While initially confident I would still win my match, doubts began to
creep into my head as I waited around for over an hour. I then got off to
a terrible start and was four down after four holes. The match remained
that way for the next ten holes when I started a comeback. I won the
15th, 16th and 17th and was fighting to push it into extra holes, but when
Ferguson tied me on the last, my run was over.

Waiting for me was my father, who let me have it for allowing
Ferguson and the officials to take advantage of me. He said something
to Ferguson, his friend, and ripped into Dominelli and other golf
association officials, but the damage had been done. It would be twelve
years before I had a chance to take the state title again. (Ironically,
twenty-five years later, Ferguson and I would be honored at the same
event for "contributions to Delaware golf" by the DSGA. It was not until

he passed away in 2016 that I learned he was awarded two Purple Hearts for wounds suffered in combat during World War II.)

A few days after this disappointment, I met with UD admissions and with the golf coach, Raymond B. "Scotty" Duncan. Scotty said a few things in our meeting that were hard to follow, but what came through was that this man seemed to really care about me. I would grow to love him; just the sight of him put a smile on my face. After taking two courses in summer school, I would become the first Riley to attend college.

Little card – great significance

It was great to be eighteen in 1964. It was the summer of the Beatles, "A Hard Day's Night," and a new wave of pop groups such as the Four Tops, The Beach Boys, and the Supremes. The world seemed to just be awakening from the nightmare of JFK's assassination, and though my high school friends and I had all registered for the draft, Vietnam was just a distant rumble. I was greatly anticipating college, as much to get out from under the harsh rule of my father as anything.

Chapter 7

Initial College Years, 1964–1966

"I've just seen a face, I can't forget the time or place where we just met …"

While I look back on the college years with fondness, I must also confess to having a certain listlessness related to academics and career goals. I had a vague sense that I wanted to become a golf pro, but if that didn't work out, perhaps a lawyer, teacher, or politician. Always looming over my head was the one post-college opportunity to which I was not greatly attracted—the draft and a stint in the military.

As a freshman in the fall of 1964, I was not eligible for the varsity golf team, so the item at the top of my list had to take a back seat. I wish I could look back and say I filled the void by pursuing higher learning with a passion but mostly I filled it with social life and a series of odd jobs, including delivering flowers for the House of Flowers in Wilmington and caddying at the newly established Biderman Golf Club. I often caddied for UD board members, such as Bruce Bredin, philanthropist Bayard Sharp, members of the Weymouth family and golf team benefactor Dr. John DeLuca.

The genesis of Biderman was said to be that "family members" like George Weymouth, son-in-law of Winterthur founder Henry F. du Pont, had become frustrated with the growth of Wilmington Country Club and wanted a more intimate club. The course was built on the Winterthur property, and many believe it simply incorporated the existing holes of Henry du Pont's private golf course. Having been one of the few who experienced both courses (I caddied for Mr. Weymouth on Henry's private course in 1962), I am certain that was not the case.

In at least one respect, my freshman year at Delaware would be different than the commuters and dormitory dwellers. Being the first year of the Baby Boomer wave, UD could not meet the demand for dorm rooms. I would be assigned to an off-campus house. I was seriously disappointed when we pulled up to the house. Above the front porch appeared the Greek letters *RHO RHO*—except someone had removed the Rs and it read "HO HO." While the origin of the Greek letters remained a mystery, my apprehension about living there quickly disappeared after I met my roommate, Phil Hickman, and three others with whom I would share the second floor. Phil was a big guy from Cape May, New Jersey who had played end on the football team but had decided to leave the program. Prior to UD, he had attended Bordentown Military Academy in New Jersey where he played football with Syracuse University star and future NFL Hall of Famer Floyd Little. Phil loved to tell stories about Little.

Other RHO RHO residents included Steve Salzenberg, the son of a senior DuPont executive, who had his own Corvette convertible and lived in a huge stone home across from the Wilmington Country Club (Steve would die in an auto accident while I was in the service); George Stamos, our hall director; Harvey Folk, a state wrestling champion from Newark; and two fellow Salesianum grads. Denny LaFazia had been a high school football All-American at Salesianum and had just transferred from Oklahoma State. James "Huck" Freebery was a starting defensive tackle on the Blue Hen football team. Huck had his own record player and a few Beatle albums that we almost wore out the needle on. I sometimes joke that the Beatles are the "soundtrack of my life," and this is where it kicked into high gear.

Huck, Denny, and the others in the RHO RHO house were quite conservative in their lifestyle. A couple of them had girlfriends from high school and would head home on weekends to see them. I never saw any of them violate a single school policy, including those regarding alcohol. Only Dennis pledged a fraternity, but after enduring some humiliating weeks, he dropped out after deciding it was an unneeded extra expense. I looked up to them as upperclassmen, so I guess I picked up a negative attitude about fraternities. The following year, my freshman roommate pledged a fraternity, but was "blackballed" halfway through the pledge period. While his disappointment and sense of humiliation soured me on the Greek system, he recovered quickly from the debacle and went on to pledge another fraternity, graduate, and become a successful lawyer.

As in my case, LaFazia joined the Army soon after graduation. He was sent to Ft. Bragg for basic training. The Army took one look at the former high school All-American linebacker and determined he was prime material for the Green Berets. After learning how to jump out of airplanes among other Special Forces training adventures, he was sent to the Army "Jungle School" in Panama to train troops. Like me, he benefited from the accelerated Vietnam drawdown and never deployed to the war zone.

After years of restrictions imposed by Catholic educators and my father, I was not thrilled with the idea of mandatory ROTC training. With my rather negative attitude I did not seem to adapt well to weekly drills and other training elements such as learning how to assemble and disassemble a WWII era M-1 rifle without catching my thumb in the bolt on a regular basis. On the other hand, I was impressed with our military science professor, Captain Bailey. He had already completed a tour in Vietnam and had returned with a high level of respect for our tenacious enemy.

Over the summer of '65, thanks to my brother Curt, I obtained my first eight-to-five job delivering office furniture for a division of the Hanby stationary stores. Wilmington was an exciting place to be that summer. The streets were jammed with people at lunchtime who poured out of the offices and into the restaurants and delis. In retrospect, I came to realize the Hanby business model was a little risky—ninety percent of our deliveries were to DuPont.

I continued to caddy off and on and played in some tournaments that summer with no notable successes. One of the tournaments was in Wildwood, New Jersey, where I partnered with Curt. To save what little cash we had, we decided to sleep in the car in the club parking lot and were nearly eaten alive by mosquitos. The next morning, walking around with our skin covered in welts and blood, a gentleman by the name of Mike Hayes took mercy on us and offered to pay for a motel room for us that night.

It turned out that Mr. Hayes owned the largest sporting goods store in South Jersey, and he offered Curt a job as store manager. I ended up working there on some future weekends and holidays. Mr. Hayes was also friends with members of the Philadelphia Flyers, so for many weekends during hockey season we would join the Flyers at the Tall Pines Golf Club across the bridge for golf. I was in for a bit of a shock in my first match against hockey All-Star Gary Dornhoefer. As first man on a fairly strong college golf team, I did not think for a moment I could lose to a hockey star. I learned the hard way that some of these guys play pretty good golf.

Back at school in the fall, I was looking forward to reconnecting with friends on campus and interested in meeting some of the incoming freshman girls. I really lacked confidence where women were concerned, but I thought that as a sophomore my chances might improve. Then it happened … September 25, 1965, an event that would change my life forever.

I was cutting through the student center when a voice called out to me. It was Mary Otteni, a girl I had met at the DuPont Country Club playing junior golf. Mary was a freshman, and she wanted to introduce me to her roommate, Sharon. It is impossible to do justice to the flood of emotions that overwhelmed me for the next five minutes. If there is such a thing as "love at first sight," then I was completely stunned by the sight of this seventeen-year-old redhead. I have no idea what Sharon and I said to each other, but that night I couldn't sleep, thinking of nothing but her face, her smile, and the fact that she had been so nice to me.

By the next morning, I began to beat back the thought of asking Sharon out. I thought that all the usual campus charmers would be lining up for her attention and I would not stand a chance. As I wrestled with these thoughts, who do I run into on my way to class but Mary. She asked me what I thought of Sharon. I had to suppress an explosion of thoughts rushing through my brain and simply said that I really enjoyed meeting her. Mary said, "Great. I suggest you call her today because she seemed to like you, too, and I think she will say yes if you ask her for a date."

That night, shaking all over, I called the Harrington dorm and held my breath until Sharon came on the phone. She said she had a date on Saturday but added that she would be cheerleading at the football pep rally Friday on the "Old College" steps and that I could walk her back to the dorm when it was over. After managing to secure a quick kiss goodnight, I headed back to my dorm, determined that I was going to do all in my power to win Sharon's heart.

Shortly after meeting Sharon and taking her out, the Beatles *Rubber Soul* album was released. I first listened to it in my friend Art Bellefonte's apartment. One song, "I've Just Seen a Face," sung by Paul McCartney, grabbed my attention. In it, McCartney sings about the chance that on another day he might have looked the other way and would never have met the face that enchanted him. Instead, he was dreaming of her that night. The song and the circumstances have always reminded me of Sharon and our early days together.

Within days of my first date with Sharon, her photo appeared on display in the student center with about eight other co-eds nominated for homecoming queen. I do not remember exactly how the voting was conducted, but I was proud to be dating a potential homecoming queen and I was certain she would win. However, when the voting results hit the school newspaper, the new queen would be a name I would hear a lot about in the future—Valerie Biden, Joe Biden's sister and campaign manager. In fact, years later I wondered if the Biden political machine had already had a sort of campaign dry-run, finding votes for homecoming queen.

During the first few weeks of school that year I had jumped back into the college partying scene, pursuing more than my share of good times, but I soon peeled off and turned my attention to Sharon. Weak grades in 1965 could be hazardous to your health due to losing your student draft deferment. It was beginning to take a toll on fellow students, including golf team friend Fred Dingle and another buddy, Bill Moeckel.

Bill had added to his academic challenges that semester by taking a job working the night shift at a motel near the Wilmington airport. It wouldn't be long before Bill ended up in the Army, where he opted for military intelligence and was later shipped out to Vietnam. Another friend, Art Bellefonte, transferred to the University of Miami, but the draft grabbed him after graduation.. Art had worked part time at a funeral home in college and when he went into the army, they placed him in

Sharon, the red headed cheerleader does not like the score

Graves Registration, identifying and preparing the remains of hundreds of soldiers killed in combat and shipping them home. I exchanged some letters with Art while he was in Vietnam and learned about his difficult experience over there.

I did not see Bill Moeckel again for forty years, but I would occasionally run into his father and his brother around town. I learned that after the Army, Bill was accepted at Cornell in their hotel management program and became a highly successful industry executive. I guess the airport motel experience had some value after all. When I reconnected with Bill on a golf trip to South Carolina several years ago, I learned we had something in common—we had both been changed greatly by our military experience. Bill credits being accepted at Cornell to his military background and the connection to a World War II veteran at the University. Today, we sometimes share stories about military veterans and heroes who have sacrificed so much to make this country great.

One of the unique experiences of the Vietnam era were the many opportunities I had to travel to Washington, D.C. on college weekends to visit my sister Bernadette. Immediately after graduating from Padua Academy, Bernadette went to work at DuPont as a secretary. With a desire to get away from living at home with my father and experience the world, she joined with some girlfriends to find jobs and rent a place in D.C. Since the drinking age was only eighteen there at the time, we would head down every chance we could.

With so many military installations in the DC area, Bernadette and her friends began to volunteer through the Red Cross at both Ft. Belvoir and Walter Reed Military Hospital. They would see the consequences of battle in the hospital wards one day and the next day head to the bars to party with other newly trained soldiers and Marines as they prepared to deploy. The bars were packed with thousands of servicemen every Friday and Saturday night, and the release of pent-up energy seemed to supercharge the atmosphere. We sometimes dodged fights when they broke out or joined in to sing the various service anthems as Marines, G.I.s, airmen, and sailors jumped to their feet to out-sing or out-shout the other side of the room.

I often wondered how many of the young men, particularly the Quantico Marines, did not survive the war and how many mothers, fathers, spouses and children would suffer from the loss for the rest of their own lives. We met dozens who were destined to serve as Marine lieutenants in the bloodiest battles of the war. It is possible that some of them were among the 498 members of officer basic class 6/67, who would have arrived in Vietnam just before the battles of Hué and Khe San. According to an article in Military.com, this class experienced a casualty rate of more than fifty percent, the highest of any class.

Chapter 8

Golf Team and Other Adventures,
1966–1967

*"Riley, you have twenty-four hours to either
pay the bill or clear out of the dorm!"*

Although only a sophomore starting my first ever college match in 1966, Coach Scotty Duncan placed me in the top position on the six man team against Penn State and Georgetown in an away match in Washington. Along with Rutgers, Bucknell, and Temple, these were our toughest opponents during my varsity years, and I was simply not ready for prime time. I lost badly to both opponents and was immediately demoted down to fourth man. I righted the ship after that and went on to have one of the best records on our winning team.

About mid-season, we played Bucknell away on their home course, and for the first time I broke 70 in competition. I was told by Coach Duncan that my 69 was the lowest score ever by a Blue Hen golfer, but I don't know if that was ever verified. Unfortunately, no one else won their match that day, so I looked a little out of place with a smile on my face at our Howard Johnson's dinner that night and team veteran John DiEleuterio let me know about it. In the small world that is Delaware, John, like Bert DiClemente before him, would one day be Joe Biden's state director. John would also spend many years in the National Guard, where he attained the rank of lieutenant colonel. After retiring from working for Senator Biden, he went back to the Guard as a special assistant to Adjutant General Frank Vavala.

The golf team came out strong for the 1967 season, winning our first seven matches including knocking off Georgetown, but for me it was the season that almost didn't happen. Paying little attention to important administrative matters during those years, I had missed the deadline to renew my National Defense Loan for sophomore year. To pay the tuition, my father secured a loan from the DuPont credit union. The deal was that I was to turn over all the money I made from summer, holiday, and weekend jobs. Everything went fine for two semesters, but then the family car broke down and dad's credit was stretched to the limit. He had to use the college funds for a car, and suddenly there was no way to pay for school.

When I got the word from home, I contacted golf coach Scotty Duncan to ask if there was anything the university could do to help. It sounded like he could work something out, but he needed to check on some details and would get back to me. Soon he called back and told me to go up to Hullihen Hall and see the dean of students, John Hocutt. I ran up campus immediately and waited for Hocutt. He asked me why I couldn't pay my tuition. After I explained the situation, he glared at me and said, "Riley, you have twenty-four hours to either pay the bill or clear out of the dorm!" Since I had been sent by Scotty, fully expecting a solution to my problem, I thought I had misunderstood him. When I asked him to repeat what he said, he stated, "You heard me—you have twenty-four hours!"

Completely bewildered, I found a phone booth and called Scotty. I said, "Coach, didn't you say Hocutt was going to help?" I explained what happened, and Scotty seemed as stunned as I was. He told me to come down to his office later that day and that he would come up with something. In the hours before I met the coach, the thought occurred to me that if this couldn't be worked out, "Uncle Sam" would not be far behind. My life was in Scotty Duncan's hands.

When I sat down in Scotty's office, in came football coach, Harold "Tubby" Raymond. Before I could say a word, Tubby began chewing me out about my academic performance. While my grades were certainly not the best, they were a little better than some of my friends on the football team, so my guess was Tubby had used this lecture before. I just didn't understand what any of this had to do with football, but then he rolled out the plan. The athletic department would arrange a loan to pay my tuition and I would work for them for the summer, without pay. I would sell football program ads up and down the state. I had no choice but to say yes, but immediately I was worried—my family counted on my summer income to pay loans and help with expenses. I was already beginning to contemplate that I would need a "night shift" job that summer.

I have thought about this inflection point in my life many times over the years. In 1967, I did not fully comprehend that it was my modest golf talent that had saved me. Not because golf was important to the University of Delaware—it was not, as Dean Hocutt had made clear. It was because golf had brought Scotty Duncan into my life and he treated me (and others) like the son he never had. No doubt he was thinking as much about my vulnerability to the draft as he was about his win–loss record; he was not going to let me down.

In late April, we would be taking our 7-0 record to play the Division I Rutgers team on their home course. The Scarlet Knights were led by their top player Dave Muraskin, described in the press as one of the "best collegiate players in the East." In addition to our perfect record, I had my own perfect record on the line as well. Muraskin was as good as advertised and I found myself one down after nine. Before heading to the 10th tee I passed through the pro shop to grab a drink when someone yelled out from behind the counter, "How many up is Muraskin?" Perhaps he didn't realize I was currently Muraskin's victim, but I sheepishly answered, "He's one up."

It is funny how little things can motivate you. I headed out to the 10th tee more determined than I had ever been in a golf match. Muraskin and I traded pars for most of the back nine before I birdied the 16th and 17th to take a one up lead. After I closed him out for the win on the last green, I marched straight past Scotty to the pro shop to find the guy with the earlier question. When I saw him behind the counter I shouted, "Hey, in case you're interested, Muraskin just lost to the Delaware guy one up!"

The fun didn't last too long. A few days later, we played the always strong Temple team on their home course, Sandy Run, outside Philadelphia. I would be clobbered by a guy named Sherm Keeney. Keeney wore a "Ben Hogan" hat and seemed to have adopted the famous Hogan demeanor. He did not speak to me after we shook hands on the first tee. In addition to the personal defeat, the loss to Keeney cost us the overall match and our dream of a perfect record. I would spend a full year thinking about exacting my golfing revenge on our home course of Louviers, where I had never lost a match. For the 1967 season, we finished with thirteen wins and two losses. I led the team with the same record.

Chapter 9

The Night Shift, 1967–1968

"Stop the belt, stop the belt!"

With having to work days for the university that summer, I needed to find a night shift position to earn cash to pay off the student loan and contribute to the family. To fill in when workers went out for summer vacation, the Chrysler assembly plant in Newark hired students to staff the night shift. I heard the work was very challenging. I was told by a couple guys who worked there the previous summer to avoid the paint shop and the body shop, if possible. Not only would I be assigned to the body shop, I was placed in a section referred to as "the jungle." The term jungle was used to describe the electrical lines attached to the welding guns that hung from the ceiling. When I was guided by the foreman to my workstation to begin my first four to twelve shift, the guy I was replacing looked me up and down and shouted over the roar of the machinery, "He's a little thin for this job, ain't he?" But there was no turning back now.

I quickly began to understand the muscular incumbent's concern. The assignment was to wield a heavy steel bar to release the locks that held the thousand-pound steel gate that hung from the ceiling, holding the frame in place while the spot welders did their work. Once the frame arrived at my station, I had to break open about sixteen to twenty locks with the steel bar, mount the side of the frame and shake it lose from the assembly. Often, melting metal from the welding guns would leach into the lock at the bottom and freeze it in place. If I couldn't pull off the gate I would have to yell for help. This would happen about fifty times my first night. With temperatures above a hundred, sparks flying and the roar of the factory never subsiding, I thought I would not survive my first shift.

I made it back for the second night driven only by the desire to pocket those $2.85 an hour United Auto Worker (UAW) wages. While they gave me a pair of gloves, it didn't take long to wear through them. I don't think I had ever quit anything in my life, but halfway through the second night a piece of sheet metal slipped and almost sliced a nearby worker in half. As he left the factory on a stretcher, I made up my mind to find another line of work. As I was leaving, I told the foreman not to expect me back. He looked me right in the eye and said, "You'll be back, I'm sure of it."

I woke up the next morning to my mother yelling upstairs that my Uncle Tom wanted to talk to me. My father's brother was almost as volatile as my father (they sometimes got in fights at family weddings) and he could back it up. He served as a Marine in the South Pacific during the Second World War, and I never heard him mention a word about it. For whatever reason, he had taken a liking to me since I was a kid. Still half asleep, I answered the phone to hear him say, "Johnny, there is a position available on the production line here at the Huber Sunbeam Bread factory if you can start today." By early afternoon that Sunday, I would be joining the United Bakers and Confectioners Workers Union, an affiliate of the AFL-CIO—my second labor union in three days.

The Huber Bakery sat at the intersection of 9th & Union Streets in Wilmington, directly across from where the Kozy Korner restaurant sits today. In 1966, the Kozy Korner was known as Goldie's Delicatessen. The old bakery building stretched over a city block, west towards the B & O rail line—the massive bread oven alone, covered half a city block. Diagonally across 9th Street was the Division of Motor Vehicles (DMV) where most of us had an opportunity to wait for hours to renew tags and licenses or have cars inspected. Like the bakery, DMV was populated by many local Italians, including several from the Rock Manor

Huber Bakery
Photo source oldwilmington.net

golf ranks. Two blocks down Union Street from the bakery was Pala's Café, home of the "World's Worst Pizza"—funny marketing angle, but the pizza actually wasn't bad. On the opposite side of the street sat "Mrs. Robino's," still a local landmark today.

The smell from the bakery ovens carried across Little Italy and other nearby neighborhoods merging with the smells emanating from the Del Campo Bakery closer to Pennsylvania Avenue and the Freihofer's Bread factory, which sat opposite Union Park Pontiac. On a ninety-degree day, if you walked by Huber's on the 9th Street side, you would be startled by the heat that pulsated through the open door. The equipment in the building was so old, the steel bore the label, "Carnegie Steel Company," which had ceased to exist in 1901.

There was one problem I did not mention to Uncle Tom when I spoke to him that morning. My hands were so raw from the previous two days on the Chrysler assembly line that I could not open them. My mother ran hot water into the sink and had me soak them in Epsom salt until I could pull them open. Off I went by bus to 9th & Union to start a staggered shift at 2:00 PM. Of course, I would be starting at the bottom of the barrel—on the semi-automated bread wrappers under the supervision of a guy named Ed. He had only one method of communicating—screaming. Ed started every shift angry, and he ended it angry.

About six hours into my shift, I started to notice blood all over the bread. In addition to the sores on my hands from Chrysler, the hardened bread crust was slowly scrapping the skin off the ends of my fingers. I have no idea how many loaves got wrapped and sent out before I was able to have my fingers bandaged. After working twelve hours, I left the plant at two AM. I called home to see if I could wake someone to come pick me up, but no dice. I walked the three miles to Pine Street and collapsed into bed. The thirty-six hours from Chrysler to Huber's would be about the toughest day-and-half of my life until I experienced Ranger Week at Ft. Benning, Georgia.

For the next several summers, plus many weekends and holidays, Huber Bakery became my home away from home. Whenever production supervisor Jack Bove called, I went. In the middle of the chaos and noise of the bakery, Jack always kept his cool and had a smile on his face. When he died recently at age eighty-eight, his obituary mentioned his selflessness and his faith, noting that he attended daily Mass.

With the bakery located near Little Italy, several production workers only spoke Italian or English with a heavy accent. We had one black employee, the janitor. Lunch breaks were on staggered schedules to ensure production continued and I noticed that our janitor always ate alone, so I would try to join him when our schedules aligned. Occasionally, someone would challenge me on why I sat with the janitor and I would get on my civil rights' soapbox. They would call me "college boy," and this was not meant as a compliment. I don't think I changed any minds, but I never felt threatened—although things got verbally hostile when the riots occurred in Wilmington after Martin Luther King's assassination.

The summer of my senior year, I was working another night shift when the bread cooler broke down for an extended period of time. I was on the back end of the line, boxing bread and placing the cartons on a long conveyor belt that reached the loading platform. The hold went on for probably an hour as the mechanics worked on it. To fill the time, I was balling up wads of bread and watching them flatten as they traveled the belt and circled the big drum near my station. For some stupid reason I decided to see if I could pull off the bread that had flattened like a pancake onto the drum. In a split second, I was lifted by the machinery out of my station and my arm was disappearing between belt and the drum with my body following. Just as my body lifted off the floor and my head and shoulder reached the drum someone screamed, "Stop the belt, stop the belt!"

Thankfully, the guy at the next station, Bob Dorris, reached up and hit the safety stop switch. A half-dozen production workers came running and together manually reversed the system and extracted me out from between the belt and drum. I had no broken bones but was diagnosed with torn ligaments and tendons in my left wrist. It would be months before I played golf again. I don't know whatever happened to Dorris, but I do know his quick thinking that night saved my arm and maybe more.

Chapter 10

The Match, May 1968

"OK, but you better win!"

Although still digging out of the academic hole I had created for myself, I was developing a love of history and political science, thanks to several talented UD professors. Professors such as my academic advisor, Ray Wolters, who focused on racial issues; David Ingersoll, a Vladimir Lenin look-alike who taught a popular course called "Communism, Fascism, and Democracy"; and James Merrill, who taught Civil War history and wrote a book on General Sherman. All stimulated in me a desire to read and learn more about our great country and the issues and opportunities it presents. As both graduation and draft day drew closer, my academic advisor Wolters planted the idea in my head about becoming an Army officer.

In my senior year, it became more challenging to hold onto the #1-man position on our golf team. Fellow team members Charlie Pinto, Tom Ciconte, and Jim Powell all challenged for the top spot. Pinto in particular was having a great year, and when the Temple rematch came around, he was #1 and scheduled to play Sherm Keeney who had humiliated me the year before. Having been named captain that year, Scotty would often review the line-up with me ahead of time to

University of
DELAWARE

1968 GOLF

The team captain mired
in another bunker

55

get my input on the various match-ups. When I saw he had me slotted to play #2 that day, I begged him for the chance to play Keeney. He agreed but delivered a strong message. "OK, but you better win!"

I first played the DuPont Louviers golf course when I was twelve. The design was extremely challenging with nine "blind" tee shots, severely sloped, treelined fairways, and tiny greens guarded by deep bunkers. The club pro, John Long, was a true character. He had "Don't Steal" printed on all the golf balls at his driving range. I never paid for a golf lesson until I was in my fifties, but I had plenty of free advice from my father and tips from Long whenever I visited Louviers. "Get over here Riley and let me see you swing," he would shout when he saw me. After suggesting a small swing change, he would admonish me with his constant refrain, "Don't tell Terl!" (Terl was the head pro at the main DuPont course in Wilmington.) When I introduced him to Sharon, he declared my golf career over. He joked, "I can tell Riley, you only care about that redhead now—you've got no chance."

I loved everything about Louviers, and I was confident the course gave me and my Delaware teammates an edge against any opponent, including Temple's Sherm Keeney. As determined as I was that day, Keeney's accurate driving and iron play through the first fourteen holes had completely neutralized my home course advantage and I found myself two down. Since that hole came back to the club house, a small gallery had gathered behind the green. As I walked towards the 15th tee, Marty Finerty, a retired Wilmington fireman who worked for Scotty, came running up to ask me how my match stood. When I told him I was two down, he looked at me and said, "Your old dad (Scotty) is not going to be happy."

I headed down the 15th fairway determined to find a way to win. I birdied that one to cut Keeney's margin to one. We both parred the 16th hole, and I found myself on the front left of the 17th green with the hole in the back right over forty feet away. Keeney was in the middle of the green, approximately fifteen feet away. At that point my goal was to two putt and hope he missed—miraculously my putt went in! Keeney then missed his putt, and our match was back to even. As we walked to the 18th tee, Keeney said to me, "I knew you were going to make that putt." That was the first time Keeney spoke to me in either match. We would both par the 18th hole to send the match into sudden death.

Because DuPont employees had begun to arrive at the club after work let out, the playoff had to be pushed up to the difficult fourth hole.

With Coach Duncan, assistant, Bill Dembrock, and others looking on, I hit a poor tee shot that stopped on the left side of the fairway nearly two hundred yards from the green. Keeney's drive finished in the middle of the fairway, well past mine.

On the fourth hole of the Louviers course, there is a very narrow gap between the out-of-bounds stakes right of the green and three tiered bunkers on the steep slope guarding the left. At a distinct disadvantage off the tee, I quickly surmised that I would have to hit the best shot of my college career or I would again lose to Keeney. Full of adrenalin and fighting to contain my emotions, I took a deep breath and swung. I felt the solid contact as the three iron met the ball and looked up to see it climbing into the sky and heading towards the flag. Seconds later, it stopped just a few feet from the hole. Obviously shaken, Keeney sailed his second shot out of bounds to the right and quickly conceded the match. I think we were both a bit shocked by the sudden turn of events.

Keeney shot a seventy-one that day, which I believe up to that point was the lowest round ever shot by a Delaware opponent on Louviers, but my three under charge on the last five holes was the best finish of my college career. I would always savor the smile and big hug I got from Scotty when it was over. Keeney would go on to a very successful career as a PGA club professional and has been elected to several golf/sports halls of fame in Pennsylvania.

A week later my college golf career ended on a negative note when I lost my last match in another sudden death playoff against St. Joe's of Philadelphia. My opponent was one of my high school teammates, Bob Murphy. Bob, a Delaware state amateur champion had also caddied at Wilmington Country Club. When the overall match ended in a tie that day, our team had to forfeit because Tom Ciconte, who played in the first man position, had left after his match to return to his job in Newark. For some odd reason, the rules did not allow teams to substitute the next player. Like myself, Ciconte would later be drafted. He was trained in military intelligence and served a year in Vietnam in a non-combat role.

The golf team finished 1968 with its third straight winning season. Later the summary in the Blue Hen Yearbook would read:

With his last putt of the year, Captain John Riley ended three of the finest years ever for a Delaware golfer. The senior's overall record of 41-10 represents the best won-loss percentage as well as the greatest number of matches for any Blue Hen golfer in history. This outstanding performance earned Riley the Three Year Award for Delaware athletes.

Scotty and his wife Jessie never had children, which I believe intensified the feelings he had towards his players. Most of us stayed in close touch with the coach long after we graduated. Whenever I had the opportunity to attend a Blue Hen football game, all I had to do was call the old coach and I would have front row seats and front row parking. If you were one of "Scotty's boys" you were on the team for life. To show our gratitude when he retired, we all chipped in to send Scotty and Jessie on a golf trip to St. Andrews in Scotland and Pebble Beach in California. Then, in 1981, I teamed up with several former UD players to organize the first "Scotty Duncan" golf outing to financially support the golf program. This effort is still going strong, more than thirty-five years later.

Another former golf team captain and patron of the program was Kevin Scanlon, who started his own golf event marketing business. During the late '80s and early '90s, Kevin ran a celebrity pro-am for McNeil Labs called the Tylenol Kids Classic, and he invited Scotty and me to announce the players on the first tee at the White Manor Country Club in Malvern, Pennsylvania. A photo that hangs on my wall from that experience always recalls one of my favorite "Scotty" moments.

In addition to top players from the PGA Tour, Scanlon and McNeil recruited other leading sports figures. The most popular attraction a couple of those years was Michael Jordan, generally considered to be the greatest and most popular athlete in the world at that time. In 1990, Jordan was lined up to play in the marquee group with baseball greats Mike Schmidt and Joe Morgan, along with former football legend and TV broadcaster Frank Gifford. While Scotty and I were positioned at one end of the first tee, Michael Jordan signed autographs for hundreds of fans about thirty feet away. People were nearly trampling each other for an opportunity to connect with Air Jordan.

Hoping for a photo with Jordan I turned to Scotty and said, "Coach, that man may be the greatest athlete in history, we should not let this opportunity pass without getting our picture with him." To my amazement, the 5' 6" Duncan walked across the tee and tapped the 6' 6" superstar on the shoulder. When Jordan turned around, Scotty beckoned him with his index finger saying, "Son, come with me, we need you in a photo." Leaving the autograph seekers, Jordan and Duncan walked back to me as Scotty yelled to someone with a camera to snap a photo. Standing at the other end of the tee with his arms folded watching this was future Ryder Cup captain Davis Love. When Scotty and the photographer had us lined up, he yelled over to Love, "Son, would you like to be in this picture?" Love trotted over and joined us.

Soon after the Michael Jordan encounter, we were shocked to receive word that the seventy-year-old Scotty had been stricken by a massive heart attack. I was one of the many "Scotty's boys" who lined up at the funeral to deliver a eulogy in honor of the old coach whom we all loved.

With Scotty Duncan, Michael Jordan and PGA star, Davis Love III

Chapter 11

Early Politics, 1968–1969

"We shall pay any price, bear any burden…"

Constantly looking for ways to earn a buck, I added waiter to my list of job skills that year. The epicenter of UD social life, outside of the fraternities was the Deer Park Hotel on West Main Street in Newark. There was talk that the poet Edgar Allen Poe had collapsed drunk in front of the hotel in 1843, never making it to his poetry reading at the Newark Academy. The restaurant section was always crammed with students, while the back-bar area was filled with locals, referred to as "townies." The townie bar looked at times like the wild west. On one occasion when I walked in to pick up a beer order, George Thompson, the balding, gravelly voiced, pot-bellied owner took out a small bat from behind the bar and knocked a guy sitting

The true center of student life in the 1960's from the Deer Park Tavern website

there out cold. He then sent me to get a mop to wipe up the blood on the floor.

Above the college conversation, the hit songs "Reflections" by the Supremes and "Somebody to Love" by Jefferson Airplane played over and over on the bar's jukebox. On many nights, a local realtor, "Doc" McClary, a veteran of the Italian campaign in World War II would join students, including future Wilmington mayor Mike Purzycki and other Theta Chi fraternity brothers, at the same table. Well known and influential around town, McClary on at least one occasion used his influence to get some of "the brothers" sprung from the Newark city jail. For my part, I would achieve my own fifteen minutes of fame when a photographer snapped a shot of me holding a tray full of beers and put it on the front page of the student newspaper *The Review*.

While a couple of us waited tables, either Bob Layton, president of the University Intramural Council or football team captain Ed "Sandy" Sand worked the front door checking IDs. Layton was a popular, handsome guy from Carney's Point, New Jersey. Commissioned through ROTC, Bob had only been in Vietnam for a month when he was mortally wounded leading his platoon in action in the Saigon region. He was posthumously awarded the Silver Star for his attempt to rescue a seriously wounded combat medic. I was in training at Ft. Leonard Wood, Missouri when I received word of Layton's death.

When Ed Sand died a few years ago, I sent an email to Mike Purzycki, his former Blue Hen teammate, telling him about my experience at the Deer Park with Sandy. I mentioned that Sandy had a certain status as captain of the football team (a team with a perfect record in conference), but he had a humble demeanor and a quiet smile, and he treated people with respect. Mike flew to California to attend Sand's funeral. He told me later that he arrived just as the service began, and Sandy's family asked him to offer remarks. Taken by surprise, Mike said he pulled out his phone and read my email to the gathering. Knowing Mike, I am sure he added some eloquent and moving words of his own.

In parallel with schoolwork, golf team, and my various part time jobs, I was ramping up my political activity that spring of 1968. Senator Eugene McCarthy of Minnesota had challenged President Johnson in '68 on an "end the war" platform. After McCarthy's strong showing in the New Hampshire primary, Robert Kennedy joined the race and shortly after, on March 31, 1968, Johnson shocked most of the country by announcing he would not seek reelection. Many of us jumped in for Kennedy because we thought he had the most realistic chance of being elected.

I had become a devoted Bobby Kennedy supporter and was certain there would be a path to end the war under his leadership. There was not much I could do at that point, though, as the primary campaign headed to California, and I was back on the night shift at Huber's. The atmosphere in the country was extremely tense following the assassination of Martin Luther King. Things were also tense in Delaware, as Governor Terry had ordered the National Guard onto the streets of Wilmington. One of the guardsmen on patrol was my brother Curt.

We were all still riding the Kennedy wave. JFK's legacy was being fed by what seemed like an endless series of hagiographies by former staffers like Ted Sorenson, Kenneth O'Donnell, and Arthur Schlesinger. Nowhere was the Kennedy aura more pronounced than on college campuses. On November 22, 1964, the first anniversary of JFK's assassination, my political science professor, Paul Dolan, entered the classroom, read Kennedy's Inaugural Address, and broke down in sobs before leaving the room. Ironically, one could point to Kennedy's Cold War rhetoric in that speech as a philosophical underpinning for the war.

Let every nation know, whether it wishes us well or ill, we shall pay any price, bear any burden, meet any hardship, support any friend, oppose any foe, in order to ensure the survival and the success of liberty.

Brother Bobby, dubbed by many as "ruthless" while serving as his brother's campaign manager and as attorney general, was elected a senator from New York soon after moving there. While scorned by McCarthy supporters as an opportunist, he emerged as a leading opponent of the war in Vietnam, a war his brother had escalated.

Whatever the contradictions, I was one of those all in for Bobby and our hopes were high that he could land the nomination if he won the all-important California Primary. I dozed off in front of the TV the evening of June 5th, while watching the election returns on television from the West Coast. When I awoke in the early hours of the morning, I heard the newscaster mentioning "assassination." Assuming they were discussing JFK's assassination, I turned off the TV and went to bed. Within hours Sharon was calling to wake me to tell me the awful news. If JFK was a shock to me at seventeen, RFK's murder was almost overwhelming at twenty-two.

Feeling the need to demonstrate our commitment to RFK, Sharon and I decided to drive to DC to attend the burial. After the funeral Mass in New York, Kennedy's remains were transported by train to Washington, but there were delays all along the route. One delay was caused when the train struck and killed a couple onlookers. After parking near the National Mall, we walked across the Arlington Bridge and waited for hours near the edge of the cemetery with thousands of others. It was well after dark when the funeral entourage brought the casket up the hill. Coretta Scott King, Dr. King's widow, passed within a few feet of us, no doubt still dealing with the grief and impact of her husband's recent assassination. It was difficult to see under the harsh television lights, but we had a sense that, for a brief moment, we were part of history.

With the exception of time spent with Sharon, the summer of 1968 had its challenges. The war dragged on, with U.S. deaths averaging more than three hundred a week. More friends were leaving for the service and more photos of our local young men killed in action were appearing in the papers. For many of us still looking ahead to our role in the conflict, it was hard to grasp the purpose for the slaughter and clear that our national leadership was either greatly confused or morally bankrupt. There was also a certain foreboding in the aftermath of the Kennedy and King assassinations and a feeling that things might get worse before they got better—if they ever did.

Largely in reaction to the civil rights movement, segregationist Alabama Democratic governor George Wallace launched a southern populist campaign for president under the banner of the American Independent Party. He selected Air Force general Curtis LeMay as his running mate and would go on to carry five southern states. There were anti-war riots in the streets of Chicago at the Democratic Convention that August. With the fresh images of what appeared to be an emerging anarchy, Nixon launched a campaign based on restoring law and order with a secret plan to end the war.

We hear about how angry and divided our country is today, but in many respects current times appear tame by comparison to 1968. And it was all playing out to political protest songs; conflict and crisis was driving art. While the lyrics of Bob Dylan captured the essence of the times for many, the screaming sound of John Lennon's voice on "Revolution" hit home with me.

To save money and help out at home, I decided to commute to school from Pine Street for my final semester (September 1968 to January 1969). Too bad I did not begin college with that plan, as I had my best semester while still working the night shift and spending an hour and half each day in the car. It also made it a little bit easier to say goodbye to the college years, although the timing of my draft notice was a bit unnerving. It said I had to report within twenty-four hours of my last exam. I quickly returned to the draft board to complete my OCS paperwork which allowed me to postpone my reporting date to May in exchange for the added one-year commitment.

In early '69, with the clock ticking towards induction day, I landed a job as a substitute teacher for a third-grade class at Forwood Elementary School in north Wilmington. The regular teacher was on a six-week maternity leave. The kids were great, and I jumped out of bed every day excited to go to work. In the final weeks before reporting for duty, I traveled to Florida for the first time—and ended up returning three weeks later. The first trip was to visit my brother Tom, who had broken his femur in a car accident while assigned to the Jacksonville Naval Air Station. My sister Bernadette and I drove straight through, while my mother came down on the train. Mom was fifty, and it was her first long distance trip. No one ever was more excited to see a palm tree.

The second trip was my first "spring break" experience. Having already completed four and half years of school and just turning twenty-three, I joined Sharon and some of the other Delaware gang in Daytona Beach. Better late than never! The most memorable part of the trip was the day Sharon and I drove down to Cape Canaveral to see the thirty-five-story Saturn V rocket that was being prepped to send our astronauts to the moon. Less high tech was our drive home to Delaware, experiencing multiple flat tires and having to negotiate with southern gas station owners to buy more retreads. After Florida, the remaining days as a civilian moved too quickly.

PART II

The *Army*

Chapter 12

Ft. Dix and Ft. Leonard Wood, May–September 1969

"You idiot, Armor OCS closed last year. Either sign the papers or get the hell out of here!"

On that early morning in May after saying my goodbyes to family and catching the train, I soon arrived at the Philadelphia Military Induction Center. To my surprise, my orders were to report to Ft. Dix, New Jersey. I had expected to go to Ft. Jackson, South Carolina, where many Delawareans were being sent at that time for basic training. I met up with a friend from grade school, Chuck Ward, who had received orders for Ft. Dix as well. We had until midnight to report. At that time, my brother Curt and his wife, Linda, were living in Willingboro, New Jersey, only seventeen miles from Dix, so I suggested we contact them to see if we might have our last meal there and report at midnight. Arriving late would prove to be a mistake, since it would cost us a night's sleep.

After dinner, Curt drove the two nervous recruits to the sprawling army post and pulled up to the sign that read, "Welcome, U.S. Army Reception Station, Ft Dix, NJ." It was about 11:45. "Reception," implying at least in my mind something positive, would prove to be a misnomer if there ever was one. For the next several hours we would be screamed at and harassed by everyone with a rank above Private, E-2. After hours of completing forms and getting multiple shots in both arms, we were funneled through a uniform warehouse having the wrong size of everything shoved into your arms—with blood running down them from all the shots. By the time we were marched to a barracks it was about 4:00 in the morning. Before being able to lay down, we received a class on how to make a bed, Army-style.

No sooner had I closed my eyes when the cadre of Reception Station harassers were screaming at us to fall-out and assemble. Immediately, we were sent to the Army barbers, who enjoyed asking how we wanted our hair styled as they took roughly twenty seconds to shave us bald. There were more forms to complete such as the one for the $10,000 insurance payment in case we were killed in Vietnam. Now that one got my attention.

After several days of "in-processing," the olive drab buses pulled up and transported us to the basic training brigade. After we formed up outside the buses, an overweight Sergeant First Class (E-7) wearing a "Smokey the Bear" hat stepped forward and said, "Which one of you lunkheads is John Riley?" I ran forward, and Drill Sergeant Crouch looked at me reading off a sheet of orders. "Riley, it says here, you are a college graduate (I was one of four in the platoon of approximately fifty trainees) and that you are headed to Officer Candidate School. You will be my platoon guide. Appoint four squad leaders and get these men into the barracks, assign them a bunk and be back here in fifteen minutes."

I stood there for a second, in shock, wondering what the hell this was going to mean for me. I turned to the platoon and asked who else had completed college. I appointed each to be my squad leaders. One of these trainees was a guy from Kansas named Leland Parks. It turned out that Lee had a masters' degree in ecology with a concentration in snakes, of all things. Lee would become my best friend for the next five months, both at Dix and at Ft. Leonard Wood, Missouri.

While in the Reception Station, I was handed a pair of boots that did not fit properly. On each of the initial days as we would march to ranges along what was known as "Infantry Walk," the pain in my Achilles grew more intense. When I reached the point of not being

Leading the platoon on "Infantry Walk"

able to take another step, I asked Sgt. Crouch if I could exchange my boots. He sent me to the supply sergeant in the building behind the barracks. I walked up the NCO behind the counter, told him Sgt. Crouch had sent me and asked if I could exchange my boots.

Before the supply sergeant could answer, we were interrupted by the company First Sergeant. I made the mistake of addressing him as "Sergeant" without adding "First." The next several minutes were a lesson in military courtesy, delivered without any courtesy. Barrel-chested First Sergeant Royos was an intimidating figure with a stern face half hidden under his drill sergeant hat. He was clearly intent on making sure I remembered him. A bit shaken by the experience, I made it a point to try to stay out of the First Sergeant's way in the coming weeks.

As we made our way through the initial weeks of basic training, it appeared that something was not right with SFC Crouch. He would show up late and leave early, and he seemed to be easier on us than what the other platoons were facing from their drill

sergeants. Frankly, he began leaving it to me to run the platoon. You could tell it was sticking deep in the craw of the senior drill sergeant, Orville Scott. Scott was a former Marine who exuded military from every pore of his body. I fixed eyes on him the minute I arrived and determined this was a man I should avoid as much as possible.

One interesting arrangement in Alpha Company was that a group of National Guardsmen and Reservists from New York City were segregated into one platoon. You could tell SFC Scott hated them as much as he did my platoon's drill sergeant. He only

A Marine at heart, Drill Sgt. Orville Scott

referred to them as "draft dodgers." Unlike the National Guard units of today, these units were typically made up of elites from certain areas around the country. In his searing 2018 history of the war, *Vietnam: An Epic Tragedy*, author Max Hastings recounts the myriad loopholes used by many to escape service or vastly lower their risk. Especially interesting was his explanation of how National Football League teams arranged to join local Guard units. "A Philadelphia footballer who likewise avoided Vietnam said, 'If we had been called up, the Eagles would have been left without a backfield,'" Hastings wrote.

In the case of our basic training company, nearly all the New York Guardsmen were in law school. No doubt the deans at New York University had rich connections with the local draft board and worked closely with the students to ensure their acceptance. Scott sometimes poured on the heat to harass the "draft dodgers." But while they resented the extra attention, they had the last laugh knowing they would soon be back on the streets of New York, starting their careers while the rest of us inched ever closer to the "two-way rifle range" in Southeast Asia.

Somewhere around week four, Drill Sergeant Crouch failed to show up, and I was ordered to meet Sgt Scott in his office. When I got there, Scott informed me that Crouch had been relieved, and he would be personally taking charge of our platoon. "Your platoon is way behind, so we will drill every night until I think you are up the standards—now get out of here."

The timing could not have been worse. I had received permission for an eight-hour leave from Crouch to go home that coming Sunday to graduate from the University of Delaware. I didn't want to mention it to Scott, suspecting that SFC Crouch had not properly cleared it. After several eighteen-hour days playing catch up with the other platoons, I decided to approach Scott about the trip to Newark, fully expecting he would tell me to get out of his sight. When I asked, he stared at me like I had two heads, finally saying he would discuss it with First Sergeant Royos. It sounded like the kiss of death.

To my great surprise, I found myself being picked up that Sunday morning by my brother and we headed down the New Jersey Turnpike. First, we would stop to see my mom, and she promised a great breakfast. I told her I just wanted to stuff myself with warm toast and drink an unlimited number of Cokes—two staples I had greatly missed during my initial month in the army.

Based on the emotions I felt when I walked in the house to hug my mom, you would have thought I had just returned from a year overseas. Those feelings would greatly escalate as I rushed from breakfast to meet Sharon, so

Private Riley joins fiancée Sharon for graduation, June 1969

we could graduate together. I probably said hello to a hundred friends at graduation that day, but I only remember one person—my beautiful fiancée. I think Winston Churchill himself could have delivered the commencement address and I would not have heard a word. (It was not the late prime minister. UD had recruited the superintendent of a Virginia women's prison.) Given only eight hours to make the round trip to Newark, Delaware, I immediately began to count the minutes before I had to head back to that charming spot we were now referring to as "Ft. Ding-a-ling."

Over my quick breakfast that morning, I glanced at the local paper and caught the news about a controversial battle for Hill 937 in what was known as the A Shau Valley along the Laotian border. The famous 101st Airborne Division had taken the hill while suffering more than four hundred casualties.

The Battle for Hill 937 became known as "Hamburger Hill." This event, along with the more famous Tet Offensive of the previous year were U.S. victories in a military sense, but they greatly fueled the country's growing anti-war fever. The stories of Tet and Hamburger Hill would be brought to life years later in literature and on film with strong Delaware connections. Mark Bowden, author of *Black Hawk Down* and "writer in residence" at the University of Delaware, authored a gripping 2018 account of Tet in *Hue 1968,* and Tim Quill, son of Delaware banker Leonard Quill, had a major role in the 1987 film *Hamburger Hill.* Tim's proud parents hosted a Delaware premier at the Concord Mall Cinema. Speaking to the packed theater prior to this unique Wilmington event, Tim's mom wanted to make everyone aware that he did not learn the profanity-laced language in the movie growing up in their home.

Tim Quill wasn't the only Delaware connection to the story that took place in the A Shau Valley. A year prior to the battle for Hill 937, brigades of the 1st Calvary Division and the 101st Airborne conducted a major assault into the valley under the code name "Operation Delaware." Although labeled a success by the military, 142 Americans died during the course of the three-week campaign.

Back at Dix, I had little time to reflect on the quick trip home as we were moving into the next phase of training—gas chamber, hand grenades, night infiltration course and qualifying on the M-14. Physical training (PT) was also ramping up. PT was led by a human push-up machine—an African-American drill sergeant named Harley, who referred to all of us as "lunkheads." Harley would do half his push-ups with one arm so he could point out those of us struggling to keep up. And feeling our unit needed remedial attention, SFC Scott was bearing down on me non-stop. Although the leadership role kept me off the dreaded kitchen patrol (KP), I was beginning to regret being picked as a leader and wanted to melt into the background like most of my fellow trainees.

At a morning roll call formation that week, several of us were called out and told to report to a building near the brigade headquarters. Once seated, in came the battalion commander, Major Collett—a man who from the moment I first saw him reminded me of the famous actor James Cagney. Collett announced that we had all been assigned to an upcoming OCS class. He stated that we would have to sign papers committing to serve an additional year and then he exited. I thought, *No surprises so far.*

When I originally met with the recruiter some months before induction, I was told I could select from two non-combat arms (I choose Quartermaster and Ordnance, knowing the chances of selection were slim to none) and one combat: Artillery, Armor, or Infantry. Of course, the advice I received from everyone was anything but Infantry! In college and during the initial weeks of army training, you heard rather intimidating statements about the life expectancy of infantry lieutenants in Vietnam, the most optimistic of which was about two weeks. Although I had no interest in tanks, I assumed they were of little use in the Mekong Delta and decided to attend the Armor School. I had signed a deal with the US Army. What could possibly go wrong?

So there I was staring down at a sheet of paper that said I had been assigned to OCS Class 7-70 (i.e., the seventh class scheduled to be commissioned in 1970, approximately nine-and-half months from that day). The class number was followed by the words: US Army Infantry School, Ft. Benning, Georgia.

As I sat stunned, guys all around me were signing their papers and leaving the classroom. I timidly raised my hand to get the attention of the officer in charge. I confidently explained to him that there was a mistake in my orders, that I had signed up for Armor OCS. He leaned down close to my face and said, "You idiot, Armor OCS closed last year. Either sign the papers or get the hell out of here!"

I signed and began counting the days.

At a morning formation during our last week, Sgt. Scott told me to report to First Sgt. Royos' office. The very sound of Royos' name made me immediately uneasy, so many thoughts rushed through my brain as I jogged to his office. When I arrived in front of Royos' desk, he told me to stand at ease as he shuffled some papers in front of him. I looked down at his tough exterior in perfectly pressed army fatigues with a Combat Infantryman Badge (CIB) proudly displayed above his breast pocket. (The CIB was the award that separated the combat soldier from those in the Army who served in a rear echelon role.)

Approaching his office, I thought I was in trouble, but Royos' mood seemed non-threatening. He looked at me and said, "Riley, the drill sergeants and I met this week and you have been unanimously chosen as the outstanding soldier in the company—in addition, you have been selected as the outstanding leader in the company. You will be presented the awards by Colonel Hadley at graduation on Saturday in front of the brigade. Congratulations and please tell your family they are welcome to attend."

Shock and relief would barely describe my state of mind at that moment.

Graduation Day was full of pomp and military precision. Some families had traveled hundreds of miles to attend and spend a few hours with their soldier before they moved on to Advanced Individual Training (AIT), wherever it might be. I was puzzled by my orders sending me to Combat Engineer training in a place I had never heard of, Ft. Leonard Wood Missouri. I would be leaving on a chartered flight the next morning from Philadelphia.

When we got back to the company area, we got some bad news. Our company commander, 1LT Monson, had rescinded our half day pass and we were ordered to stay in and clean until lights out that night—just more Army harassment. Sharon had driven up from Delaware with my mother and a couple dozen hard-shell crabs and we had planned a picnic. I hated to tell them that I couldn't leave. I did not even know when I would see Sharon again. Before I could tell them, my friend Lee Parks approached begging me to do something—his wife, Emily had flown out from Kansas to catch a few hours with him. The only chance for both of us was Scott, the former combat Marine I thought had a heart made of stone.

I caught Scott near his office and asked if I could speak to him. I told him Lee's story and threw in my own for good measure. At first, he said there was nothing he could do about it, the company commander had issued an order. As I started to turn around, he said to wait. He then picked up the phone and called Royos. Hanging up the phone, he looked

straight at me and said, "You and Parks find a way to get out of here so
that no one knows you left—be back by 2100 hours."

While I would go on to be impressed by other military leaders with
whom I came in contact over the next two and a half years, none would
surpass the high esteem I felt for Scott and Royos. In eight short weeks,
I had moved from an initial fear and loathing of these two men to a state
of respect and admiration. They were both as hard as nails and no doubt
had fought valiantly in the jungles of Vietnam. They had a rather minor
role to play in the grand scheme of a war involving millions, but they
performed their work with pride and dedication. I was truly the reluctant
recruit as I headed off to Ft. Dix in May of 1969, but by July I began to
think of myself in a different way—as a soldier. I knew I was a product of
Rojas and Scott; I would never forget them.

As the war grinded on that June and July, more politicians, mostly
Democrats, added their voices to those of the protesters. At first, the
conflict was JFK's war; it was he who raised the number of U.S. military
advisors to 16,000. But it was Johnson who deepened the American
commitment, sending in the ground combat forces that General
Westmoreland and others said would be needed to defeat this determined
enemy. In addition to the thousands of college kids protesting the war,
the media, led by Walter Cronkite, "the most trusted man in America,"
had turned against the war and U.S. policy. As I was completing basic
training, *LIFE* magazine published an issue with the face of a young
man on the cover, Army specialist William C. Gearing, Jr., who was
one of the 240 American soldiers who had been killed during a single
week in June. His penetrating eyes stared out at the nation in a way that
seemed to ask, "Why?" The issue was entitled *Faces of the American Dead
in Vietnam: One Week's Toll.*

Since the timing of that cover story coincided with reporting on the
losses at "Hamburger Hill," many believed all the soldiers featured had
died in the battle for Hill 937, a hill that was immediately abandoned
after being taken. Some believe this *LIFE* issue did as much to sour
middle American on the war as any other event. President Nixon had
been elected in part that previous November on his so called "secret plan
to end the war." Americans were getting impatient, but I couldn't think
about that—I was headed to my next training stop in Missouri before
continuing to Officer Candidate School.

Promoted out of basic training to the rank of E-2, I naïvely assumed
some of the petty harassment would subside. However, upon our

arrival at Ft. Leonard Wood on a hot humid July night, we had NCOs shouting at us from all sides. Following the standard Army long wait we would endure the standard drill sergeant "Your ass is grass and I'm the lawnmower" welcome speech.

Leaving Ft. Dix, I was feeling pretty good about myself. I had not only weathered my first nine weeks in the Army, I had excelled. Expecting the worst from the Army, I was pleasantly surprised by the quality of some of the cadre I had encountered. Suddenly, the depressing feelings from the initial days at Ft. Dix were returning. I worried I was about to enter a darker phase at Ft. Leonard Wood. This would prove to be correct.

Several aspects of Leonard Wood would bother me. First, the drill sergeants, particularly the senior drill sergeant of unit A-1-1 (Alpha Company, 1st Battalion, 1st Brigade), ruled almost exclusively by intimidation and punishment. Second, our sleeping hours were reduced to six hours every night—lights out at 2200 hours and back on at 0400. I had no leadership opportunity—platoon guides and squad leaders seemed to be assigned randomly or because the drill sergeant thought they might be physically intimidating.

The biggest issue, however, at Leonard Wood was racial tension. It was 1969, just a year since the assassination of Dr. Martin Luther King, and the rumor was that the courts in Detroit and Chicago had sentenced most of the young black men in my Ft. Leonard Wood AIT company to the Army. It was hard to blame these guys for some of the anger at white America that seethed out of them, but it was not a problem I had much control over. My immediate problem was that I had an angry 6' 8" black man in the bunk next to mine nicknamed "Big Evil."

By the end of our first week in AIT, I was mentally and emotionally exhausted and counting the days until it would be over. In these down moods, I would often dream that there would be a change of thinking by the politicians in Washington and Hanoi and peace would break out. One positive development from Basic to AIT was that you were generally deemed "off duty" from about midday Saturday until Sunday at 5:00. The first weekend, I went down to the service club on main post to find a phone to call home. Typically, we would wait an hour or more to use a phone and the calls were restricted to a few minutes. It always seemed to me that the juke box in these centers only played the song "One" by Three Dog Night. Its message of loneliness was reflective of my mood during my first Army summer. Try as I might, I could not shake the lyrics from my head.

During our second week at Wood, I received a message to report to the company clerk. I don't remember his name, but he was a pleasant young guy from the Northeast, and I would soon learn he was the post golf champion. He said, "I see you were captain of the University of Delaware golf team. Any chance you could have your clubs shipped out? I have a car and can keep them in my trunk. We can head out of here to the post course on Saturdays after you get off. And by the way, there are some serious golf hustlers on this post."

The course had a great name, Pine Valley. Although not to be confused with the #1 course in the world located in Clementon, New Jersey, I have wonderful memories of my time there. The clerk was correct about the golf hustlers. I was probably the lowest handicap of the bunch, but this was a cash hungry group of NCOs who would work every angle to win a buck. On Sundays we would play thirty-six holes, a normal round in the morning followed by a rather athletic endeavor in the afternoon—eighteen holes with only one club while sprinting between shots. One day I won a month's pay (about $90) in the morning round, only to lose it all back in the afternoon.

Located near the Ozarks in the Mark Twain National Forest, "Lost-in-the-Woods" as we referred to it, was teeming with wildlife. One night on bivouac, I was driven out of my tent by marauding skunks; on guard duty I had an encounter with a bobcat; and every time you turned around someone was killing a moccasin or a rattlesnake. My friend Lee Parks would always try to rescue the snakes, admonishing the troops to leave them alone. When someone would yell "snake!" Lee would come running and not hesitate to snatch it up with his bare hand, poisonous or not.

On the evening of July 20, 1969, the company hooked up a small TV on the back step of our barracks, and we all watched the grainy images in amazement as Neil Armstrong became the first man to walk on the moon. It was a moment of tremendous pride for everyone. We were at a point where our country was greatly divided, but at least for a shining moment, on a barrack's step in the back woods of Missouri, we were all together.

As we moved through August, the blazing Missouri heat was starting to moderate and with some rainy days, the thick dust that hung in the air and filled your eyes during 0430 PT (physical training) also began to disappear. Unfortunately, the racial tension continued, and you held your breath as threats were fired back and forth through the ranks. Word of serious incidents, including use of weapons were common but unconfirmed. The irrational conduct of the company drill sergeants also continued. You could smoke on breaks, but you could not drink water. One day about fifty of us answered the call to give blood for the troops in Vietnam. When we returned to the company area, they accused us of trying to dodge training and proceeded to put us through an hour of PT, including low crawling through the mud and dirt until we nearly passed out.

In early September, course completion day finally arrived, and we were told to assemble to receive our orders. Drill Sergeant Biggs stood in front of the formation and began to read off the next duty station for every soldier by alphabetical order—it was going to be a long time before he got to the Rs. I think I could say with some certainty, that the first forty to fifty names were followed by, "Vietnam!" Biggs made it as dramatic as he could. He seemed to take pleasure in delivering what most felt was very bad news. The few of us going to OCS or expecting a special duty assignment (my friend Lee Parks was expecting orders for Ft. Devins, Massachusetts for a research project) were beginning to fear our orders were not going to materialize and we would be headed to Vietnam. Finally, they got to the first officer candidate and the words, "Infantry OCS, Ft Benning, Georgia" rang out. I never thought I would be glad to hear those words.

I had received the correct orders, but the OCS start date would not be until the end of September. This being the Army, I would not have time to relax or enjoy extra leave. I was placed on fourteen straight days of dreaded KP duty—the final Leonard Wood insult.

Chapter 13

Officer Candidate School, Ft Benning, Georgia, September 1969–March 1970

"So, what can they do about it, send us to Vietnam?"

The following passage appears in *The History of the Infantry Officer Candidate School, Fort Benning, Georgia.* It is the best explanation I have read about the stressful, often petty and irrational, but sometimes exhilarating twenty-four weeks I spent at Ft. Benning, Georgia.

> *The OCS system is designed to place the candidate under physical, mental, and emotional stress to simulate, as closely as possible, the stress and fatigue of combat. Only in this way can the candidate receive an evaluation as to his ability to work and react under such pressure …*

To get to Columbus, Georgia, I had teamed up with two guys I met at AIT, Dick Bennett and Larry Miles. Bennett was from Connecticut, and one day following our commission, he announced to our eternal disbelief that he had been granted conscientious objector status and was free to go home. There was no doubt in our minds that it was a "con-job," but Dick was not the only one working the system like this.

A graduate of Lafayette College, Larry was smart, talented, and confident, but he was as apprehensive as Dick and I were about what we were about to face. A good athlete in college, Larry liked to say that his greatest accomplishment was holding basketball star Bill Bradley to thirty-six points when he guarded him in a game against Princeton. In our Army competition, Larry would easily lead all scorers, sometimes pouring in thirty-six points himself.

After arrival at the OCS Brigade, we were ordered to change into our fatigues and quickly join a formation where there would be a roll call followed by further instructions. While standing in formation, TAC (Training, Advising, and Counseling) officers swarmed through the ranks, examining every inch of us from boots to haircut. They did not like anything they saw and within minutes most of us were responding to the command, "Drop and knock em' out" (that is, do push-ups until your arms burned).

The majority of military personnel who deployed to Vietnam served in rear echelon roles that supported the actual combat infantryman in the field. So if you simply allowed the draft to take you, there was a chance you would not be fired at in anger and you would complete your obligation in only two years. However, if you attended Infantry OCS, there was near zero chance you would avoid combat. Every day of OCS was concentrated on the task of getting you ready for the real thing. Through basic training and AIT, I had harbored thoughts that maybe I would escape this fate, but now I was in an environment that told me my deployment was inevitable—so inevitable, that when we anticipated the wrath of our TAC officers to one of our minor acts of rebellion, everyone would shrug and say, "So, what can they do about it, send us to Vietnam?"

At times, it was difficult to see the connection between the program and the task of getting you prepared to fight. Take mealtime, for example. I vividly recall my first experience at the mess hall. After struggling to complete the required chin-ups on a cross-bar before the entrance, I was staring up at Lt. Bailey. I had been watching him perform his near sadistic ritual, screaming into the face of the 54th Company candidates as we worked our way towards him and lunch. About 6'4" and 200 lbs., Bailey was a loud and intimidating figure standing a step above me. As I dropped from the chin-up bar I shouted out as required, "Sir, Candidate Riley requests permission to enter the mess hall."

Bailey leaned down in front of my face and while scanning my uniform announced, "Riley, who the hell do you think you are, Ben Hogan!"

My mind raced. *How did he know I played golf?*

I answered, "Sir, Candidate Riley—no, I do not think I am Ben Hogan."

He responded, "Well, Candidate, why are you wearing a golf suit?"

What the hell is this man talking about, I thought. No time to answer, I was sent to the end of the line to start over. I was soon tipped off that the term "golf suit" referred to a fatigue shirt not having the same fade as the pants. Since we had to don a freshly starched, clean uniform each day we were not in the field, it could be tricky to get the shirt and pants to match.

After finally getting past Bailey, I got my first glimpse of the mess hall—TAC Officers darting from table to table accusing candidates of the minor offenses such as the fork or spoon being in the wrong position, or barking out the constant refrain, "Are you eyeballing me candidate?" I was rapidly losing my appetite, but no problem there—as soon as I sat down someone yelled out, "Candidates, clear the mess hall!" *Dear God*, I thought, *six more months of this*!

Every day we were handed multiple tasks with only enough time to complete half. Part of the game was to determine what the priorities were and what were the things you could postpone. We learned to rise after lights out and find a way to prepare for the next day. If reveille was scheduled for 5:30, you got up at 5:00. I spent many an evening sitting on a toilet with my bayonet slicing the stubborn Georgia red clay from my boots and applying a spit shine, because TACs would meander through the early morning formation checking every pair. The toilet stall also functioned as study hall.

Another game with the TACs and OCS was to "expect the unexpected." TACs were primed to fill each day with unwanted surprises. Exhausted after day one, we turned out the lights, craving a full night's rest. While we were told that reveille would not be until 0530, the next morning the lights came on before 0500 and TACs were screaming at us to be outside for a run in five minutes.

Across the street from the 5th OCS Battalion stood the famous airborne jump towers. These crane-like devices would lift a parachute and paratroop trainee straight up 250 feet and then drop them. It was the last step before paratroopers made their first live jump. The jump towers were surrounded by the "Airborne Track" where troops could be seen and heard on an almost continuous basis making the loop. Their cadence rang out across the field and it was not an optimistic tune.

The Jump Towers

If I die in the old drop zone
Box me up and ship me home
Pin my wings upon my chest
Then bury me in the leaning rest

As we stood in the dark that morning, we heard the voice for the first time of Lt. Colonel Charles Mendoza. Mendoza could have been the model for the pinnacle of military bearing and everything Ft. Benning stood for. The young, tall, handsome, Airborne/Ranger/Special Forces veteran was bedecked with awards for valor and Vietnam service. He was also in great shape and could run like hell. We were about to join him for the first of many trips around the Airborne Track.

I always hated my skinny body, but today I would thank God for it and for my ability to run (Scotty Duncan required that we stay in shape for golf by running and playing pick-up basketball against the UD coaching staff). By the time we had completed our first trip around the track, bodies were everywhere. Guys were throwing up on themselves and tumbling out of the ranks onto the ground. Just when you thought it was over, you could hear panicked voices from ahead—"we're going around again!" More bodies fell out. By the time we finished that morning I was one of less than half the company still standing in the formation, our chests heaving as we bent forward with our hands on our knees. After barely breaking a sweat, Mendoza let us know he was not impressed with our performance and that we could look forward to many more mornings of the "Mendoza Mile!"

Some of those who had trouble that morning and would continue struggling with the "Mendoza Mile" (which was actually two to three miles at near sprint speed) in the weeks ahead were what was known as the "prior service" candidates. The very NCOs that could have been training me only days before were now peers, but they did not have the advantage I had of having been physically conditioned by eighteen weeks of Basic and AIT. On the other hand, they knew far more about the Army than the TAC officers who ruled over us.

These men, mostly sons of the South, quickly became the go-to guys for answers and advice. Several of them had been in the Special Forces and all had been in combat. In addition to Green Berets, there were veterans of the 101st Airborne Division, the 1st Infantry Division, the Americal Division, and the 1st Air Calvary. A few, like Clarence "Ranger" Dodd, Don Richards, Mario Peterson, and Al Hecker could have run the company. (During his tour of duty in Germany, Hecker was a guard at Spandau Prison whose sole occupants were Nazi war criminals Albert Speer and Rudolf Hess.) There was something reassuring to the college kids like me that these men had been under fire in the much-hated

Vietnam War—and were still willing to go through the challenge of OCS and go back to "Nam" again and take on even more responsibility.

Soon, sporting "Win in Vietnam" stickers on our clipboards, we were off to our first leadership class. We settled into the classroom for the normal challenge of fighting to stay awake, when onto the stage walked Lt. Col. Weldon Honeycutt of Hamburger Hill fame. The embers of that fire were still smoldering as Senators Kennedy and McGovern had recently taken to the floor of the Senate to directly criticize the military leadership for unnecessary casualties. Honeycutt used his time that day as much to attack Kennedy and his other critics as to discuss leadership. All I remember was that by the time he finished, I was convinced I was not going to live more than a year.

The focus of much of the criticism of Hamburger Hill was that commanders abandoned Hill 937 after it was taken. In retrospect I believe the critics missed the point. Under General Westmoreland a strategy was implemented not unlike that at least partially deployed by Grant and Sherman in Virginia and Georgia during the Civil War—make the war so cruel and devastating to the enemy that they determine the price is too high to continue. This was manifested through the rather morbid scorekeeping method of "body counts." In the case of Hill 937, Honeycutt and other commanders touted a body count of 630 with vastly higher overall battle casualties due to the concentration of air strikes and artillery bombardments. I can assure you that the Colonel was not about to apologize that day at Ft. Benning.

As OCS training kicked into high gear, we faced critical milestone tests. If you failed, you were out and on the next plane to Southeast Asia. Already losing candidates based on test failures, we were soon introduced to the student evaluation system. Basically, this was a forced self-policing system, dubbed the "Top 5 and Bottom 5."

At the end of every month, we were handed a sheet of paper with ten blank spaces—we had to fill in the names. The Bottom 5 would immediately be "thrown off the Island" and in every case I was aware of, sent to Vietnam. Although we were warned not to discuss our selections, it was inevitable someone would approach you. I remember being shaken in the middle of the night one time, and hearing my name whispered, "Riles, Riles, who did you put on your bottom 5?" It was a dirty game of survival, but probably did weed out some of the less qualified. And we all worried a group might silently collaborate and you would find yourself on the way out the door.

We received little information about the outside world, but word had leaked that President Nixon was going address the nation on the evening of December 15, 1969 to announce troop withdrawals as a part

of his "Vietnamization" strategy. This was a plan where U.S. forces were to gradually transition from a direct combat role to more of a support and training role for the ARVN (Army of the Republic of Vietnam). As part of the company area clean-up crew that December night, I decided to risk turning on the TV in the "Day Room" (a recreation room that was never available except for cleaning).

Was this the break we were all hoping for? I wondered. Would Nixon announce a significant reduction?

As with most American youth in 1969, I was not a Nixon fan. US deaths that year were running up to a thousand a month and more than ever, it was hard to see the purpose. While I was disappointed by his announced reduction of 50,000, to below 500,000, the fact was this may have

Wishful thinking – Candidate Riley flashing the peace sign in front of the 54th Company barracks

ultimately saved my life. This would be small comfort to the 10,000 who would die in the difficult years ahead.

By time Christmas rolled around, we were in our twelfth week and had achieved a status called "Intermediate Candidate." It did not mean much, other than the fact that OCS was basically shutting down for two weeks and I would receive my first extended leave. After a short visit with the family in Wilmington, I flew out on Christmas Day to spend a week with Sharon and her family in Clinton, Iowa. It was a rare white Christmas in Delaware and we had to put chains around my father's bald tires (a common practice before snow tires) to gain traction on the unplowed roads. Dad had his flaws, but he was determined that day to get me to the Philadelphia airport. After changing planes in Chicago, we landed on a snowy runway at the Quad Cities, Illinois airport that night. I was thrilled to be with Sharon and her family, but I would soon be counting down the days to when I had to return.

The time came quickly, but I had not been able to get a flight. I was finally able to book a train from Clinton to Chicago to New Orleans to

Columbus, Georgia. It would be a twenty-five-hour trip. I kissed Sharon goodbye at 4:30 in the morning and, with her stepfather at the wheel, set out across the frozen Iowa landscape to find a rail siding outside of town. As we drove away, I could hear the voice of Mary Travers of Peter, Paul, and Mary on the radio singing, "Leaving on a Jet Plane." My spirits sank deeper as she sang about leaving her love, and about how they would marry when she returned. To this day, the beautiful melody written by John Denver takes me back to that early morning drive.

While mostly hating to leave Sharon, I was down again on my overall predicament and worried that I was facing disciplinary action if I arrived late. How did I get myself into this situation? *Pay attention to detail, Candidate,* a constant refrain of the TAC officers rang in my brain.

There was one delay after another as we headed into the deep south. By the time the taxi dropped me at the company area Sunday morning I was six hours late. I didn't know what would happen, but I feared the worst—expulsion or a recycle back to the beginning of the program. As I started up the walk to the front door of the barracks, I heard Lt. Barron coming from behind scream,

"Riley, you are AWOL—get down and start knocking them out!"

He then walked right past me and into the barracks. With my duffel bag beside me, outfitted in my dress green uniform, I looked a little out of place on the sidewalk in what we referred to as the front leaning rest, the starting position for a push up. I continued in that position for more than an hour, suspecting that Barron or another TAC was watching and ready to pounce if I attempted to move. Finally, I decided to risk getting up and tiptoed into the building. I never heard another word about my AWOL status.

We were soon headed to remote parts of the sprawling Ft. Benning military reservation for training on more complex weapons such as artillery, armor, personnel carriers, heavy machine guns, helicopters, and close air support. Everything seemed secondary, though, to the looming thought of Ranger Week. In week seventeen, we would be turned over to Ranger instructors for seven days and placed on continuous patrol. This exercise was designed to be the closest simulation possible to what a sustained mission would be like in Vietnam. We were to go through a series of role plays where each of us would assume a leadership position. We could expect to move cross country non-stop, with approximately two to four hours sleep a day with limited water and rations. It would all culminate with a "quick time" march to Victory Pond at the Ranger Camp where we would have to complete the Ranger Water Confidence Test. Again, failure to complete meant being dropped from the program—a cruel fate after eighteen weeks.

It had been intermittently cold or wet throughout Ranger Week. Another cold front blew in just in time for our February swim. After an exhausting seven days, we arrived at the Ranger Center and were placed in the bleachers as instructors explained the purpose of the Water Confidence Test. The idea was to instill confidence in you by having you overcome or at least face your fear of heights and water.

Ready for Ranger Week

While listening to the orientation, we were looking at a thirty-five-foot telephone pole. From the top of the pole, a log with two steps in the middle stretched out above the lake, followed by a rope that stretched thirty feet to another pole. Near the end of the rope, the famous Ranger Tab was blowing in the wind. Our objective was to make it to the tab and then drop into the lake.

As I sat there, my mind was so focused on the problem before me that I lost track of the wind and cold. I did not react when the officers started calling for the student executive officer. It had been a week since I was in that position, assisting the student company commander Mario Peterson. It so happened that Peterson had been injured that morning on the demanding march and was taken back to main post. Since leaders always go first, the Rangers were looking for the top guy to kick-off the Confidence Test. Peterson wasn't there so now they wanted number two. Al Hecker was sitting next to me calling, "Babe, Babe … that's you—you're the XO—you're going first!"

As I was trying to catch my breath and get my legs under me, Al grabbed me and said, "Babe, don't look down when you climb the pole, and when you drop, look up at the sky or you will tip over and land on your face." Al knew what he was talking about—he had taught small unit tactics for the Rangers and served many times as a demonstrator for the confidence test.

Every step of the process required that you ask for permission from the Rangers. I started, "Sir, Candidate Riley requests permission to climb the pole."

"Climb the pole, candidate," the officer-in-charge shouted through a bull horn. As I tried to stabilize myself at the top of the pole, I requested permission to walk the log.

Next thing I heard was, "Goddamit Riley, sound off like you have a pair!"

At that second, I nearly slipped off as a gust of wind hit me while I was trying to figure out which foot to put on the log first. Finally, I made it and soon dangled from the rope.

Then I heard, "Drop candidate!"

Hitting the water wearing fatigues and combat boots sent me straight to the bottom of the lake. The shock of the forty-degree water jolted my mind and body. I remember looking up from the bottom of the muddy lake as I squatted my legs to spring myself off the bottom. I gasped for air when I cleared the surface. After a short swim to the dock, I slipped on the ladder climbing out of the lake and banged my body on the rungs as I headed again to the bottom. But at that moment I only cared about one thing, I had cleared the last big hurdle of OCS. I had been dreading Ranger Week and the Water Confidence Test for months and I had met the challenge. Most importantly, I had met it under the intense gaze of my 120 remaining fellow officer candidates. (We had begun our quest with 200.) As I headed towards the exit, someone handed me a towel before I jumped on the heated bus that was waiting. I never felt better in my life.

For the last phase of OCS, we carried the title of senior candidates. We were identified by the white scarf we wore around our neck. Junior candidates, or "smacks" as we called them, saluted us on post. We were allowed civilian clothes in our lockers and had weekends free from noon Saturday. I played golf one weekend in what was essentially a showdown. For months, several guys in the company had been taking bets as to who would win a match between myself and an officer candidate from Boston. He had also played in college and talked a good game. Wearing army dress shoes and using borrowed clubs, I shot a 73 in my first round of golf in seven months. I won by sixteen strokes. My old coach, Scotty Duncan, would have been proud.

At formation a couple nights before graduation, they read out our orders for our first duty assignment. As the names were being called, I was excited to learn that twenty-five of us were ordered to Ft. Knox for Armor Officer Training. With Armor on my original recruitment papers, I was certain I would be on that list—especially after they had just called Bennett and Miles' names, two college-op guys I had started with. But when they got to my name it was announced that I would be assigned as a TAC Officer, back at Benning Infantry OCS. I couldn't believe my ears. I didn't know if I was more upset about missing the Armor opportunity or that I would be going back through OCS again.

After breaking formation, I charged into Captain West's office. He was not around, but I was told to talk to First Sergeant Quattrociocchi, or "Q" as we called him. He tried to blow me off, but I stood my ground, figuring I would outrank this guy in twenty-four hours (which is only technically correct—1st sergeants command a lot of respect in the Army). I argued that based on my original recruitment papers and my status on the Commandant's List (top 10% of graduates), I should have been the first one selected for the Armor School. He told me he would look into it, but he didn't sound convincing. I then did something risky and probably stupid—I told him if the orders weren't changed, I would contact my congressman. I didn't have a clue how I would do that, and he was clearly pissed that I said it. I held my breath for a few hours.

Finally, word came that the First Sergeant wanted to see me. When I walked into the office the angry "Q" threw my new orders at me. But I was happy; I was headed to the land of the tanks. Only on this trip I would have a companion along, my new wife. There was only one week to go before the big day back in Wilmington.

As OCS Class 7-70 closed out, we each received a cycle book. It was similar to a high school or college yearbook. On the page before the patriotic congratulatory letter from LTC Charles Mendoza was an unsigned poem penned by one of my classmates. As I look back on his words, they seem to capture some of the growing divide in our country and the bitterness some in the military felt towards the anti-war movement.

We fought for freedom while over there
So that our country would have no fear
But while we fought through mud and dust
The people back home didn't care about us
They carried signs like "Ban the Bomb"
And "Don't send us to Vietnam."
At first it didn't bother me none
But I've seen my buddies die – one by one

Now I'm still fighting – but just to live.
My life for them, I'll never give.
My friends and family I wish well
But all those others can……...!

The poem was followed by a reminder of where we were headed:

During our training at OCS we faced many obstacles, but none so large
as those which challenge our fellow soldiers in Vietnam. Take time and
think of your future years, for soon their obstacles may be yours.

As I was going through OCS, I did not like it at all. There was no question, though, that I had a strong sense of pride after making it through. In time I began to understand the impact it had on me. It was no doubt a life changing event. It gave me an emerging sense of confidence that I could lead troops in combat if I had to and meet new challenges, both in the Army and the world beyond.

Postscript: A Return to Ft. Benning

On September 27 and 28, 2018, I had the opportunity to return to the Ft. Benning Officer Candidate School for a two-day visit. It had been more than forty-eight years since my graduation. I was invited to attend the OCS graduation of Class 502-18 and also had the opportunity to attend a Ranger School graduation. The current OCS battalion commander, LTC Matthew Chitty arranged to have Captain Jose Elizabeth, an OCS graduate, provide a tour and a briefing on the current program.

Joining the captain and I were two recently commissioned second lieutenants. On our way to the Ranger graduation at Victory Pond, one of them turned to me and said, "So sir, what will your speech be about today?" I glanced over at Captain Elizabeth, who had a big grin on his face. As I explained that I was not the speaker, we pulled onto the site and were stopped by security. A sergeant leaned into the window to tell us the parking was reserved for VIPs, such as the commanding general of the 82nd Airborne, and that we would have to turn around and park back along the approaching road. With a straight face Elizabeth responded, "Sergeant, this man is the Governor of Delaware." I cringed but didn't say anything. This whopper by my escort did greatly improve our parking spot but made me a little nervous that the next person we met might be from Delaware and actually know my former boss, John Carney. I asked the captain to switch my title to "author."

OCS has changed dramatically since 1969-70. The school is only twelve weeks instead of twenty-four; candidates have substantial freedom and privileges; and the constant harassment, particularly during mealtime, is gone. Also, since OCS is now generic to all branches, candidates do not face the hurdle of Ranger Week or the Ranger Water Confidence Test. The most dramatic change I observed, though, was the presence of a sizeable number of female candidates. I don't recall seeing a woman on the post in 1970, but today it all seems perfectly normal.

Considering the reduced length of the new OCS and other changes, the obvious question would be: How does today's OCS compare to 1969-70? Based on my limited observation, I would say today's OCS is less challenging in many respects than what I experienced, but that should not imply it is less effective. Clearly the officer candidate of today is highly motivated, while many of the future officers of my time were basically coerced due to the draft. Maybe that was why OCS in 1969 had a planned attrition rate of half the class. Today's candidates are carefully selected, treated with greater respect, and then sent on for focused training in the branch of their choice.

Four OCS grads: Ft. Benning, September, 2018

Chapter 14

Ft. Knox Days,
April 1970–November 1971

"Sir, when you go over there and face what we have faced, then come back and tell us. We think you will see things differently."

I remember very little of my OCS graduation day at the end of March 1970. I know I was very excited to see Sharon for the first time in three months—and, to my disbelief, my father made the trip to Georgia. In his fifty-five years, he had never been more than 150 miles from Wilmington. Sharon and I were married on April 5th and enjoyed a short honeymoon trip to Virginia Beach and Williamsburg. Father Robert Kenney, my high school mentor, performed the ceremony at Christ Our King Church. He blessed our union and fittingly told a golf joke during his homily. Father Bob had moved from Sallies to become principal of Father Judge High School in Philadelphia, but we stayed in touch. I still have some of his letters urging me to improve my grades and receive the sacraments.

Mr. and Mrs. James Gerald Putman
request the honour of your presence
at the marriage of her daughter
Sharon Jean Tollett
to
John Steven Riley
Second Lieutenant, United States Army
Sunday, the fifth of April
at three o'clock
Christ our King Church
Wilmington, Delaware

Back from Williamsburg, we packed our new Union Park, Pontiac Tempest T–37 and headed to Kentucky. The car was purchased from the father of a Sallies classmate, John Renzetti. At the time, John was serving as a helicopter pilot in Vietnam. For his years of service, he would later be inducted into the Delaware Aviation Hall of Fame. Pilot or crew member on a helicopter in Vietnam was a risky business, and I think a case could be made that many belong in a hall of fame somewhere.

While I had orders to report in forty-eight hours to the Armor Officer Basic course, there were no other instructions. We rolled into beautiful downtown Radcliffe, Kentucky, needing a place to live. Before the day was done, we were moving into a furnished half of a sixty-foot trailer. After settling in, our first stop was to visit the famous Ft. Knox Gold Vault, most recently elevated in pop culture by the James Bond movie *Goldfinger.* The cramped and fragile trailer would be our home for the next six months, and we would be fortunate to dodge a couple tornados that blew through the area.

Every new second lieutenant could expect to move from final training to a stateside period of "troop duty" prior to deployment overseas. Many tagged along as training officers in Basic Training companies. There were hundreds of those positions at the huge war prep factory that was Ft. Knox. My friend Larry Miles and I heard about a couple openings running weapons' ranges and thought that sounded like more fun than restraining overzealous drill sergeants and waking up the basic trainees at 0500. We also heard you had a better chance of staying in that job because they didn't like to train new trainers.

I was thrilled to get the assignment as the Officer in Charge (OIC) of the U.S. Weapons Range, known as Easy Gap, several miles out into the Kentucky boondocks. The range became a mini arsenal every day as we would set up about 50 M-60 Machine Guns, M-79 Grenade launchers, M72 LAW anti-tank rockets, and Claymore anti-personnel mines. My chief assistant, or non-commissioned officer in charge (NCOIC), Dewey Ponds, was a career soldier (a "Lifer") and veteran of both the Korean War and Vietnam. Sgt. Ponds could have been a stand-in for "Gunny" (R. Lee Emery), the former Marine and star on the Military Channel.

Soon, I was teaching my first class, and took my rotation in the firing demonstration at the end of the four-hour segment. I got pretty good with both the M-79 and the LAW and was thankful that the targets I shot at every day were not firing back. We would save a belt of M-60 ammo for the final "mad minute" of the demo and fire several hundred rounds from two guns in about 30 seconds to the rising cheers of a bleacher full

M-60 Machine Gun class,
Ft. Knox, winter 1970

of basic trainees. That moment never failed to touch a button somewhere in the DNA of a nineteen-year-old male.

When the Army launched a new weapon that combined the M-16 rifle and M-79 Grenade Launcher into one weapon, the M-203, I was sent back to Ft. Benning for a two day "top secret" briefing. Soon after I returned from Benning, a LAW blew up on the shoulder of a trainee on another range, killing three. It was a hell of a reminder that these weapons were not toys. We never fired another LAW during my time at Easy Gap.

During lunch breaks, I would listen intently to our training team and the drill sergeants discuss their experience in the war zone. They had their own language—a mixture of G.I. slang, Vietnamese expressions and locations, and frequent use of the French word for many, *beaucoup*. I hung on every word, hoping to discover tips on survival when and if I was deployed. When the story on Lt. Calley and the My Lai massacre broke, I was a bit stunned when they all defended Calley, saying he was being railroaded by the army and the press. When I took the other side, indicating that My Lai was a stain on the U.S. Army, they shot back, "Sir, when you go over there and face what we have faced, then come back and tell us. We think you will see things differently."

As summer faded into fall that year, the adrenal cortex portion of my brain would activate anytime a call came into the range and SFC Ponds would yell out, "Sir, it's for you." I was approaching the end of my "troop duty" time, and although officer assignments to Vietnam were scaling back due to Nixon's troop withdrawals, some of my fellow lieutenants at Knox were receiving orders. Every week, someone was either arriving new at Committee Group or heading out—sometimes with orders for "the Nam." We would gather on Friday after work at the Ft. Knox Officers' Club for what was known as the "Hail and Farewell" and toast those who were moving on.

It was on one of those officers' club evenings when I first caught sight of our new deputy post commander, Brigadier General George S. Patton. He was a highly decorated combat veteran who greatly resembled his famous father. It seemed rather fitting that the Pentagon would assign him to the home of the Patton Museum at the time of the release of the movie *Patton*. Sometime later he would sign my Army Commendation Medal, which still sits above my desk in my home office.

With officers either deploying overseas or mustering out of the army, assignments changed on a regular basis. In late 1970, I was reassigned to take over the Gas Chamber, the Hand Grenade Range, and the Night Infiltration Course, the only "live fire" exercise faced by basic trainees. Each of these activities were full of adventures that ranged from dropped or lost grenades to tear gas trapped in the fabric of my fatigues that would release into the apartment when I arrived home from work. Soon Sharon demanded that I take my uniform off outside.

At the end of March that year I would have only one year remaining on my commitment. Most of the informal chatter among the junior officers was that given the troop withdrawals it would be unlikely one would receive orders for Vietnam if he had less than a year to go. Between the years I worried about the draft and the couple years I had already served, it seemed that Vietnam was always out there, and I would end up going one day. Now, as each month ticked off the calendar, it was becoming apparent I would not deploy to the war zone after all. While it was certainly a relief for me, the war in Vietnam continued to dominate the news every day.

Throughout my time in the Army, I would try to stay in close contact with my family, particularly my mother. She would never complain or ask for help, but I knew she was under great strain trying to work full time; manage my father and his issues; and make a decent life for the remaining kids at home.

Mom never learned to drive, so she would take a bus or grab a lift with family or friends whenever she could. While returning from church one morning that spring, a guy ran a red light and crashed into my sister's car. My mother was thrown against the metal dashboard and broke nearly every bone in her face. That afternoon, I got the call that she had been taken to the hospital. I contacted my commander and was granted emergency leave. I drove all night long from Kentucky to Wilmington.

When I saw Mom's broken, swollen, black and blue face, I nearly passed out. My brother Curt grabbed me as I looked for a place to land. I stayed home for several days as she went through surgeries to fix her broken nose, repair her shattered eye socket, and realign her broken jaw. It was agony for her, and it tore our hearts out to see her suffer so much. Life, as I was beginning to realize, can be terribly unfair.

In mid-1971, I was selected to be the Officer in Charge of Instruction at the U.S. Army Training Center (USATC). My job was to "train the trainers" in Army teaching techniques. I also spent part of that summer teaching basic infantry tactics to ROTC cadets. The hours were such that I had some extra time for golf. In 1970, I had finished second in the

Ft. Knox Open, so heading into the summer of '71, I was determined to take the title.

Ft. Knox, which based on population would have been the fifth largest city in Kentucky at that time, had two golf courses: Lindsey (part of the officers' club) and Anderson. The Ft. Knox Open was held around mid-summer at Anderson. (On a return trip there a few years ago, I learned that it had been closed and homes and office buildings erected on the site.) After three rounds, I was tied for the lead. In the last round I fell behind on the front nine but made two eagles (that is, two under par on a hole) down the stretch to win by one. I have made an occasional eagle in competition over the years but never two in one round—in this case, two in the last four holes. It seemed like a touch of fate that I would win the Ft. Knox Open.

Spending most days in front of officers and NCOs teaching instruction techniques renewed my interest in education. The University of Kentucky offered courses at the post so I started attending night classes. Somewhere around October, word came down that several of us were eligible to be released four months early from the Army; there were just too many lieutenants. My discharge date moved up from March 26, 1972 to November 26, 1971. Sharon and I suddenly began thinking about life after the Army.

I had been a reluctant, but fairly successful, soldier. My commanding officer and others tried to talk me into making the Army a career, but I wanted no part of it. The Army in 1971 was not in good shape. Discipline had been eroded, driven in large part by an unfair draft in an unpopular war. The ugliest manifestation of the decline was the escalation of what was known as "fragging" incidents. The term was derived from the fragmentation grenade. In Vietnam, disgruntled troops would simply eliminate a hated NCO or officer by rolling a grenade into their sleeping area. There was concern about it at Knox, although I don't recall any incidents. In addition to evidence that drug use was proliferating, signs of decline were manifested by troops not being in proper uniform; graffiti appearing on government property; reluctance to respond to anything a soldier deemed petty; and just an overall malaise about service. On the other end, the NCOs and career officers constantly expressed a distain for the troops serving under them. Their view was that the country and American youth in general were in full decline.

Ultimately, the answer to this problem would be the creation of the professional Army. Although not fully implemented until 1973, the big change was already under way during my final months. Signs began popping up all over post featuring the term VOLAR (meaning, all-volunteer Army) as they were preparing for the day with a well-planned communications strategy. I have always found it more than ironic that the man most hated by America's youth, Richard Nixon, would be the president who ended the draft, ultimately got us out of Vietnam, created the Environmental Protection Agency, opened up China, pursued détente with the Soviet Union, helped to secure the right of eighteen-year-olds to vote through the Twenty-Sixth Amendment, and implemented the federal policy of affirmative action to advance minorities. He would also become deeply respected by America's Vietnam POWs for "bringing them home with honor."

In the middle of the turmoil of 1971, though, you could not convince me that Nixon was good for the country. While I was fortunate not to lose a family member in Vietnam, I did know some of those who had fallen in a cause so many believed was a terrible mistake. Two deaths that hit home for me were Curt Brown and Bob Layton. Curt was the son of the future CEO of Hercules, where I would work one day. I had met Curt through some golfing friends during my senior year of high school. It was unusual for the son of a prominent family to serve in a combat role in this war, so it was shocking when we learned of Curt's death. Handsome and outgoing, Curt was a lot of fun to be around. Bob Layton, who worked with me at the Deer Park Tavern, was discussed earlier. Both Curt and Bob would have almost certainly gone on to good things in life.

While the war had been initiated based on the fairly noble intentions of preventing the aggressive advancement of communism and defending the people of South Vietnam, it became seriously corrupted under Lyndon Johnson, beginning with the much discredited Gulf of Tonkin Resolution. This resolution by Congress gave a green light to LBJ to escalate the war, based on an incident that either never occurred as described or had been exaggerated. Nixon had successfully exploited the great divide in the country to beat Hubert Humphrey in the tumultuous presidential campaign of 1968. Humphrey never righted his campaign ship after the wild events at the Chicago Convention that year. Nixon talked about "peace with honor," but many thought he meant the honor of politicians whom they felt were lying about the war. Some of their suspicions were confirmed when in June of 1971, the *New York Times* began to publish the "Pentagon Papers."

I had been a volunteer in the anti-war campaign of Bobby Kennedy in 1968. Now I was poised to muster out of the Army, three and half years later, with the war and the ugly debate over its purpose still ragging. Already attracted to politics, I determined that one of things I wanted to do when I got out was to work for a presidential candidate in 1972 who would beat Nixon and bring the remaining troops home. I didn't know who that would be, and I didn't know how I would do it.

My upcoming work in Delaware politics was going to connect me with some interesting people, especially a twenty-nine-year old running for the U.S. Senate, Joe Biden. But more than politics or career, the one thing I was determined to do upon re-entry was to find some help for my father, help that he had no interest in accepting.

PART III

Adventures

in Politics, Business, Sports, and Fundraising

Chapter 15

Candidate for Congress, 1972

"Of all the stories that came out of the Democrats' trenches before, during and after the state convention, the one that seized me the most was about John Riley."

My friend Larry Miles and I headed to our last "Hail and Farewell" at the officers' club the day before leaving the army to discover no one was there. We didn't have time to figure out if that was an omen of sorts or we just didn't get the message it had been cancelled. While enjoying our final beer at the club, post commander General Patton walked through the bar. Out of habit I froze for a second, worried he might have something unpleasant to say. A second later he was gone.

Sharon and I traveled west out of Ft. Knox to spend a few weeks with her family in Topeka, Kansas, where her stepfather, Put, had been sent to supervise another DuPont expansion project. We enjoyed Thanksgiving with them and made it back to Delaware in time to spend Christmas with my family. The situation had continued to deteriorate with my father, but the question remained as to what exactly we could do for him. Fortunately, during my mother's recovery from her injuries in the car accident, she was referred to Dr. Janet Kramer. While Dr. Kramer's specialty was adolescent medicine, she also worked with state officials in drug rehabilitation. (An incredibly bright and caring physician, Janet would go on to establish the trailblazing First State School at Christiana Care for children with chronic and terminal illnesses.) Mom and I met with Dr. Kramer to discuss Dad's symptoms and she suggested an intervention plan that would include Dad spending up to a month in a detox facility. While it was a plan, the challenge was how it would ever be implemented; there was no chance my father would agree to such a thing.

Uncertain about my career direction, I enrolled in a couple of courses at UD under the G.I. Bill, an education course and a graduate history course. Sharon landed the job she hoped for as a physical therapist at the Delaware Curative Workshop in Wilmington and we moved into the Town Court Apartments in Newark, off Elkton Road. My high school mentor, Father Kenney, was back at Salesianum after a stint as principal at Father Judge High School in Philadelphia, and he brought me on at Sallies in a substitute teaching position for a couple of months (I guess everyone had forgotten the Ring Mass beer party my senior year). And in addition to the G.I. Bill income, the Delaware Military Pay Commission sent me a check for $300 for having served and I was able to receive unemployment benefits for a period of time.

Still passionate about doing something to help end the war, I decided to head to New Hampshire for a week to see if I could volunteer for one of the anti-war candidates and to experience what the political world would be like. I was joined by one of my college buddies, Greer Firestone.

Our first stop in the state was to visit Susan Greatorex at the *Manchester Union Leader*. Susan was on our Model UN team in our college days and had taken a position with the famously conservative newspaper right out of school. She gave us her perspective on the candidates then trudging through the New Hampshire snow. I was impressed by former Marine and Korean War hero Congressman Pete McCloskey. He had great credibility on the subject of the war, but his campaign appeared nothing short of quixotic as a Republican seeking the nomination against Nixon. We settled on World War II B-24 pilot, Senator George McGovern, since he seemed to have the best shot at a nomination against Democratic "establishment" candidates such as Hubert Humphrey, Ed Muskie, and Henry "Scoop" Jackson.

Other than briefly meeting McGovern and some of his campaign team, we didn't accomplish much of value, but they did give us the name of their Delaware campaign chairman, Wilmington lawyer, Ernie Wilson. Ernie and his wife Kendall were champions of various liberal causes in Delaware, including the ACLU and prison reform.

The finances of the McGovern state campaign were a mystery to me, but I believe at least one staffer was being paid, and it wasn't me. In addition to the political volunteer work and my courses at the University, I was also spending time on my job search. As a true '60s idealist, I had confined my search to positions I thought would help make a better world. I eventually landed a job as a Child Protective Services worker that July, with an annual salary of $7,721. I would also be joining my third union, AFSCME. This social worker experience had a significant impact on me and would sow the seeds of my philosophical conversion to the conservative side.

During this time, we continued to wrestle with the situation with my father. Thanks to Janet Kramer, we had a plan, but I just could not gather myself to face the day of reckoning. Then it happened. One Sunday morning, I picked up the phone to hear my sister Becky in distress on the other end. She said that my kid brother Denis had intervened to defend my mother when my father flew into one of his rages. Phyllis, the youngest, was also home and I could hear her crying in the background. I dashed out of the house and sped north on I-95 knowing today had to be the day. I overpowered my father and restrained him, while mom called the number Dr. Kramer had given us. The crisis team arrived in about thirty minutes, and by then Dad was resigned to let events take their course—he was going to rehab.

The treatment program involved introducing new drugs with a new set of side effects. It was not a perfect solution but better than the status quo. Dad was only fifty-eight at the time, so Mom and I worked to gain him an early retirement from DuPont. Eventually, after hiring a lawyer, we were able to secure his Social Security disability benefits. What we had to share with the hearing officer to gain approval was dehumanizing for him. From that day forward he was weak and listless and slept half the time. He would succumb to a massive heart attack at age sixty-two, on November 11, 1976.

As another unfortunate footnote to this tragedy, we discovered that Dad had not paid any Delaware income tax for nearly ten years. Even with very little income and numerous dependents, he owed more than five thousand dollars, including interest and penalties. With nowhere to turn for the money, my mother had to use her very small settlement from the 1971 accident to pay the debt. Not that we were in much of a position to help, but Mom insisted on using her only retirement nest egg to settle the matter.

Traveling in Democratic Party circles that spring I met the state chairman, Mike Poppiti. Perhaps since I was a veteran, Poppiti took an interest in me and asked if I might like to run for office myself. I said yes, but assumed he was talking about the future, certainly not during the current election cycle. Missing the first signal, only days later I received a call from Ken Boulden, the executive director of the party. He said Poppiti wanted to specifically discuss my becoming the Democratic nominee for U.S. Congress that year. Not having a clue about what running for Congress would entail, I agreed to meet with them the next day to discuss it.

At Democratic state headquarters the next morning, Poppiti extended the offer for me to be the candidate for Congress, and they wanted to move quickly. He said they would like to schedule a press conference that coming Monday, the same day I was due to tee off in the Delaware State Amateur Golf Championship. I told him I would have to think it over and seek some advice. I guess my body language said I was running because, unbeknownst to me, Poppiti alerted the press that the party would be introducing its candidate on Monday morning—right about the time I would be on the ninth hole of the tournament. Instead of thinking about golf, I was suddenly focused on the biggest development of my life to date.

I called family and friends to get their advice. The problem was, they were about as naïve as me when it came to politics at this level. The one person I could trust, who actually knew something about running for Congress, was retired Lt. General Joe Scannell, former adjutant general of the Delaware National Guard. Joe had run for Congress in 1952 and was a former Wilmington Democratic chairman. Joe had become a mentor to me since I left the service. (I was in the same OCS class as his son.) He didn't tell me what to do, but he did tell me to expect the worst. I guess that made me nervous enough to keep my Monday golf date.

The golf championship was being held at Wilmington Country Club, and I was paired with Rich Osberg, who went on to win the tournament. To ensure that there would be no press conference, I left a message with Poppiti and Boulden at Democratic headquarters. Apparently, the message never got delivered or they decided to ignore it. When the press arrived, Poppiti told them I was running but decided to pursue the golf title first. Not satisfied with a simple comment from the state chairman, a reporter set out across the golf course to locate me without success. We spoke later on the phone and I came up with a brilliant response about running—that I was ninety-percent sure. The headline in the *Newark Weekly Post* read, "Riley Flubs Tee Shot, Bogeys Press Conference." Not exactly an auspicious start to my short-lived campaign.

My name being floated as a candidate caused several reactions. One was that Wilmington attorney and Democratic activist Arlen Meckler announced he was running. In the same article, Democratic county chairman Ed "Pete" Peterson said I would make an excellent candidate, while never mentioning Meckler. It seemed like Poppiti had his party luminaries lined up for me. The other reaction was from county councilman and U.S. Senate candidate Joe Biden. An article in the paper said, Biden was "rumored to be unhappy" with my candidacy but that he had "spoken to the golfer and was satisfied that he was viable." Obviously perturbed with party leaders, he added, "I don't like backroom decisions."

The next day, Joe said he wanted to talk to me. We met on the sidewalk in front of the old Kozy Korner Restaurant at 10th and Washington Streets. Although Biden's published comments were negative, I was surprised by how hard he pushed back against my candidacy. He said that our combined campaigns would be dubbed the "kiddie campaign," and people would not take us seriously. It was basically a one way discussion and he added that I should think about joining to help his campaign.

When I told Poppiti about the Biden meeting, he became angry, or at least feigned being angry. He said Joe had little chance in the race against a respected Delaware leader like Cale Boggs and that he had no right to try to talk me out of running.

Worried that I had gotten in over my head and a bit shaken by the Biden experience, I went off to the Democratic convention that weekend as a possible candidate—at least Poppiti was pushing me to keep my name in the mix. What I did not understand was that negotiations had been going on behind the scenes with Newark Mayor Norma Handloff to get her into the race. Apparently, she agreed at the last minute and I was out. Although I felt embarrassed by the way it happened, the party bosses did me a favor. Handloff was a credible candidate, though she would go on to lose to future governor and incumbent congressman Pete du Pont by a very wide margin. I also came to respect the seriousness of Biden and his candidacy, as he had an extremely well-run campaign and knocked off an admired leader in Cale Boggs.

While Biden didn't run as an "anti-war" candidate, at least in the McGovern or McCarthy sense, he no doubt benefited from the strong opposition to the war by young voters. Riding a wave of "old enough to fight, old enough to vote," the Twenty-Sixth Amendment was ratified in 1971. So 1972 was the first national election where Americans between the ages of eighteen and twenty-one went to the polls. Cale Boggs was recognized as a WWII war hero, but his support of Nixon's "Peace with Honor" policy did not endear him to young voters at the University of Delaware or other campuses where Biden campaigned heavily. Still, Biden's victory by only a few thousand votes was a remarkable achievement considering the total rejection of McGovern at the top of the ticket. Joe carefully positioned himself as a moderate, new generation leader, thereby not alienating the conservative Democrats in the southern part of the state.

As Delaware and the world now know, Joe Biden, elected to the Senate before being old enough to serve, was struck by tragedy when his wife Neilia and one-year-old daughter Naomi were killed in a car accident that seriously injured his two sons. Sharon and I joined hundreds of mourners at a packed St. Mary Magdalen Church in north Wilmington for the funeral. Sadly, forty-three years later we would stand in line with thousands of others from around the state and the country to pay our respects to Vice President Joe Biden on the loss of his son Beau to brain cancer. Beau, an Iraq War veteran had been elected Delaware's Attorney General in 2007 and had a bright political future.

Following my less than satisfactory sojourn into elective politics and disillusioned with McGovern and the Democrats, I decided to step away from the game and concentrate on my family and career. This dedication was nearly compromised about a year later when Biden asked me to consider joining his staff. While somewhat in awe of the man at that time, I resisted the temptation. When I finally got back into politics, it would be to work for a Republican.

Just when I thought the drama surrounding my fledgling congressional campaign had subsided, the great Delaware sports editor and columnist Al Cartwright decided to have a little fun at my expense. And all things considered, I was a pretty easy target. After all, to the outside world it appeared that I had ducked out of an announcement to run for high political office to go play golf. Cartwright's headline read, "What if McArthur Had Lived the Life of Riley?" The column started out:

Of all the stories that came out of the Democrats' trenches before, during and after the state convention, the one that seized me the most was about John Riley.

He went on to write:

But I think Riley blew a great gimmick, in addition to his niblick. He had the greatest setup in the world. What he should have done, once he surprised himself by passing the qualifying test, was schedule the press conference for the first tee the next morning. Think of the publicity value. Anybody can make an announcement at party headquarters. If nothing else, it would have shook-up Osberg, his match-play opponent.

Cartwright then posed hypothetical situations of various leaders following my example at important times. In addition to Philadelphia Mayor Frank Rizzo, Vice President Spiro Agnew, and even General McArthur, he imagined Governor Russ Peterson being absent from the signing of the "Delaware Coastal Zone Act" because he decided instead to locate a rare "double-breasted, yellow bookmaker."

Chapter 16

A New Career Path, 1972–1973

Saving the world!

In July 1972, I started my new position working in the field of child abuse. The office for the State Division of Social Services (DSS) was located on Governor Printz Boulevard in northeast Wilmington, in the middle of one the city's most challenging neighborhoods. The DSS office could be described as the Delaware nerve center of former President Johnson's "War on Poverty." On the one hand, social workers spread out to inform the public what benefits were available to them such as "Aid to Families with Dependent Children" (AFDC), food stamps, vocational rehabilitation services, and children's health programs; on the other hand, social workers were involved in ensuring that rules were being followed such as children being properly cared for. As a Child Protective Services worker, I was on what I would call the "compliance side."

It was very rare that I would have a conversation with a father about problems in the home, since in order to receive an AFDC payment (commonly referred to as a welfare check) the presence of a man complicated things for the mother and she could lose her payment— although I never saw that rule actively enforced. What became clear to me over my year in the social work trenches was that there was a significant culture of dependency on government among a segment of the population. While the largest concentration of cases could be found in the Wilmington public housing projects, the problems extended out into the suburbs as well. Most of the families reported to Child Protective Services fell into the public assistance category because social workers tracked their cases and reported them if they felt the children were abused or neglected.

It did not take all that long to gain an understanding of how intractable some of the issues were for the people we worked with. While our job was to change the family situation (typically just a young mother or young grandmother with children) and improve things for the children, in most cases the mother's energy seemed to be devoted to maintaining the status quo. This was especially true when drugs and addiction were in the picture.

When serious neglect or abuse was uncovered, we would take the parent or parents before a judge to have the children removed from the home and placed into foster care. This step was emotional and potentially risky due to the reaction of the parents or children, and because the placement in foster care often failed. While there were some great foster parents who were highly motivated to make a difference in children's lives, it was still not the child's home. The Delaware Family Court was the venue we used to gain custody for a placement or in the worst cases to terminate parental rights.

My first trip to Family Court was a memorable experience. I been alerted by the worker helping to train me that the court clerk, Mr. Boeck, ran the place like a drill sergeant and could be hard on social workers. When we arrived, some people had been waiting for hours in the almost chaotic environment where children were crying, angry spouses glared at each other, and lawyers paced back and forth. To keep things moving, the clerk was barking orders at everyone. I couldn't place the name or the face, but he looked familiar. Suddenly, he yelled for me to come forward. He leaned down from his position above me and said, "Riley, you won't have to wait. I'll get you in front of the judge next. Nice to see you again." Then it hit me. Bill Boeck was the man responsible for the Salesianum football programs that I sold on Friday nights at Baynard Stadium more than ten years prior. After the brief exchange, Boeck went right back to yelling at everyone. The other social worker who had been coming there for years looked at me in disbelief.

There was a significant difference in the demeanor of the Family Court judges. By the time I came before the court, Roxanna Arsht had been appointed as the first woman judge in Delaware, and I had several cases before her. Judge Daniel Kelleher, though, was the judge I hoped would be assigned. He was very sensitive to the children and their plight, once musing about taking a child home with him rather than placing him in an emergency shelter.

It was logical to anticipate the possibility of suddenly finding myself in a dangerous situation. Most of the social workers were women, and they sometimes would ask me or one of the other men to go with them when they had concerns about a family. In my own caseload, I had a volatile family situation outside the city and was alerted that the father had a gun. I called State Police youth aid officer "Hap" Crystal, and we went to the home with another officer. It was the most intensive five minutes of my year in the Child Protective Services, but Hap kept everything under control. It proved to be a false alarm; no arrests were made.

While I had started out with that youthful, "save the world" attitude, I soon came to realize that my efforts were unlikely to put a big dent in the problem. The most frustrating aspect of the job was coming to grips with the fact that people are not going to change just because you provided a little guidance. This was not the U.S. Army, where the soldiers I gave orders to typically obeyed, even if they disagreed. Most of the DSS clients not only would not follow your guidance or the rules of the system, they put enormous energy into being manipulative. People were simply not going to share all the facts because they didn't trust the "man" from the government. My year as a social worker would have a significant impact on my view of the role of government. While I was still a Democrat when I moved on, I found myself questioning the value of big government solutions to society's problems.

Chapter 17

The Corporate World, 1973

"If you don't get out of here, I'm calling the police."

After leaving the service, my friend Bill Wheeler had gone to work as an office equipment salesman at National Cash Register (NCR) and was extolling the virtues of sales to me for some time. I never thought of myself as a salesman, but thinking back on it, I had been selling all the time—in the Army, in politics, and even in social work. We had learned during my year working for DSS that Sharon was pregnant with our first child (daughter Amy) and earning $7,721 a year was not going to cut it much longer. One day, while waiting at the office copier, I met our Xerox salesman, Bob Defino, and he mentioned that Xerox was hiring. Fortuitously, the hiring manager for the regional office, Steve Epp, happened to have also graduated from Ft. Benning OCS. I was hired within the week, in July 1973.

Xerox had ridden Chester Carlson's invention of the plain paper copier to the pinnacle of the office equipment market. In 1973, only IBM was a bigger brand. The company's success was also facilitated by their approach to marketing, which included reliance on a thoroughly trained sales force and the strategy of renting their products instead of selling. The running joke in my early years at Xerox was that the multi-billion enterprise was only thirty days from bankruptcy, since every contract at that time was month to month.

Xerox invested heavily in research, although for years it could not seem to solve the problem of copying blue ink or paper jams in our copiers. We learned to blame the jams on the customer's paper quality and counseled them to use black ink. The company opened an innovation center (PARC) in Palo Alto, California in 1970 that would eventually become famous for fumbling the future to none other than Steve Jobs and Apple Computer. Xerox scientists had invented the key elements of modern personal computing, such as the mouse, the "desktop," networking, and, most importantly the graphical user interface (GUI) to replace command lines and DOS prompts. After seeing a demonstration of the technology, Jobs would incorporate Xerox's ideas into the development of Apple products in what biographer Walter Isaacson refers to as "one of the biggest heists in the chronicles of industry."

Isaacson's description of a confrontation between Bill Gates and Steve Jobs over their agreement related to the Xerox technology was one of the great exchanges in the book:

> *They met in Job's conference room, where Gates found himself surrounded by ten Apple employees who were eager to watch their boss assail him. Jobs did not disappoint his troops.*
> *"You're ripping us off!", Steve Jobs shouted, raising his voice even higher. "I trusted you, and now you're stealing from us!" Hertzfeld recalled that Gates just sat there coolly, looking Steve in the eye, before hurling back in his squeaky voice, what became a classic zinger.*
> *"Well, Steve, I think there's more than one way of looking at it. I think it's more like we both had this rich neighbor named Xerox and I broke into his house to steal the TV set and found out that you had already stolen it."[2]*

The experience moving from state social worker to a position with one of the country's most successful companies was energizing in every way. Everyone was positive and supportive, seemingly driven for both their own personal success and the success of the company. While the training program was renowned and thorough, I believe I was learning as much associating with the talented people around me. At least initially, one of the most appealing aspects of the job was the fact it was as close to a meritocracy as I had ever been exposed to—very much like competitive sports. If you could sell, or if you could manage others effectively to sell, you were going to get ahead. To some extent, my perception would change over time, as I began to realize that corporate politics, personal relationships, and broader policy goals played a role in career and promotion decisions.

One salesman I met after joining Xerox, Bob Berman, became one of my closest friends. But Bob was more than a friend, he was extremely

2   Walter Isaacson, *Steve Jobs* (New York: Simon and Schuster, 2011), 178.

bright and someone I would learn from every day. A New Yorker, Bob was a trained geologist who had graduated from the Bronx High School of Science. His fascinating background included time spent exploring future development opportunities for John Rollins in Haiti and moonlighting as a restaurant reviewer in New York. Since we had adjoining sales territories, we would meet early in the morning and double-team prospects most days. We often would spend an hour or more on the phone at night analyzing what we learned and determining strategies for the future.

Our favorite meeting spot in Wilmington was the Sherwood Diner, near the train station. Owned and operated by a Greek family, they would welcome us each day with their latest kitchen creation and once a week, bake the best cheesecake south of New York City. After much begging they finally divulged the secret cheesecake recipe to Bob, just to get him off their backs.

Following the completion of the Xerox training program, it was in many respects a shock to transition out into the "real world," particularly the business of "cold calling." Not only were many businesses not interested in what I had to sell, they were downright hostile. All dressed up in my business suit, I bounced into one of my first calls on Market Street in Wilmington. As I tried to introduce myself to the owner, he looked at me and said, "If you don't get out of here, I'm calling the police." This was not a response that was covered in Xerox sales training. Teaming up with Bob Berman on a call, the customer fell sound asleep in the middle of our pitch, his head nearly hitting the desk. Bob has been retelling the story for more than forty years.

Nearly at the point of desperation during my first year for some business, I received a call from the Teamsters Union office in south Wilmington. The rather intimidating looking gentleman in charge asked me the cost of the recently introduced Xerox 4000 copier. Before I could reach into my bag for a price sheet, he pulled a gun out of the desk, slammed it down in front of us and said, "First, we have to negotiate." Looking back, I believe that man was Frank Sheeran of *I Heard You Paint Houses* fame (the title of a book by Delaware attorney Charles Brandt, which connects Sheeran to the disappearance of Teamster boss Jimmy Hoffa). Fortunately, he began to laugh and then put the gun away. It would be one of my first orders.

Bob Berman was quickly promoted to sales manager, and he soon would become my boss as district manager. My career moved along one step behind him as I was promoted to sales manager and then the number two position of district sales manager. Most of these years we were enjoying continuous growth and I was involved in recruiting and hiring dozens of new sales reps. One rep Bob and I both were excited about was Senator Biden's brother Frank.

Handsome, charming, and quick witted, Frank looked like a sales star waiting to happen. To our disappointment, Frank's interest waned quickly and he spent less than a year with the company. I would not see Frank again for over thirty years—until the day Sharon, Carie, Kevin Reilly, and I stood in line for nearly five hours to pay our respects to Vice President Biden on the loss of his son Beau. As our position in line approached the church door, I spotted Frank working his way down the line thanking everyone. When he saw me, he came straight over and to my surprise gave me a hug recalling his ever-so-brief Xerox days.

One of Xerox's benchmarks of success was an annual sales incentive award known as President's Club, which included a five-day trip to a resort location. Along with other Xerox friends and spouses Joe Teti (Barb), Dave Jenkins (Rowena), and Kevin Reilly (Cathy), we celebrated success in places like Hawaii, Florida, the Caribbean, and Mexico. Whatever the corporate trip planners put together was not enough for Berman, and he always led the way planning the trip within the trip. His specialty was figuring out the local food delicacies and best restaurants wherever we traveled—sort of a "Tripadvisor.com" before the Internet.

Bob Berman and I became such close friends that we bought homes a block from each other. When his brother couldn't make it for his son's "Brit Milah" (circumcision), I was asked to fill in as "sandak" (Jewish godfather). Often engaged in political campaigns in my spare time, Bob would jump in to help whenever he could. During the campaign to elect Tom Evans to Congress in 1976, political consultant Mike Harkins simply referred to him as "Kissinger." But good things do not last forever, and Bob was offered a great position on the West Coast and moved to Laguna Beach. One of the best trips we ever took as a family was the trip out to see the Bermans when the kids were teenagers. Today, Bob is retired and living with his wife, Phyllis, in Florida. We connect from time to time.

Kevin Reilly and I have been so closely connected over the years that people have asked, or sometimes simply assumed, that we are brothers. Actually, I met Kevin in 1977 when he walked up to my sales desk at Xerox and introduced himself. He was a local celebrity due to his athletic prominence, including two seasons with the Philadelphia Eagles, so I knew all about him. As a 6'2, 240-pound NFL linebacker, he was an impressive sight. Maybe there was something in the name, regardless of spelling, but that moment was the beginning of the closest friendship I have ever known. Kevin and I worked together at Xerox; our children grew up together; we became partners running a major charity golf tournament; we briefly managed Delaware boxer Henry Milligan; and most recently we collaborated on his popular memoir *Tackling Life*. But the best part about Kevin Reilly is he is always there for you. He gives of himself to family, friends, good causes, and people in need he has never met—and we still laugh about our old Xerox days.

Book signing with Kevin Reilly
at Stanley's Tavern, 2017

Xerox recruited a number of professional athletes and even more military veterans. In addition to Kevin Reilly, our office hired former Eagles Willie Tolbert and John Land (who played for the Delaware State Hornets and became the leading rusher for the Philadelphia Bell in the World Football League). Former Pittsburgh Steeler and UD star fullback Dan Reeder was on my sales team, and Washington Redskins All-Pro running back Larry Brown worked out of our DC office. From the college ranks, NCAA swimming star and Villanova University coach Jane Ackerman joined our team, and Olympic diver and Penn coach Rob Cragg worked out of our office as well. On travel days, Jane would share stories with me about the strange venue where the Villanova team held their practices: Foxcatcher Farms, the estate of John du Pont in Newtown Square, would later become infamous as the site where du Pont murdered Olympic wrestler Dave Shultz.

The veterans were less celebrated but included a number of guys who had fought through many of Vietnam's toughest battles. Mike Popen, who worked for me for several years, had been with the 3rd Marines. He was one of the nicest men I met at Xerox, so it was hard to picture him running a platoon during some of the most intense fighting of the war.

Another vet I got to know was a service technician by the name of Jim Dolan. Jim had grown up in Newark and graduated from Brown

Vo-Tech in Wilmington, where he played varsity football. A tough kid, Jim played both ways for Coach Jim Buchanan, a WWII Marine Corps veteran. Jim himself was attracted to the Marine Corps and volunteered at nineteen.

In Vietnam, the Marines were concentrated in "I Corps," in the northernmost part of the country, closest to the DMZ and the enemy infiltration routes. Dolan served with the 1th Marine Division in 1968 and 1969. His unit, A-I-I, was located near Da Nang and a "free fire" zone they called "Dodge City." Jim had been trained in demolition, so while on "search and destroy" operations he was one of those assigned to clear tunnels. He received the first of his two Purple Hearts as a result of shrapnel from a mine that mortally wounded a South Vietnamese soldier (ARVN) assigned to their platoon.

While at Xerox, I had never talked with Jim about his service, but I noticed he joined with other Vietnam veterans on November 11, 1983 when we dedicated the Vietnam Memorial in Wilmington. (This is discussed in greater detail in Chapter 21.) While doing research for this book, I met Jim for breakfast at the Kozy Korner in Wilmington. He told me how after being blown into a ditch by the blast from the landmine and bleeding from shrapnel wounds to his head and legs, he waited for the medevac. On the first attempt, the helicopter took fire and had to pull off. Finally, they were able to land and lift Jim and the dying ARVN aboard. He recalled with admiration how the pilot and a corpsman, who attended to the dying Vietnamese soldier, remained focused on doing their jobs although in mortal danger themselves.

Jim Dolan spent two weeks at the Naval Support Activity (NSA) Hospital Da Nang surrounded by the wounded and the dying. Fifty years later, just the mention of his time in the hospital gives him pause. He told me if I wanted to learn more, there was a video available about the hospital on the internet. He warned me it was hard to watch—and it was. Sent back to his combat unit, Jim was again wounded by a mine. This time the Marines evacuated him to Camp Smith in Hawaii where he recovered and then served out the balance of his thirteen-month rotation. He had spent seven hard months in Vietnam. While the Army death toll of 38,000 was the highest of any branch in the war, the Marines lost more than 13,000—a rate of loss nearly double that of the Army.

My Xerox years allowed us to live a suburban middle-class life and meet many friends and interesting people. Having to constantly meet new people and persuade them that I and my company offered the best solution for their business needs was a great confidence builder. But as the years passed, I found the work less and less fulfilling. After all, selling machines to make copies faster was not exactly going to change the world. So I began to become more involved in politics, community activities and even looked around for other business opportunities. I would waste a year's worth of work and thousands of dollars trying to get into the restaurant business and put down payments on a couple rental properties, only to eventually pull out. For a year I was part of the side business with Kevin and attorney Murray Sawyer managing boxer Henry Milligan, but when I finally got into business full time on my own, it would be out of necessity.

Concentrating on being a new father and on my Xerox career, I had stayed away from politics since my brief time as a Congressional candidate, but when an old friend, who happened to be a Republican, announced a run for Congress, I felt the pull of politics again. This event would be the catalyst that caused me to finally change from being a Democrat to a Republican.

Chapter 18

The Other Side of the Aisle, 1976

"Hey, Riles, want to have lunch at the White House?"

I opened the paper one morning in 1976 to read that Tom Evans was running for Congress. I met Evans when I caddied for him as a teenager. He was a fine amateur golfer, but more importantly he was a gentleman who always treated me with kindness and respect. As national co-chair of the Republican National Committee (RNC), I had been following him in the news for years. When he announced for Congress, I jumped at the chance to help him. Although still a registered Democrat, I would soon become a key advisor. I still had a lot to learn about running political campaigns, however. I was about to be educated by Delaware's top political brain.

Mike Harkins' political smarts are legendary. He came to some prominence working in Republican Bill Roth's campaign for Congress and Hal Haskell's campaign for Wilmington mayor, but before anyone paid him for political consulting, he was palling around with Joe Biden at Archmere Academy, an elite private Catholic school in Claymont. While Mike was a brilliant campaign consultant, his unique style sometimes clashed with the candidate.

The people and relationships at the top of the Republican Party establishment in 1976 were far more interesting than what I had experienced in the Democratic Party, and Evans and Harkins transcended both worlds. On one end of the spectrum, where much of the money and influence resided, were the "good government" types like former congressman and Wilmington mayor Hal Haskell, and former Delaware attorney general W. Laird Stabler Jr. On the other end of the spectrum (self-made, non–du Pont family lineage) was the "Big Daddy" of Delaware politics, former lieutenant governor John Rollins, the millionaire entrepreneur who became national finance chair of the Republican Party. It seemed like everyone associated with the GOP in those days had been on Rollins' payroll at some point.

One day, Evans invited me to attend a meeting at his home with Stabler and his campaign chairman, George Jarvis, state senator and soon to be Delaware's secretary of transportation under Governor du Pont. They had brought Harkins with them, and clearly the deal was already cut for Mike to run the show. Harkins began firing questions at everyone, much of it related to how much money had been raised and spent. He was blunt and critical. Every once in while he would glance at me as if to say, *Who are you and what are you doing here?*

I was soon working side by side with Harkins whenever I could break away from my Xerox day job. My major campaigns with Mike (in addition to my own for New Castle County Council in 1982) were that first Tom Evans run for Congress (1976), and Rick Collins for county executive (1980). On a less intense level, I worked with Mike on helping elect Rich Gebelein as attorney general (1978), Rita Justice's campaign for county executive (1984), and several of Mike Castle's campaigns. My role was always in a volunteer capacity.

Like many campaigns, a regular feature of the Evans' race were parties or random gatherings at the candidate's home. Present were staff, contributors, party officials and even reporters looking for a story. At an Evans' party on the first of August that year, there was a short interaction we have been talking about in our family for the past forty-plus years. Several of Evans friends, including Dr. John Gehret, a Wilmington gynecologist, were in attendance. As with Evans, I caddied for Dr. Gehret as a kid. Sharon was approximately seven months pregnant with our son Tim, and Gehret was holding the door as we were heading out that evening. He asked Sharon when she was due, and she responded, "October 1st." We all laughed when the Doc said, "Based on my experience, you look like you could deliver that baby tonight." About 2:00 a.m. Sharon poked me in the side, "John, I think my water just broke! We have to get to the hospital." That day, October 2nd, 1976, Timothy James Riley arrived in the world, weighing just over five pounds.

On another evening at Evans' Westover Hills home, a couple of reporters were grilling Evans as I sat off to the side. One of the reporters, Curtis Wilke, who sported a massive mustache, would go on to some renown as a reporter for the *Boston Globe*, as well as an author and college professor. His book *Fall of the House of Zeus* chronicles the life of

Mississippi plaintiff's lawyer Dickie Scruggs, a book that would involve commentary on Joe Biden and other Delawareans. What I remember from that conversation was an exchange where Evans went "off the record," with Wilke taking notes. When he was challenged that that segment of the interview was off the record, Wilke responded, "You should know with me Tommy, nothing is off the record!"

While out on the campaign trail with Evans, I met the young guy the Democrats had put up to run for state treasurer. Tom Carper was new to Delaware; he had a quirky sense of humor and seemed quiet and a bit naïve. Unlike Joe Biden, who knocked you over with ego and charisma, there was no aspect of the Carper persona that would give anyone a clue that he would win statewide elective office more than any politician in Delaware history. He would also be the leader that would bring much needed reform to the Democratic Party and mentor an array of ambitious young men and women to future electoral success. Although I immediately liked Carper, I would never have suspected he would eventually have a significant influence on my life and future career.

Election nights in the '70s and '80s in Delaware were Harkins' nights—the man lived for these moments. At Republican state headquarters, the mad genius created a huge scoreboard covering every wall with the 237 election districts laid out. With no instant statewide computerized returns, Mike would send out volunteers to every polling place to collect the votes and have them brought back or called in. As election night 1976 progressed, it was becoming evident that the Watergate legacy and Ford's pardon of Nixon were taking a toll. Nationally, Jimmy Carter and other Dems were winning, and Evans was in a holding pattern for hours, several thousand votes behind Democratic candidate, Sam Shipley. With the trend not looking good, Harkins studied the board intently. Suddenly, his fist shot up into the air, and he turned to me and the others, saying, "Break out the champagne, Evans is the new congressman from Delaware." Everyone in the room thought Harkins had lost his mind. But no one knew the election districts and voting patterns like Harkins—he knew where the votes were, and he knew how to count them. Evans snuck by Shipley with fifty-one percent of the vote.

That night, Evans asked me to meet him the following morning at his insurance office in the Delaware Trust Building to discuss the first steps of the transition (Evans would be taking over from Pete du Pont, who had been elected governor). I was both surprised and excited when Tom offered me the position as his chief of staff. I immediately accepted, but I was soon struggling with my decision, realizing I was not fully prepared for this big step and worried about putting my career into the hands of just one man. Besides, I felt I had a good position with Xerox and was in line for a promotion.

The next month was a whirlwind for me. I notified Xerox that I was resigning to take the congressional staff position, and I took some vacation time to work on the transition. Just a couple days into the process I got a call from Harkins, "Hey Riles, want to have lunch at the White House?" I had been to the White House once in college—passed through outside the ropes after standing in line for a couple hours. Mike proceeded to explain that President Ford's chief of congressional relations, Bill Kendall, was a good friend and could offer advice on both people and policy. If nothing else, Harkins said, lunch in the White House Mess would be an experience to remember. (The White House Mess is an exclusive U.S. Navy-run restaurant for White House officials, cabinet members, etc.)

As I continued to work on the Evans' transition, including recruiting staff for the Capitol Hill office, I began to realize there was a lot I needed to learn about life on "the Hill." I had discussed my concerns separately with Harkins and the idea began to emerge of hiring a DC chief of staff, while I would become the state director. (Evans and Harkins had a strained relationship during the campaign and while Mike was not directly involved in the transition he did help me as I struggled through the transition process for the first time.) The day we traveled to have lunch at the White House, Harkins mentioned that Kendall was looking for his new role, so maybe he could be a potential candidate.

As it turned out Bill Kendall and I really hit it off, and he was definitely interested in heading up Evans' DC operation. (Bill had formerly been chief-of-staff to Congressman Peter Frelinghuysen of New Jersey.) I raised the possibility of a Riley-led Delaware office and a Kendall-led Washington office with Tom, and he said he would think it over. Meanwhile, I continued to travel to DC to interview staff. One member of Pete du Pont's staff who was interested in staying on with Evans was Rick Eckman. Rick would remain with Evans for several years and later become a successful Wilmington lawyer.

After further discussions with Evans about Kendall, he agreed to meet him at the White House, but he also wanted to see President Ford while he was there. I called Kendall to make the arrangements. Of course, the appointment with lame-duck President Ford would take some work, but he said he would try to make it happen. A few days later we arrived at the West Wing, where Kendall welcomed us and said the president was unable to meet with us, but we would instead meet with his chief of staff, Dick Cheney.

I do not remember much about our discussion with Cheney that day, though I am certain that part of it was focused on the political picture in the wake of the 1976 election. As a kid from Wilmington's Pine Street, I was a bit in awe of the situation I found myself in. Cheney, true to the form we would later see when he served as vice president, never cracked a smile and seemed to have little interest in the meeting. The office itself was very impressive, a beautiful view of the south lawn with a crackling fire only a few feet away.

About fifteen minutes into the Cheney meeting, there was a knock on the door, and in came Donald Rumsfeld, then secretary of defense. Rumsfeld quickly mentioned the NATO meeting he was returning from, indicating all was well with the alliance. As Cheney walked him back to the door, I reached across the cocktail table and stuffed my pockets with packs of matches with the White House logo.

Back at my Xerox day job, I learned more about the pending opening for a new senior sales specialist position and it was growing more tempting. At the same time, although things had worked out well with Bill Kendall coming onboard, I was struggling with my feelings about moving full time into the political realm. Our second child had just arrived, and it was clear I would need more time at home to help out. Also, during that Thanksgiving week my father had passed away.

It was a time of deep reflection for our family as we struggled to come to grips with the impact Dad had on our lives. No doubt my father had some fundamental flaws. He had a fierce temper and almost immediately resorted to physical confrontation to solve problems. Perhaps this was due to being raised in the household of a tough cop during the Great Depression. On visits to our grandparents' home as a child, I never noticed any signs of affection, but I remember Dad cried for days when his parents died. Whatever the origin of his issues, you couldn't help but wonder what his life could have been with proper medical care. Any chance he had was destroyed by extreme medical malpractice. Soon after Dad's death I told Sharon of my doubts about taking the Evan's job and together we thought through the next steps.

I started with Harkins to get his advice on my dilemma. At first, he tried to talk me out of it, but he could see my mind was made up, "Well, you better tell Evans soon, and you should bring him an idea on who can backfill you." After a brief discussion, we settled on Bill Wyer. Bill had moved to Wilmington after working for Evans at the Republican National Committee. He was the classic political operative, and Evans liked him. Bill agreed to be considered, so I went off to meet with Evans. Tom seemed shocked, and although I felt disloyal regarding my change of heart, I was convinced it was the right move.

While career, politics and a growing family dominated my life in 1976, I continued to dream about one day winning the state golf championship. In August 1975, I had a top ten finish in the Delaware Open (includes both amateurs and professionals) so I felt I had as good a chance as anyone for the State Amateur title in June of 1976. But my mediocre performance the first two rounds over the difficult Pike Creek Valley course (the club was later taken over and renamed The Three Little Bakers) left me eleven behind my former UD teammate Jim Powell, who was having the best performance of his golfing life. For the third round of the tournament, officials stretched the course to its maximum length. Paired with an old friend, Steve Kostow, who cheered me along the way, I shot a 69 on a course described as "gruesome" by the media. With only one other score under 75 that day, I made up eight shots on leader Powell, who ballooned to a seventy-seven.

The sports page the next morning featured the headline, "RILEY'S 69 FAILS TO NARROW POWELL'S 3-SHOT MARGIN." Mixing golf and politics the reporter added that I had to "hurry from our conversation to go to work at the GOP Convention in Dover for former golf association president, Tom Evans, who was running for Congress."

My older brother Curt (who had missed the thirty-six-hole cut) offered to caddy for me the last round, confident that together we could bring home a state championship for the first time in the family. But my youngest brother Denis (age twenty), who did not play golf, had carried my bag for me the first three days, and I did not want to hurt his feelings, so I declined Curt's offer. Perhaps due to competing in only one or two tournaments a year, I handled the stress and adrenalin of the last round poorly. Powell easily won his only amateur title, while I fell to fourth.

I have sometimes wondered if having the big brother on the bag that day would have made the difference, but I have never regretted the decision. Denis had been seriously injured in a car accident his senior year in high school and underwent several difficult and unsuccessful facial surgeries. No one, except perhaps my mother, knew how much it affected him and eleven years later he took his life. We had our difficulties as a family, but this would be a shock like no other.

The nicest thing that happened to Sharon and me during and after the Evans campaign was our introduction to Phyllis Wyeth and her artist husband, Jamie. In the days before the '76 election, Phyllis invited us to a small dinner party at their farm in the Brandywine Valley. Sitting across from us at dinner was Jamie's famous father, Andrew. That was the first of many social events at the Wyeth home during the balance of the '70s.

While Phyllis was working in the Kennedy White House in 1962, she was severely injured in a car accident near her Virginia home. She was partially paralyzed but was able to walk with the aid of leg braces and crutches. Although the Wyeths were nationally connected to Democratic presidents (Jamie had been asked by Jackie Kennedy to paint JFK's official portrait, and he spent days with Jimmy Carter painting him as well), they were friends of the Evans and other leading Delaware Republicans, particularly those in the du Pont family.

Being "on the list" for Wyeth art events and social gatherings was about as "uptown" as a kid from the East Side could aspire. We attended dinner parties and art openings with the likes of Andy Warhol and Rudolf Nureyev, but the kindness of Phyllis and Jamie did not stop there. Jamie casually autographed various posters and prints of his art for us, and even took the time to draw new images of his famous "Portrait of Pig" on one of them. Forty years later, that poster is still prominently displayed in our home, along with an autographed photo of his 1976 painting "Wolfdog," my all-time favorite. But their nicest gesture was to support the developing art career of my sister Becky, including

inviting her Maryland College of Art and Design (MCAD) class to visit their home and Jamie's studio. Today, I believe I can say without reservation that Rebecca Raubacher is one of Delaware's finest artists, no doubt due in part to the encouragement of the Wyeths and Tom Evans' wife, Mary Page.

We rarely saw the Wyeths after those heady days but cheered our hearts out when

With Sharon, Carie, and sister Becky at the Rehoboth Art League, Rebecca Raubacher Retrospective, September 2017

Phyllis' horse Union Rags took the third leg of the Triple Crown just a few years ago. Phyllis died on January 14, 2019 and was remembered for her many philanthropic endeavors and her success as a breeder of thoroughbred horses.

I remained friendly with Evans and helped with his re-election campaign against Bob Maxwell in 1978. Later I would serve on the county council with "Max," who is a great guy. During that campaign, Tom asked me to be the "advance guy" for a special attraction coming to Wilmington to kick off the re-election and help him raise some money. Forty years later, my photo shaking hands with Ronald Reagan as he stepped off the jet is still hanging in our den. At the time, I had mixed feelings about the former actor, but I have to say he could not have been more friendly and charming. Like many Americans, I came to admire Reagan for his role in ending the Cold War, rebuilding our military strength, and improving the outlook in the country overall.

Joining Tom Evans to greet Ronald Reagan
at the New Castle County Airport, 1978

Chapter 19

Rick Collins and County Politics,
1980–1984

"The only thing missing from that movie was the smell!"

During the Evans race, I met state auditor Rick Collins, who had just been elected to his second term. With his movie star looks and engaging manner, we expected it was only a matter of time before Collins ran for higher office. Rick had originally come to Mike Harkins' attention through Democrat Jim Soles. A UD poly sci professor, Soles had run for Congress in 1970 and had become an advisor to political leaders and aspirants. Soles in many respects would embody what is often referred to as "the Delaware Way"— the ability of Democrats and Republicans to work together to solve problems. A student in Soles' class, Collins told him he wanted to work in Republican politics, so Jim sent him to Harkins who hired him. Just prior to their 1974 convention, state Republicans had no one to run for state auditor, so Harkins turned to his young staffer and said, "Rick, want to be state auditor?"

With our mutual interest in politics and golf, Rick and I became good friends. He did not talk about it much at first, but as the years went by, I learned more about his experience with the 1st Infantry Division in Vietnam. He said he was trained in military intelligence and fully expected a rear echelon assignment when he got to Vietnam. Instead, when he arrived in country, the assignment NCO stamped his papers and said, "Collins, you are on the next chopper out to the 1st Division firebase." He said, "That night I was on patrol and walking point!"

The 1st Division saw some of the most intense fighting of the war and, according to their website, they suffered more than 20,000 casualties in Vietnam. When the movie *Platoon* was released in 1987, Rick (who had been awarded a Bronze Star for his service) and I went to see it together. Afterwards, as we sipped a beer in a nearby pub he said, "John, the only thing missing from that movie was the smell." It wasn't just his words that shook me that night, but the fact that the normal cheery disposition had given way to a distant stare I had not seen before.

Harkins and Collins asked me to chair Rick's 1980 run for county executive with the idea that I would become the chief administrative officer (CAO) under Rick if he were elected. Having recently been promoted to Delaware sales manager for Xerox, I would not commit to CAO but did agree to the campaign role while fully understanding that it would be a Harkins' show. Unlike the '76 Evans campaign, where he mostly worked alone, Mike would be aided by a recent addition to his staff, Mike Ratchford. "Ratch," a native of Mississippi, had met Harkins when Mike was running Republican Gil Carmichael's campaign for Governor in 1979. No one ever assimilated into the Delaware culture and political scene better or faster than the well-liked Ratchford. He would go on to be chief of staff to Governor and Congressman Mike Castle for many years and later lead W.L. Gore's government relations.

Rick Collins defeated Democrat Joe Farley in the general election and soon after I was named chairman of the transition team. The most important function of any transition is recruiting the best people to staff the senior positions in the government. This is also the time when you begin to realize that you don't know what you don't know. While we knew there was a union representing the line staff in the county, we did not realize that the management union covered every other employee except the department directors appointed by the county executive. When we met with the human resource staff to discuss sensitive personnel questions and the state of union negotiations, we were shocked to learn that these same managers would be sitting on the other side of the table in the negotiations.

Aside from the position of county executive itself, the most important job in the county was the CAO. While I was flattered to be asked to serve in that capacity, I did not feel it was the best career step for me. After days of discussions, Harkins agreed to put his political consulting business on hold and assume the position.

On January 16, 1981, shortly after Collins was sworn in, I was asked to attend an early afternoon meeting with the leadership team in the county executive's office in the City County Building downtown. It was snowing that day and schools and businesses had closed early. I left my

Xerox office on Silverside Road and set out on the slippery roads, turning onto Shipley Road above the Springer Middle School. The events over the next fifteen minutes were unforgettable—an example of how life can change in an instant.

As I started down Shipley Road, I could see smoke rising above the trees just past the school. As I got closer, I realized that it was a car fire, and I could see that a car was smashed against a tree on the right ride of the road. I felt like I was having one of those out-of-body experiences as I pulled over and approached the burning car, praying there was no one was inside. The windows were black!

I cautiously touched the door handle on the driver's side hoping it did not burn my hand and pulled the door open. I was horrified to see a large man slumped unconscious to the right of the wheel. I struggled for all I was worth to pull his heavy body out of the dark, smoke-filled interior. With my feet braced on the side of the car we landed in the snow together, his body on top of mine. As I turned him over, I could see he had stopped breathing. At the same time, I noticed the engine was still running and the wheels were churning deep into the mud and ice. After pulling the victim about ten feet from the car, I reached in to turn off the ignition, praying the vehicle didn't blow up.

My knowledge of CPR was limited, and I never thought of it as something I would ever use, but immediately began to apply pressure to the center of his large chest. After a few minutes I looked up, and a man approached and I screamed at him to call 911. Unfortunately, my attempts to revive the driver were unsuccessful.

Forrest C. "Babe" Ridings was only fifty-seven years old. While I had never met him, it turned out that he lived near me and worked for Young Lumber, which was owned by the Shea family, whom I knew. His son and friends called me that night to thank me for my efforts. Since I was unable to save him, it did not feel like a heroic deed, but soon I was contacted by the Delaware State Police. State Superintendent Norm Cochran held a small ceremony at the

With Amy, Tim, Sharon, and State Police Superintendent Norm Cochran for award presentation, January 1981

Penny Hill station (incidentally, the same one I was marched into by Officer Jester after the high school drinking incident) and presented me with a citation for my efforts.

In parallel with the Collins' race, we assisted friend Murray Sawyer in his race to represent the Third District of County Council. Murray was a smart, young, idealistic Wilmington attorney who took everything including his service on council very seriously. While we didn't have to exactly twist Murray's arm to run, he was clearly not as captivated by the political world as some of the rest of us. Murray became a solid ally for Collins on council, but he was always his own man—not a vote that could be taken for granted by Harkins, whose job it was to chorale the votes for the administration.

After a couple years helping Collins run the county, Harkins left to manage legislative affairs for Governor du Pont. Rick had developed a close relationship with the public safety director, John McCool, so he would appoint McCool to be his new CAO. Rick then decided to not seek reelection and was offered a position as lead Delaware representative for Citibank. They had built a new facility at the New Castle Corporate Commons, the development project started during his term.

Chapter 20

County Council, 1982–1985

"Congratulations on being elected to my old seat. I have to tell you, being a U.S. senator is a hell of a lot easier than being a county councilman. Good luck!"

Due to the census that cycle, Sawyer's term was only for two years. With his term expiring, he wanted out, and along with Harkins and Collins, set out to convince me to run for the next two-year term. It was not a hard sell. I had always wanted to run for office some day and with council being a part-time position, I thought I could make it work with my day job and family commitments. Of course, it was not as simple as originally suggested. Others were interested in the Republican nomination and there were some tense moments getting things worked out. Through it all, Harkins was effective working behind the scenes, but his sometimes, heavy-handed methods left resentment with some of the party regulars.

Running in the once-heavily Republican Third District, which covered the western portion of the county from Brandywine Hundred to the Newark line, we did not expect strong opposition. We planned a few low-cost ads and a couple direct mail pieces which required a budget of around $15,000. To begin to raise the money, Harkins handed me a list of names of prominent Greenville Republicans. "Riles," he said. "To get started, you need to go see Harry and Laird"—

John Riley • County Council

As Chairman of Rick Collins' County Government Transition Team 1980-81, John learned firsthand about the past and present of New Castle County Government. He helped lay the groundwork for many of the present programs of the County Administration and will continue to work with County Executive Collins as our County Councilman. County Government continues to be faced with new challenges and with John's experience, independence, determination and knowledge, the people of the 3rd Council District can be assured that their voice will be heard.

A lifelong resident of New Castle County, John is a graduate of Salesianum and the University of Delaware. While working his way through college, John distinguished himself as a member and Captain of the Delaware Golf Team. Upon graduation in 1969 he enlisted in the United States Army. John was commissioned Second Lieutenant in 1970 and currently holds the rank of Captain in the Army Reserves.

John is presently a marketing manager for the Xerox Corporation for whom he has worked since 1973. He formerly worked for the State of Delaware and as a child abuse investigator.

John serves as the Vice Chairman of the Leukemia Society Fundraising Committee, member of the Delaware Sports Hall of Fame Committee, member of the Congressional Military Academy Review Board and serves on the Xerox Community Involvement Program Committee.

John, his wife Sharon and their three children, Amy (8), Tim (6), and Carrie (5 mos.) live in Devonshire.

R JOHN RILEY
COUNTY COUNCIL

Paid for by the Riley for County Council Committee

Candidate and family

that is, former Wilmington mayor and U.S. congressman Harry G. "Hal" Haskell and former Delaware attorney general W. Laird Stabler Jr.

I had met both gentlemen previously (I had caddied for Haskell as a kid), but I had never asked them for political contributions. Along with John Rollins, they were two of the real "rainmakers" on the Republican side. The affable Stabler was most encouraging and wrote out a check for $500 (the maximum allowable donation) as we spoke. He also referred me to other major Republican funders and agreed to sign a letter on my behalf. My meeting with Haskell was a bit more challenging.

Harkins had worked for Haskell as mayor, and they seemed to have a unique relationship. Haskell obviously respected Mike's political talents but spoke about him as if he were a wayward child. Haskell went by "Hal," but Harkins always referred to him as Harry. When I walked into his office (at the time he owned and was president of Abercrombie and Fitch) in the old Beneficial Building at 13th and Market and asked for "Harry," his personal assistant immediately set me straight. "Whatever you do, don't call him 'Harry'—he hates it!" I decided on "Mr. Haskell."

The first thing that struck me that day were the holes in the former congressman's sweater. I thought, how can such a wealthy man, who owns an American fashion symbol, have holes in his wrinkled sweater? I stumbled through my county council "elevator speech," fully expecting the same positive response I had received from Laird Stabler. After rambling on for a while about issues unrelated to the county, Haskell asked me how much I was looking for. When I said the maximum allowable contribution was $500, he said he did not have that kind of money in his bank account and would have to sell some stock. Could I come back in a week?

Several years ago, as I was exiting the Acela train at the Wilmington Amtrak station after a day in Washington, I encountered the ninety-year-old Haskell at the bottom of the stairwell with a large suitcase. Typical of Amtrak, the escalator was under repair, and he was clearly contemplating how he would get the suitcase up to the platform level. I ran down the stairs to help him and inquired about his trip. With a twinkle in his eye, he told me he was on his way to New York to see a childhood sweetheart. Hal's wife had died a few years before, and the two of them had become reacquainted after so many years. It turned out that the "sweetheart" was Ruth du Pont Lord, the last of Henry F. du Pont's children to live at the Winterthur estate. (Mrs. Lord died in 2014 at ninety-two.)

In the weeks after I agreed to run, there was not a whisper of activity on the Democratic side. I began to believe I would cruise to an election win without an opponent. That would have made life easier that fall, but it was not to be. For whatever reason, a guy named Kilroy entered the race. He never appeared at a single candidate event with me and spent very little on the race. Early on election night it was announced that I was easily elected to the Council seat recently held by none other than Senator Joe Biden.

One of Delaware's great traditions is "Return Day." With roots dating back to colonial times, winners and losers from across the state travel to Georgetown (the county seat for Sussex County) to hear the final vote tallies and to at least symbolically "bury the hatchet." I traveled to Georgetown the Thursday after election day but thought it a bit presumptuous to ride in the parade after being elected to a lowly county council seat. So I decided to line up with the other spectators on the parade route. Soon I would be watching fellow councilman Dick Cecil drive by waving to the crowd. When a smiling Joe Biden appeared, he noticed me and came over to the rope line. I have never forgotten our brief exchange. "John," he said. "Congratulations on being elected to my old seat. I have to tell you, being a U.S. senator is a hell of a lot easier than being a county councilman. Good luck!"

Wow, I thought, *did he really mean that?*

Mike Purzycki was also elected to council in 1982. I had known Mike to say hello to in college and ran into him from time to time in the ensuing years. The handsome former football star would be representing Newark, and although we were on opposite sides of the aisle politically, he would become one of my closest friends. On more than one occasion over the subsequent years, we have looked back on our early council days and lamented how ill-prepared we were for our new roles. But like many other things in life, there is no substitute for experience, and we would enjoy plenty of "on the job" training in the months ahead.

In my first week as a council member, I agreed to meet with civic association activist Joe Kelly regarding one of the many projects they were opposing in the Pike Creek Valley area. I must have missed the message that he would be bringing at least twenty-five of my very passionate new constituents with him. I would learn they did not like the morning traffic on Stoney Batter Road. Although I had been warned by Murray Sawyer that everyone with open space near them would fight to keep it "open" forever, I did not realize exactly how this opposition would be manifested. Soon it became evident that all the political energy in suburban New Castle was being focused on fighting "growth" in nearly all forms. While Pike Creek or Hockessin might turn out to fight a dentist expanding his parking lot by four spaces, the big battles would be fought out against planned shopping malls in the north end of my district and the man all the "civics" loved to hate, John Rollins.

The day to day business of county council focused on land use (primarily the efforts by developers to increase the density and value of the land they brought through the rezoning process), taxes and the allocation of resources (the budget). Council met every two weeks and the planning department (today known as the Land Use Department) would typically put forward a half dozen or more rezonings for consideration.

The constituents of the Third District clearly believed my job was to stop all the rezonings proposed for our area. If I agreed and wanted to stop a project, I had to get fellow Republican Dick Cecil to support me, along with at least two Democrats. It was not always easy to determine what was driving Democrats on council. Sometimes they might be in favor of a project because their union constituents would let them know they were interested in the potential jobs. Other times they would join me in opposition because they planned to run for higher office at some point and did not want to get on the wrong side of the civics.

Democratic councilman Joe Toner of New Castle let me know when I arrived that he considered it a courtesy to follow the lead of the councilperson from the district on zoning matters. Joe was the dean of council, having served since the county was reorganized into the county executive, council form of government. Joe was the personification of what is referred to as "blue collar." A straight-talking veteran with tattoos on his thick arms, his day job was as a painting contractor. As a Republican representing the wealthiest part of the state, I was probably the cultural antithesis of all that Joe stood for. But Joe loved golf and seemed to give me a pass because I was Irish Catholic and I had grown up blue collar.

I guess because we seemed to have a connection, Joe took everything personal in our relationship. When he ran for county executive in 1984, he was crestfallen when I went on the radio to endorse his Republican opponent, Rita Justice. "How could you do this to me, Riley?" he asked. When I tried to explain that it was my duty to support the Republican, he wouldn't hear of it. "I thought you were my friend," he said.

Toner sometimes had a funny and colorful way of making a point. There was a particularly controversial rezoning on the agenda one evening, vehemently opposed (all rezonings in my district were "vehemently" opposed) by the Alapocas Woods civic association. Alapocas was a beautiful, affluent neighborhood off Augustine Cut-Off just outside the city. Residents included many DuPont executives and Wilmington professionals. Their president, a Wilmington lawyer named Nardy Ableman, had a reputation for being eloquent but long winded. The night of the vote, Ableman was particularly loquacious, and Toner's patience had run out. As our eyes were glazing over, Toner's shadow suddenly hovered over my desk. I looked up to see his tattooed arms folded across his barrel chest. He leaned down so close to my face I could see the paint splatterings all over his glasses. He said, "Riley, when this guy started talking, you had seven votes. You are now down to four, and if you don't shut him up, you're going to lose me too!" Needless to say, I interrupted Mr. Ableman and called for a vote.

During the first year of my term on council, we moved a short distance from our home in Devonshire to a slightly larger home in Chalfonte. This would be our home for the next eighteen years. During these years our children would complete grade school (St. Mary Magdalen) and high school (Amy and Carie, Ursuline, and Tim, Salesianum), and we would become very close to our neighbors, Dick and Eleanor Lewis. A waist gunner on a B-17 in WWII, Dick had survived a crash landing in France in 1943, interrogation by the Gestapo, and two years in Stalag 17B in Krems, Austria. He would write about it in his book *Hell Above and Hell Below*. No one ever had better neighbors than the Lewises.

During the first morning in our new home the phone rang. On the other end was the Republican state representative, Mary Beth Boykin, who announced, "John Riley, you have moved out of your district!" She repeated the concern a couple more times as I tried to respond. I told her I had checked the district lines carefully, and we only looked at homes in the district. She continued to insist I made a mistake and hung up the phone. Hanging up, the thought entered my brain that I made the political blunder of the year. I was already imaging the front-page headline about the stupid county councilman who accidentally moved out of his district. My heart suddenly pounding, I looked up the district lines again to confirm what I already knew. I called Mary Beth back to let her know she could rest easy, but she didn't sound convinced.

Chapter 21

The Vietnam Memorial, 1983

*".... and it was a thousand acts of courage by American
service men and women every day."*

L and use and issues related to county infrastructure were about
as mundane as public service gets. My two most memorable
experiences on council were unrelated to the regular business of
council. One was the placement
and dedication of the Vietnam
Memorial in Brandywine Park
off Baynard Boulevard and the
other was the renaming of the
Greenhill golf course in honor of
Delaware Hall of Fame golfer Ed
"Porky" Oliver.

Just like the Vietnam
War itself, the memorial was
controversial from the start.
There were questions about
the design of the Charles Parks'

Wilmington Vietnam Memorial,
dedicated November 11, 1983
Photo courtesy of Carie Riley Sweet

statue, the location of the memorial, the cost and who should pay, and
finally the lack of a woman in the design. A neighborhood citizen's group
filed suit to block the location.

The gender issue was raised by the women on council, president
Karen Peterson and Mimi Boudart. One day, a Democratic member
of council alerted me to the fact that Karen intended to use her council
president powers to appoint Mimi Boudart to be chair of the memorial
committee, replacing former council member Francis Schneider. In the
middle of the memorial design issue, I was concerned about Mimi and

Karen's motives, so I objected. The argument was settled behind the scenes by the appointment of council attorney Mike Reynolds, a Marine Vietnam combat veteran. Mike did an outstanding job. As the day of the dedication approached, prominent *News Journal* columnist Bill Frank started his editorial page column with the words, "At last, bickering is over, controversy, we hope forgotten."

Karen Peterson and Mimi Boudart had a valid point about recognizing women who served. The issue from my perspective and that of the veterans was mainly the timing and the concern that the issue was politically motivated. While it was true that only eight women had died in the war, and all the names on our Delaware memorial were men, an estimated 11,000 women served with honor and their contribution deserves to be recognized as it has been at the national Vietnam Memorial in Washington.

My primary role on the memorial committee was to recruit a keynote speaker for the dedication. Suggestions included everyone from President Reagan to General William Westmoreland. Since I was familiar with the story of Pittsburgh Steeler Rocky Bleier, who was awarded the Purple Heart for wounds suffered in the war, I suggested to the committee that he be considered. The committee loved the idea, so I called on my friend Kevin Reilly to see if he could help. Bleier had counseled Kevin after his amputation three years before. As one of the very few NFL players who served in Vietnam, Bleier had great credibility and appeal to the veterans.

After retiring from the Steelers, Bleier became a sports broadcaster on Pittsburgh television. When Kevin called to invite him to speak, he immediately said yes. With anticipation building for the dedication on Veterans Day, about a week before the event Kevin checked back in with him to confirm his arrangements. At that point we realized we had a problem. Living outside of Pittsburgh, Bleier thought the dedication was in New Castle, Pennsylvania, only a short drive from his home. He would have to be back in the TV studio the afternoon of the dedication, and there were no flights out of Philadelphia that would fit his schedule. I called several companies with corporate planes without success. Fortunately, Bleier was able to rent a private plane. He did not receive an appearance fee for coming to speak, but we did manage to cover the cost of the flight through private donations.

Rick Collins, Kevin Reilly, and I met Bleier's plane at New Castle County Airport. The weather was so bad that morning that there was a serious question as to whether it could land. After the brief introductions at the airport, we drove to the Hotel DuPont for a short breakfast reception to introduce Bleier to the media and some of the dignitaries attending that day. Part way through the reception, a man tried to get my attention at the door. It was Harry Alexander, a well-known Salesianum football star who had played with Bleier on perhaps the most famous Notre Dame team of all time (the 1966 Notre Dame-Michigan State game that year is still considered one of the greatest in college sport's history). Harry asked if it would be OK for him to come in a say hello to his friend and teammate. They had a brief, poignant reunion.

You could feel the emotions building every day up to November 11. Ten years had passed since the U.S. withdrawal from Vietnam, and there had been no parades, recognition, or welcome home events for Delaware's warriors. While the overwhelming majority of Vietnam vets had assimilated successfully back into society, many carried their scars in a visible manner. A popular logo emblazoned on jackets of many vets at that time said, *When I die, I'll go to heaven because I've spent my time in hell.* It was typically followed by the name of a province in Vietnam along with the years they had served there. Those likely suffering from PTSD, along with the well-adjusted who seemed to have put the war behind them, lined up in old fatigue jackets to march in formation from Warner School to the site where the statue would be unveiled near the Washington Street Bridge.

Due to the stormy weather that November morning, part of the ceremony was moved inside to the Warner School, two blocks from the memorial site. As we exited down the school steps, Rocky Bleier noticed the vets and immediately dashed across 18th Street to ask if he could march with them. They cheered and shouted out, "Rocky is with us." This would only get more emotional.

With keynote speaker Rocky Bleier

Bleier clearly understood his audience, and he poured his heart into his speech. The most emotional part of the program, though, was the reading of the names of the 166 young men from Delaware who had died in Vietnam. This part of program was led by retired Army colonel Ed Jentz, who broke the war down into its various campaigns. In a moving and creative fashion, he tied each phase to the rock n' roll songs that were popular with the troops at that time. Among those who read the names of the dead were county executive Collins and the president of Chapter 1 of the American Gold Star Mothers, Pauline Anderson. Mrs. Anderson would read the name of her son, Lt. Charles R. Anderson who died March 3, 1971.

Prior to introducing Collins to read the names of Delawareans who died in "Counteroffensive Phase II," Jensen reflected on what our troops faced during the period of July 1, 1966 to May 31, 1967:

It was days of Claymore mines, flak jackets, boonie hats, airboats, and sampans.
It was sniper holes and rain and Kool Aid.
It was names like Perfume River, Union I and II, Kingfisher, and Cedar Falls.
It was "pop smoke" and, "I roger yellow smoke – is the LZ hot?"
It was deep reconnaissance by Green Berets on Teams Alabama, Colorado, and Nevada of the "Shining Brass" and "Prairie Fire" operations.
It was cities of Tay Ninh, Nha Trang, Bong Son, Qui Nhon, Chu Lai, Phu Loc, and Quang Tri.
It was the songs, "Parsley, Sage, Rosemary and Thyme," and "The Universal Soldier."
It was the Supremes, The Beatles, The Temptations.

Through eight segments before he introduced the different name readers, he would repeat the refrain:

….and it was a thousand acts of courage by American service men and women every day.
Reading the names of those honored Delaware comrades from that campaign is: Mr. Rick Collins, County Executive … a Vietnam Veteran.

As the reading of the names was ending you could hear the thumping sounds of helicopter rotor blades in the distance. All eyes turned south to see the Hueys (UH-1 helicopters) break through the clouds above the Brandywine building and head directly at us. Veterans in the crowd put their arms around one another and many lowered their heads and wept. One could only imagine some of the memories resurrected by these iconic symbols of the Vietnam war. The dedication was all we hoped it would be and more.

Chapter 22

Ed "Porky" Oliver Golf Club, May 1983

"Don't you turnover left hand!"

I am not sure what triggered my desire to rename the county-run Greenhill Golf Club in honor of Ed "Porky" Oliver, but I recall that when I mentioned the idea to fellow council members Joe Toner, Bob Maxwell, Dick Cecil, and Mike Purzycki, they immediately embraced it. Oliver was a legend in the Delaware golf and sports community, and I had grown up listening to stories about the golfing hero from my father and friends, particularly the Rock Manor players I once caddied for. Many of them had caddied with Oliver at the old Wilmington Country Club, now known as Greenhill Golf Club. In addition, I had attended school and played on the Salesianum golf team with Oliver's son, Bobby. Although I saw Oliver several times as a child, including on the dais at the St. Anthony's Sports banquet, the one encounter that has stayed with me was seeing him struggling to breath while lying on the couch in the Oliver living room on West 31st Street.

Tips from a hometown hero

143

He had just been released from the hospital after having a cancerous lung removed.

A heavy smoker, one could add lung cancer to a list of hard luck experiences for Oliver and his many Wilmington fans. His career included tying the record for the lowest four rounds in the history of the Masters in the same year Ben Hogan would shatter the record. In his great biography of Ben Hogan, James Dobson described the confrontation between Oliver and Hogan at the 1953 Masters.

> *The Hawk's personal gallery had swelled to over 10,000 people, and during round three both Hogan and playing partner Porky Oliver treated them to an exhibition of shotmaking. "Putts dropped everywhere," remembered an Augusta member who followed the pair around the course that afternoon. "When Ben wasn't making one. Porky was. It was like watching golf's version of a heavyweight boxing title. Little man versus big man."*
>
> *By the end of their two-man exhibition match, Oliver had assembled nines of 34-33 for 67, but Ben did him one better, going 32-34—66, his lowest round ever at the Masters.*

In addition to losing the Masters to Ben Hogan's record setting performance, Oliver also finished tied for first in the 1940 U.S. Open, only to be disqualified from the playoff for teeing off too early in the Saturday afternoon round. (Until converting to its current four-day format, the Open had previously concluded with a thirty-six hole final on Saturdays). Oliver won eight times on the PGA Tour and played on three Ryder Cup teams. As he chronicled another Hogan-Oliver confrontation, Dobson presented a colorful description of the Wilmington sports hero.

> *In contrast to the gray and buttoned-up Hogan, Pork Chops was a friendly ape of a man who dressed himself almost clownishly. But as Ben knew from painful experience, there was nothing the least bit funny about Oliver's tournament game. He was prone to patches of brilliant play and putting streaks that could knock the breath out of you. Five years before at the Western Open of 1941, for instance, Ben finished the tournament with a three-stroke lead over the field, not unreasonably assuming he'd won, only to see Oliver come blazing home with a back-nine 28 to beat him by a stroke with 275.*

As one of only two Republicans on council, it was never easy to gain support for legislation, but this idea was immediately embraced. The only question was the exact name: would it be the more formal "Ed" or "Edward Oliver" or include his PGA Tour nickname, "Porky," a moniker renowned to have been provided by golfing legend Sam Snead. The consensus was to include "Porky" since that was the name by which the outside world knew him.

After the resolution passed council changing the name, we planned a dedication for May 23, 1983. I wrote to the PGA inviting any old Oliver friends from his PGA Tour days to either come to Wilmington for our planned May dedication, or to offer a written tribute. We received letters full of Porky Oliver stories from many of the famous names of his era, including Arnold Palmer.

Two pros, former U.S. Open champion Tommy Bolt and Charlie Sifford, the "Jackie Robinson of golf," agreed to come and play an exhibition. In front of hundreds of spectators, county executive Collins, councilman Joe Toner, and I joined the pros for the rain shortened event. Following golf, we gathered with the Oliver family, newly appointed club pro Jimmy Robinson and other dignitaries for the ribbon cutting and remarks. It was evident that Oliver meant a lot to Sifford and that he considered his trip to Wilmington a payback for supporting him during the days he fought to be accepted in professional golf.

Having helped to lead the Leukemia Golf Classic for ten years, I have had experience working with sports agents and negotiating appearances with many PGA Tour players. Charitable golf events are first and foremost a business opportunity to the athlete and his or her management team. But with Bolt and Sifford, they did not even raise the subject of an appearance fee. It was an event to honor their old friend, so both future members of the World Golf Hall of Fame flew to Wilmington.

Tommy Bolt was one of golf's biggest stars in the 1950s. During the decade, he won fifteen times, including the 1958 U.S. Open, finishing four strokes ahead of a young Gary Player. Bolt played on two Ryder Cup teams and also won the PGA Seniors Championship and the Liberty Mutual Legends of Golf in 1980, just three years before his Oliver dedication appearance. Equally renowned for his hot temper and throwing clubs, he was labeled by the media "Terrible Tommy." One of the more famous Bolt stories involved Porky Oliver throwing his club for him at the Colonial Invitational in Ft. Worth, Texas, so that Bolt would not suffer another fine. There would be only smiles and laughter at the dedication that day, especially after Bolt birdied the first three holes on the rain-soaked course.

While Sifford's winning record was less impressive than Bolt's, his career took place against a backdrop of segregation and racial injustice. His 1992 book *Just Let me Play: The Story of Charlie Sifford, the First Black PGA Golfer* sits on the shelf in my home office. Often referred to as "bitter" or "surly" due to years of fighting for his fundamental rights and to end the disgraceful "caucasian only" clause in the PGA's charter, the only Sifford Wilmington saw that day was a gracious man, still loyal to a friend who had died more than twenty years before.

I suppose another reason for the cigar chomping Sifford's good humor that day was the fact that he had finished second the day before in the Senior Hall of Fame Classic at Pinehurst, North Carolina. His second-place check was the biggest payday of his pro career. Following golf, several of us joined Wilmington restaurateur Davis Sezna for dinner at the Columbus Inn, where the sixty-one-year-old Sifford described for Tommy Bolt how he won his biggest check by holding off rival Don January with a par on the last hole. He said, "Tommy, when I want to fade the ball, I shift my cigar to the right side of my month, and I say to my left hand, 'Now don't you turnover, left hand!'"

In recognition of his pioneering struggle and accomplishments, Sifford would be awarded the Presidential Medal of Freedom in 2014—an honor only bestowed on three other PGA professionals: Arnold Palmer, Jack Nicklaus, and Tiger Woods. Inspired by Sifford's life, Woods named his son "Charlie" after Sifford.

Oliver dedication day: to my left, Joe Toner, Tommy Bolt, Charlie Sifford, and Rick Collins

Chapter 23

Suing the *News Journal* for Libel, 1984

"I doubt that many citizens would want to spend half a day playing golf with some minor politician…"

The shadow of corruption always seemed to hang over New Castle County government. The fact was that a change in zoning was often a high stakes game where a fortune could be won or lost. A previous county executive, Mel Slawick, had gone to prison on corruption charges, and there would be more trouble down the road. In New Castle County, the word "developer" was seen as a pejorative term, synonymous with corruption. It made no difference that many developers were honest, took risks, created jobs, and built the homes and businesses that supported our quality of life. Activists in the county assumed that council members were selling their vote, and at least one local columnist for the *News Journal* used the power of his pen to imply corruption at every turn.

Early on the morning of November 18, 1983, I was awakened by a call from Kevin Reilly, who said I needed to read Ralph Moyed's column that day in the *News Journal*. He added, "You're not going to like it." I could not fathom why Ralph would have me as a subject of a column. The day before, when I had returned to the Xerox office after making sales calls with a member of my team, I picked up a message that said to call Moyed. I had never met or spoken to him in my life. Nevertheless, I had a begrudging respect for the work that he did trying to keep politicians honest. His columns were acerbic, caustic, and amusing—as long as you were not the object of his scorn. The thought never crossed my mind that he would turn his fire on me. I assumed he was just checking into something he had heard about some doings on county council. I called his number, but he did not pick up.

While the headline, *Scourge of familiarity fells Toner's big bash* attacked Joe Toner directly, Moyed quickly turned his attention to me, focusing on the highly controversial effort by a local developer, Albert Marta, to rezone the Brandywine Country Club to allow for a regional shopping mall. Moyed wrote, "Riley played golf with developer Albert Marta and as a result became 'more understanding' of Marta's desire … to turn Concord Pike into a parking lot." To add insult to injury, it was blazoned on the front page of the News Journal's local news section.

His column dripped with scorn as he continued to rail against county politicians, implying that many were corrupt. Again, targeting me towards the end of the column he could not help but belittle me further:

> *"I doubt that many citizens would want to spend half a day playing golf with some minor politician … but hundreds of voters have thousands of things they would like to say if politicians ever stopped talking to special interests and started listening to constituents."*

The problem with Moyed's column was that I had not played golf with Al Marta. I had never even spoken to him—or to anyone that worked for him—about his effort to rezone the country club property. While that upset me, I was equally infuriated by the arrogance Moyed displayed, writing his accusations without even talking to this "minor politician." I thought to myself, he would never do this to Joe Biden or Pete du Pont. OK, so even if I were a lowly county official, did I not deserve the courtesy of responding to his allegation before it went to print?

To say I "lost it" would be putting it mildly. I quickly got dressed and sped downtown to the *News Journal* offices. When I entered the building, I asked where publisher Brian Donnelly's office was located. They told me to have a seat and they would check to see if he was available. "Never mind," I shouted, and dashed up the stairs to the second floor looking for a big office across the room full of desks and a scattering of reporters. I found Donnelly and charged into the office, slamming the paper onto his desk and demanding he print a retraction. Eyes bulging and lurching back in his chair, Donnelly was clearly stunned, as the receptionist and the security guard arrived right after me. We had a further brief exchange, where he said he had faith in Moyed's reporting but would give me the courtesy of checking with him about his sources. I called Moyed a liar, said his column was libelous, threatened to sue them if they didn't print a retraction, and stomped out of the building.

Feeling like everyone on the streets of Wilmington were looking at me like I was a crook, I decided to walk over to my friend Murray Sawyer's nearby law office to see what he thought. He asked me if I had played golf with Marta and if I had discussed the zoning with him. When I said no, Murray replied, "if they don't print a retraction, then you should think about suing." I had no idea what that would entail, but we decided to wait to see how the paper responded. If they printed a retraction, we would just let it go.

During the course of the day, Moyed and the *News Journal* attempted to confirm their story with no success. In those days they had a morning and evening edition, so they decided to remove my name from the later edition of the paper. Of course, by then, the damage had been done, but they still refused to print a retraction. We sued.

Later, as the suit moved to the discovery phase, we learned that on the day the column appeared, the *News Journal's* attempt to independently confirm Moyed's source was a "Keystone Kops" endeavor. In a room full of *News Journal* lawyers, Sawyer asked Moyed to identify his source. He declined to answer, citing Delaware's Reporter's Privilege statute. Murray then asked what attempts Moyed had made to verify the accusations made by his source. After a long sidebar among Gannett's lawyers (Gannett had acquired the *News Journal* in 1978), Louis Finger, a prominent partner at the firm of Richards, Layton, & Finger, told Moyed that he had to answer. Moyed took a deep breath and sheepishly said, "I asked Mel Slawick."

Murray and I looked at Moyed and his lawyers with disbelief. Even Finger looked shocked. So Moyed admitted to contacting a Democrat who didn't know me, a former county executive who had been sentenced on obstruction of justice charges in 1976, to attempt to verify false information from a source he would not divulge. To add insult to injury, Moyed then said that Slawick could not confirm the information. Thus, Moyed had no corroboration for my accuser's lie. Still the newspaper printed it.

Moyed was not assigned to cover county politics, so he had no personal base of county political knowledge. At a later deposition, Merritt Wallick, the reporter who did cover the county, was asked if he knew about the column before paper printed it. He explained that he told Moyed to call me first, "Because that does not sound like Riley."

The uphill battle in the lawsuit was primarily that Delaware has a very strong "Shield Law," allowing reporters to protect their sources. In addition, as a public figure you only have protection from libel if you can prove actual malice. Although Murray and I were certain that in the partisan atmosphere of county government the source acted with malice, we could not prove it unless the source were revealed. At the Superior Court level, our case was rejected due to the Shield Law protection. But Moyed and the *News Journal* had not made many friends among the Delaware political class, and, as the case proceeded, a bill was introduced in the Delaware House of Representatives by Speaker Chuck Hebner to strip reporters of the privilege. Hebner specifically cited our case when advocating for his bill. The bill passed the House 30–9 and went to the Senate, where the Gannett lobbyists pulled out all the stops to ultimately defeat it. Committed to see things through, Murray appealed the decision to the State Supreme Court. Much to our surprise, they agreed to hear the case.

It was at this point we received the only real settlement overture from Gannett. Incredibly, it was an offer to apologize, but the apology had to remain confidential. That was almost as laughable as Moyed trying to confirm his libel by calling Mel Slawick. So Murray proceeded to prepare for arguments before the court. His team, including Bruce Herron and Dan Losco did a great job presenting the case in the intimidating Dover courtroom, as Moyed and I sat across the room from each other.

As things turned out, the court ruled in Gannett's favor. Justice William Duffy, who served as a B-24 bomber pilot during WWII, wrote the opinion. It concluded that Moyed's column was not defamatory. But the most interesting statement from my standpoint was Duffy's final paragraph which read:

> *Riley has argued, vigorously and with some persuasion, that the defendants are liable for defamation and that they acted with actual malice by New York Times standards (this refers to a previous case considered a precedent). I have concluded that defendants are not legally liable for defamation and, therefore it is unnecessary to consider whether they acted with actual malice. But it does not follow that Riley's arguments are devoid of merit. On the contrary, there is significant support for Riley's complaint in the record and in the briefs of counsel. For example: the only persuasive evidence in the present record is that Moyed's statement that Riley had "enjoyed a golf outing with" Marta was false. And that statement was the only basis on which Moyed wrote the cynical and disparaging remarks about Riley which followed. Moyed published his column without*

making any attribution about the (false) statement and without making any reasonable attempt to communicate with Riley. In thus attacking a named person Moyed appears to have violated Gannett's journalism standard. After Riley complained, Gannett withdrew the references to him from the later editions of its newspapers, but by then, of course, Moyed's column had been published. And defendants refused to publish a retraction. Under the governing law, there is no legal liability. But there surely has been unfairness to Riley.

Some years ago, Murray gave up his law practice and started his own investment advisory firm, Westover Capital Advisors, LLC. Sort of a serial entrepreneur, investment advisor fit nicely with his existing incorporation business and the trust services he had been providing to clients over many years. But suing the *News Journal* would not be the last crazy deal I got Murray involved in. We would soon be entering the wacky world of professional boxing.

As a father of children then aged eleven, eight, and two, I was finding it increasingly difficult to balance my career as a Xerox sales manager and service on county council with my kids' ever-expanding number of activities. And while there was a pull in the direction of home and career, I was also getting more frustrated with the land use game and being in the minority on council. So, like my predecessor, Murray Sawyer, I decided to leave council when my two-year term was up. In discussions with political friends and allies, I decided to endorse a local insurance executive, Rick LaPenta. Almost overnight, we were getting pushback, and a primary fight soon broke out.

LaPenta's opponent in the primary was Wilmington lawyer G. Thomas Sandbach. I knew Tom from our days at the University of Delaware, where he was active in student government. This wasn't Sandbach's first foray into county elections. He had also run and lost a primary battle in 1980 to Murray. The primary was more about personal political ambitions than any difference on the issues. As was sometimes the case, a minority group of Republicans saw LaPenta as another Mike Harkins' protégé, so they jumped in to help the Sandbach campaign.

Primaries can be hard to gauge so there was a certain amount of concern when Election Day arrived. I planned to vote early afternoon and then settle in for one of my least favorite tasks— calling our identified favorable voters to ensure they made it to the poll. The minute I walked into the polling place, Wilmington lawyer Rich Levin, who was working

for Sandbach as a challenger, jumped up and announced loudly that I was
an ineligible voter. He based his challenge on the fact that he knew I
had moved from the address on the rolls. This was a technicality since
I was still in the district and eligible to vote from either address. While
arguing with the local polling officials, I immediately thought back to
the scene Mary Beth Boykin had made the day after I had moved a few
months before. Levin had to have been tipped off to the fact that I had
recently changed addresses.

Angry and frustrated by this turn of events, I tried to reach the
election commissioner without success. I also turned all my energy to
personally calling more than a hundred identified voters during the
remaining hours before the polls closed. I don't know exactly how many
votes I turned out, but I was certain I had made up for my non-vote
many times over. That night we celebrated LaPenta's victory, and I had
an added sense of satisfaction.

Chapter 24

The Leukemia Golf Classic,
1983–1996

"Pitching a World Series is fun. I was just happy to be alive!"

In his book *Tackling Life*, Kevin Reilly describes part of the story of our partnership in both the Leukemia Golf Classic and Pro Management, Inc. It is not my intention to cover that same ground, but rather to share a few anecdotes that made these two experiences unforgettable in my life and a few others.

After playing in the Getty Celebrity Pro-Am at Cavaliers Country Club in 1982, I was approached by Dave Press, the local public affairs director for Getty. Dave shared with me that Getty had been spending about $25,000 a year and raising far less for the charity. He was worried that the event could not be sustained and wondered if I might like to get involved. The event was fairly unique at the time, with golfers paying to play with a local or national sports figure, and I thought it had significant potential both as charitable fundraiser and as a venue for corporate client entertainment. I also saw it as a chance to bring the PGA Tour to Delaware, something that rarely happened since the days of Porky Oliver and a couple exhibitions at Wilmington Country Club in the '60s.

The first suggestion I had for Dave was to recruit Kevin Reilly as chair. Kevin had name recognition, as well as great sports contacts and media relationships. We would form a committee of various business leaders with an interest in golf (Tom Ciconte, Charlie McDowell, and John DiEleuterio would all take turns chairing the event in the future). One of those who agreed to serve was Mike Harkins. At the initial organizing meeting in Kevin Reilly's basement we were discussing whether we could raise the cost of sponsorship from the current level of

$300, when Harkins, who was laying on his back on the floor, looked up at everyone and said, "if we can't sell this out at $1,000 per sponsor, we should fold it right now!" Dr. Bill Medford leaned over to me and whispered, "Who the hell is that guy?" Harkins was right; we sold out the first year and for many years after.

We made a series of other immediate decisions, including moving the tournament to the Hercules Country Club and the addition of PGA pro and legendary showman Chi Chi Rodriquez. Chi Chi was the perfect focal point for the program in 1983, wise-cracking his way through golf tips and eye-popping trick shots that amazed the crowd. I was sitting with Chi Chi in the club lounge a couple minutes before the program was to begin. A young girl with Down Syndrome was cleaning tables nearby. As Chi Chi got up to leave, he headed straight towards the girl and spoke softly to her. After a minute or so she removed her apron, and Chi Chi took her by the hand. As we started out the door, he looked at me and said, "This young lady will be my special guest." He walked out with her and had a seat placed immediately behind the roped off area, where he announced to the crowd that he was dedicating his golf exhibition to his new friend. The smile never left her face.

In the days before Christmas that year, a package arrived at my house from Cleveland. I recognized the name on the return address as Chi Chi Rodriquez' agent. I opened it to find a cocktail table book of the illustrations of Norman Rockwell. Inside the cover was a note. *To John & Sharon, two incredible people. God Bless, Chi Chi Rodriquez.*

With the addition of Arnold Palmer and Fuzzy Zoeller to our golf line-up, and regular appearances by celebrities such as baseball greats like Joe DiMaggio and Warren Spahn and acting personalities Richard "Shaft" Roundtree and George "Spanky" McFarland, the Leukemia Classic was gaining significant recognition in the region and nationally. In her book *The Last Boy* about Mickey Mantle, author Jane Leavy describes an exchange between Mantle and some Atlantic City casino high rollers.

"So Mick," he said. "*You gonna play in that leukemia thing in Wilmington?*"

"The leukemia thing" was a golf tournament. Whitey Ford was scheduled to be there.

"Very good lobster in Wilmington," Mickey replied.

Based on the success of golf we decided to add a tennis component, which would be led by Delaware tennis champions Gretchen Spruance,

Jeff Olmstead, and Cindy Pendergast. As with golf, they booked tennis pros such as Marty Reissen, Bobby Riggs, Dennis Ralston, and Tim Gullickson to headline the event each year. Participants also enjoyed playing tennis with Richard Roundtree, Franco Harris, and Governor Mike Castle.

Spanky McFarland and Warren Spahn would always come to town the weekend before the event, and Kevin Reilly and I kept them occupied for a couple days. It was on one of these evenings when we learned about Spahn's experience with the 276th Combat Engineers at the Remagen Bridge in World War II. Although wounded, he was one of the survivors when the bridge collapsed into the Rhine River. Spahn was awarded the Purple Heart and Bronze Star and would earn a battlefield commission—all before returning home to become the winningest left-handed pitcher in the history of baseball.

Pitching legend Spahn meets golfing legend Palmer at Winterthur

One night we were having dinner with the Cy Young Award winner at Kid Shelleen's in Wilmington, when Mayor Dan Frawley came through the door. Leave it to sports nut Frawley to be the only person in the restaurant to recognize Spahn. We had a great conversation that evening about Spahn's career, including pitching victories over the Yankees in the World Series. One quote I recall from our discussion had to do with performing under pressure. He said, "People ask me how I coped with the pressure of pitching a seventh game against the Yankees in the World Series. My answer—that's not pressure—pressure is trying to fight and live another minute in combat. Pitching a World Series is fun. I was just happy to be alive!"

In 1986, we decided to attempt to recreate the famous Winged Foot show-down for the U.S. Open between Fuzzy Zoeller and Greg Norman, the #1-ranked player in the world and the man who reveled in the nickname "The Great White Shark." After booking the pros, Tom Ciconte and I saw PGA pro Peter Jacobsen entertain a corporate crowd with golfer impersonations, so we decided to add him into the mix. The tournament would be expanded to two days, with an eighteen-hole shoot-out on Monday and the pro-am to follow the next day. In addition to tournament sponsorships, we sold about two thousand tickets for the golf match, and the three pros did not disappoint. There was an incredible chemistry between the stars, and they kept up the chatter from tee to green. For an added bit of fun, Tom Ciconte, Charlie McDowell, and I donned Masters' caddy outfits and carried their clubs.

Caddying for Fuzzy Zoeller was an adventure. He was one of the best players in the world, but he is unfortunately more famous today for putting his foot in his mouth at the 1997 Masters by making a crack about what Tiger Woods might order for the annual champions' dinner. I learned that day that the Fuzzy shtick is humor with an edge, and I was often the foil. On our sixth hole (Fuzzy and Norman were tied at three under par), Fuzzy asked me the yardage for his second shot. When I answered, "Play it 165," he responded for all to hear, "I'll decide how to play it, you just give me the yardage!" On the 13th I gave him the line for a blind tee shot. When Jacobsen hit it right of the line and I said, "Nice shot," Fuzzy approached his drive announcing to crowd that I had "no idea what I was talking about."

Norman, who Fuzzy called the "Blond Bomber," was Zoeller's primary target—and he was clearly enjoying the upper hand based on his easy win against Norman in their recent U.S. Open play-off. Norman, who could be distant and a bit prickly when off stage, seemed to enjoy the give and take, and he typically followed the barbs by blasting the ball past both his playing partners. About forty yards out from the 8th tee, a spectator leaned over the ropes to look back at Norman as he got ready to unleash his power on a drive. Seeing the spectator in harm's way, Norman announced, "Son, if you are going to stand there, you better spread your legs." He barely pulled back as "the Shark" let it fly.

Later that night at our Longwood Gardens' tournament dinner, Zoeller talked Norman out of his white sport coat as he was leaving. As we were closing out the evening, Zoeller offered a few comments on the match that day and then took out a black felt pen and autographed Norman's white jacket. After adding autographs from DiMaggio, Spahn, and some others, he auctioned off the jacket for $2,000.

I have been asked many times over the years what we paid for the various celebrities who participated in the Leukemia Classic. We only paid appearance fees for the PGA and tennis stars, which ranged from $3,000 to as high as $25,000. (Arnold Palmer was more, but he cut his fee in half as a favor to his friend Howdy Giles.) We booked all the pros through their sports agents, such as IMG and Leader Enterprises (golf) and Advantage International (tennis). We tried to align our tournament with the LPGA McDonald's Championship and worked through players like Cindy Figg-Currier to recruit as many as twenty pros a year. There were no contracts or agents involved and all the ladies were paid a modest stipend of $300. We never paid a fee to other celebrities or sport's stars but did pay travel expenses for Spanky McFarland and a few others.

In 1986, we arranged a partnership with the LPGA McDonald's Championship. Basically, we agreed to assist with introductions to Delaware companies in exchange for a donation of $100,000 from the McDonald's proceeds. This was reduced to $50,000 the next year and then the deal expired. The year 1986 was our most successful financially, with our tournament contributing $200,000 after expenses to Leukemia research.

The McDonald's Championship had a terrific run in Delaware. While golfing great Betsy Rawls was the face of the tournament, the event was controlled by Herb Lotman, a supplier to McDonald's from Pennsylvania. Lotman lined up other McDonald's suppliers from around the country which formed the financial platform for the tournament. While certainly a mainstay on the LPGA Tour calendar in nearby Malvern, PA, when it moved to Wilmington it was bolstered by a significant DuPont investment of money and people and reached the top echelon of national sporting events, raising a record $2 million a year for McDonald's Children's Charities. When DuPont began to pare back its participation due to global pressures on the company, Lotman made the fatal mistake of

moving the tournament to Havre de Grace, Maryland. It went into rapid decline and folded four years later.

Mickey Mantle's comment in *The Last Boy* was not the only book where the Leukemia Classic was mentioned. Soon after Payne Stewart's appearance in 1988, I received a call from writer Allan Zullo, who was writing a book entitled *The Golf Hall of Shame*. Zullo said he had been told that Payne Stewart had lost

The day Payne Stewart lost his knickers, left to right Mike Osberg, me, Payne Stewart, Charlie McDowell and Tom Ciconte

his knickers in a golf match in Wilmington and asked if I might have a photo. It was true, we did have a photo of Payne standing next to LPGA player Cindy Figg-Currier in his jockey briefs and one of him posing with our committee. Zullo and co-author Bruce Nash wanted to prominently feature the story and photo in their book. I promised him I would get back to him.

While Payne was surely one of the golf world's more colorful characters, I wasn't sure he would want the photo without his knickers "going viral." I called Payne's agent, Robert Fraley, to ask him. Fraley, who would later die in the same plane crash that killed Stewart, said he would mention it to Payne and then get back to me. Much to the delight of Zullo and Nash, Stewart said OK. The authors highlighted the incident on the cover of the book and quoted me. They decided to use the photo with Figg-Currier, and I had never thought to check with her before giving them the photo and permission to run it. A few years later while playing in the area, Cindy, her husband and baby stayed at our home. The subject of the photo never came up.

After John Daly shocked the golfing world to win the 1991 PGA Championship, several Classic committee members immediately raised the idea of bringing him to Wilmington for our event. Recognizing that Daly was a different breed of player compared to the country club types we had worked with previously, some of us worried about what we might be getting into. Daly's representative turned out to not be the easiest person to work with, which added to the uncertainty around our planning.

In May of 1992, only weeks before Daly's appearance in Wilmington, his future wife was about to give birth to their daughter. Following events in the national media, it appeared to be a complicated relationship (Daly would later be accused of assaulting her), and rumors were rampant about Daly's difficulties with alcohol. It would turn out that the countdown to the birth of their baby and the date of our event were running in parallel. Another complication with Daly was his fear of flying. With forty-eight hours to tournament day, Daly did not have a flight booked, and we had no back-up plan if he failed to show. The night before the tournament when I spoke to the agent, he informed me the birth would happen at any moment and he "hoped" to get John on a plane right after.

Early the next morning I got a call from the agent telling me the baby had been born and Daly was on a flight to Philadelphia. Checking the times, it was clear he would arrive at least an hour late for our planned schedule, and if we had traffic issues on I-95 to the Philadelphia airport, he might miss half the day. I called some contacts and was soon in a police cruiser on the way to the airport. When a disheveled John Daly exited the plane, he looked at me with bloodshot eyes, hands shaking, and said, "Do you think you guys can take me straight to a McDonald's? I'm desperate for a Big Mac!"

After driving the nearly comatose Daly to the Hercules Country Club, we pulled in with an informal greeting committee gathering around the car. Looking around, Daly turned to me and said, "I need a couple Buds, real bad." As someone ran off for the beer and we collected Daly's clubs to put them on a cart, I turned to a tournament committee member, Jim Eversman and said. "This guy is a wreck. I think his life will have a bad ending."

Daly continued to slump in the cart as we drove him out to the seventh fairway. The plan was to have the long-hitting man with the mullet haircut hit a shot with every group, pose for photos, and then drive on to the next group until we had worked our way through some forty fivesomes. To my complete surprise, as we pulled up to the first gathering of players and spectators, Daly jumped out of the cart and glad handed everyone saying, "Hi, I'm John Daly. Want to see me hit one?" He then blasted a three wood off the grass, higher and farther than I had ever seen a golf ball fly. And he continued that act for the next five hours, knocking down Budweisers the entire time. When Daly flew out that night, I was in awe of his talent but worried his life might have a bad ending. Daly has had his struggles since (including losing millions gambling), but he managed to shock the golf world again by winning the Open Championship at St. Andrews in Scotland. The members of the "Royal & Ancient" are still trying to understand what happened.

Recently, Town Square Delaware publisher and business executive Michael Fleming stopped by my house to give me a copy of a book by a former congressman from California, James Rogan. The book's title was *And Then I Met…*. It was Rogan's personal story about his boyhood obsession of meeting and having his photo taken with famous people. When I opened up the book, the first chapter I came to was about child actor George "Spanky" McFarland. As I looked at photos with Spanky on the walls in my home, the thought crossed my mind that maybe I should think about my own book. Mostly, though, it caused me to think about the years of friendship with the little fat man known to generations of kids as Spanky.

With help from Leukemia Society executive director Laurie McArthur, Kevin Reilly and I would sign letters to various celebrities and sports legends inviting them to our tournament. Many would go unanswered. One particularly memorable response was a multi-paragraph letter from football legend "Broadway" Joe Namath. Joe thanked me for the invitation, wished us luck raising money for a worthy cause, but ended with the line, "John, I don't even like golf!" We received surprises when stars like Richard Roundtree (*Shaft*), Dale Robertson (*Death Valley Days*) and Dennis Frantz (*Hill Street Blues*) said they wanted to join us. But Spanky was the one who went all in. Wilmington was not just a stop on his schedule. He enjoyed meeting new friends here, especially *Our Gang* fans, including former Eagle Bill Bergey, dentist Howdy Giles, and patrons of Stanley's Tavern in north Wilmington.

Although he was only sixty-four when he passed away in 1993, Spanky was one of the last survivors of the *Our Gang* cast. Spanky would become emotional anytime he heard mention of Buckwheat, Darla, Stymie, or Alfalfa. He would also defend their reputations as if they were family members, and he objected to others using the *Our Gang* label, which was never trademarked

Our favorite "Little Rascal" in knickers

We had some great personalities headline our event for more than a dozen years, but not every PGA professional can light up the room like Payne Stewart or entertain like Peter Jacobsen or Chi Chi Rodriquez. Fuzzy Zoeller could charm an audience, but shortly after we first booked him, I saw him at a PGA event and he went out of his way to warn me that he was just a golf pro. "John, I can't do that shit Chi Chi does," he said. Johnny Miller, Fred Couples, Ben Crenshaw, and Craig Stadler all could hit a golf ball, and John Daly was a truly unique athlete, but it was becoming clear we were running out of the entertainers.

In 1996, we booked PGA champion and future Ryder Cup captain Paul Azinger. Zinger had been diagnosed with cancer following his win that year, so we felt his story of recovery would be a good fit for our event. The challenge with Zinger was his schedule, and the only way to make it work was if we could arrange for a private plane. Since the Wilmington-based credit card giant MBNA had a jet for every day of the week, I contacted my friend Ken Boehl and asked if the company would donate a flight. MBNA agreed, and I traveled as the only passenger to Bradenton, Florida—basically for the purpose of identifying Azinger at the airport. He arrived with agent Robert Fraley and immediately began his own inspection of the corporate jet. He walked around it at least two times, asked about the company and talked to the pilots. He told me on the flight he just wanted to make sure everything was safe. It was sadly ironic that Paul Azinger was Payne Stewart's best friend on the PGA Tour and that Stewart and Fraley would die on a similar plane five years later.

The other interesting encounter with Azinger occurred the day after the tournament when committee member Charlie McDowell hosted us for golf at the famed Pine Valley Golf in Clementon, New Jersey. Zinger lived in the area during his teens when his father was stationed at nearby McGuire Air Force Base, and he had always wanted to play the course. As we finished our morning round and headed into the club house, we ran into former President George H.W. Bush. The former president was as excited to see Paul Azinger as we were to see the president. He was very gracious and spent time having his photo taken with each of

Golf with PGA champion Paul Azinger and a chance meeting with the 41st president

us. When the always animated and outgoing John DiEleuterio stood next to Mr. Bush he said, "Mr. President, I'm a Democrat, but I voted for you in the last election." (Bush, of course, lost to Clinton in 1992.)

President Bush turned to John and said, "John, if half the people who have told me that since the election actually voted for me, I would still be president!"

The next time I shook hands with President Bush would be at a Mike Castle fundraiser at his Kennebunkport home fifteen years later … and he was wearing a Pine Valley blazer.

Chapter 25

Henry Milligan and Pro Management Inc. (PMI), 1986

"White can't fight"

A lthough boxer Henry Milligan did not like to play golf (perhaps the only sport the Princeton sports phenom never mastered), he would appear at the Leukemia Classic every year. Neither Kevin Reilly nor I knew the former national amateur heavyweight boxing champion well, but we would quickly come to know his brother Michael, who walked into our Xerox office one day looking for a sales position. This connection led to a year-long crazy ride like no other. It turned out that at that time, Henry and Michael were discussing changing Henry's boxing management. When Michael mentioned this development to me, I suggested having a meeting to include Murray Sawyer and Kevin Reilly. Before long, we formed Pro Management Inc. (PMI) to support Henry's boxing career. We didn't know a lick about boxing, but Henry needed help and we were willing to try.

Henry Milligan is certainly one of the most unique figures in Delaware sports history, and it was a thrill be part of his journey for that brief time. Thanks to the man who slugged it out with Mike Tyson and Evander Holyfield, we entered a truly different world to include the sparring gyms of Philadelphia, the offices of New York promoters, the glitz of Atlantic City casinos, and eventually the frenzied world of sports agents and the NFL Draft.

The most fascinating aspect of the boxing world from my perspective were the characters we encountered: colorful figures like our boxing consultant, Pat Duffy, promoter Bob Arum of Top Rank, Inc., his matchmaker, Teddy Brenner, our "cut man," Eddie "the Clot" Aliano, our security man "Mountain" (former heavyweight champ Joe Frazier called him "a mean looking dude"), and an assortment of managers and potential sparring partners hanging around the Philly gyms. Pat Duffy's original claim to fame was managing the U.S. Boxing team that included a young fighter named Cassius Clay (later Muhammad Ali). Over dinners in Philadelphia, he would regale us with stories about his glory days with Ali, George Foreman, and Sonny Liston.

While Kevin Reilly concentrated on helping Henry prepare mentally for his fights and managing the sports media, Murray Sawyer and I focused on the business side. With Henry's star rising in the sport, we went to New York City to negotiate a contract with Top Rank, Inc. Top Rank was a boxing promotion business run by Bob Arum, a former Bobby Kennedy Justice Department prosecutor who became the promoter of Muhammed Ali's fights. In addition to promoting high profile battles with legendary fighters like Ali, Marvin Hagler, Sugar Ray Leonard, George Foreman, and Evander Holyfield, he had a regular show on national television from Atlantic City's Resorts International Casino on Friday nights.

All smiles at the Irish Pub after a big Atlantic City win

We believed Bob Arum saw our handsome, Princeton pedigree, heavy-hitting Henry as a guy who could fill seats, excite crowds and bring in new fans, but on our visit to discuss a contract we first had to talk to Arum's "matchmaker." Teddy Brenner was a cynical character who was skeptical about white boxers. "White can't fight," he pronounced, as we tried to discuss Henry's prospects for a title-fight. A bit deflated, we headed into Arum's rather spartan office for a meandering discussion about his experiences with Muhammed Ali. He invited us to continue the discussion over sandwiches at a neighborhood bar, but it remained hard to see where our conversation was leading. Back in his office, we were surprised when he handed us a one-year contract culminating with a title fight paying $500,000. All we needed was for Henry to win his next three fights.

As we were closing out the meeting that day, we told Arum we expected a signing bonus (our only real leverage was the possibility of approaching Arum's archrival Don King, which we were not excited about). Arum objected, stating he did not give signing bonuses. After a minute of silence, he asked what we had in mind. We said $25,000 and he immediately responded, "I'll give you $10,000." After he wrote the check and handed it to us, we dashed out of the building and jumped in a taxi before his man Brenner could talk him out of it.

While Kevin Reilly, as a former NFL linebacker and sports commentator, seemed to easily fit into the boxing scene, Murray and I, often attired in business suits or golf shirts, were looked at with some skepticism. In the gyms, they didn't know if we were from the FBI or refugees from a local country club. On one occasion, the police stopped us outside of Champs' Gym in North Philadelphia in what I could only describe as "suspicion of being culturally confused." Later, in a profile piece on Milligan in *Philadelphia* magazine, the author referred to us as "looking like a couple of ministers in the middle of a gang war."

When I published a series on Milligan and PMI in Town Square Delaware back in 2015, I received numerous calls and comments from friends and contacts developed since the 1980s who never knew about my fight management days. One friend from New Jersey joked that I should have been sued for malpractice. But the fact was that Henry knew what he needed to do to be successful (not many fighters have a Princeton engineering degree and membership in Mensa), and if anything, he expressed gratitude for the support he received.

Boxing for PMI ended on a bloody night in Atlantic City when Henry met a quick tough fighter from Detroit named Frankie Minton. Henry had been sick in bed with the flu the week prior to the bout, but we could not talk him out of fighting. Minton's record included strong performances against some of the great boxers of the era, such as James Kinchen and Iran Barkley. While the fight was close, Minton caught Henry with a shot that broke his nose. Eddie "the Clot" tried to work his magic to halt the bleeding, but the referee stopped the contest. Soon Henry hung up the gloves (though he would later make a

Familiar pose with Henry, ringside at the Roy Jones Jr. fight in 2016. Event coordinator Carie Riley in background

comeback) and pursued his MBA at New York University. While there, he was cast as a boxer in Robert De Niro's film *Night and the City* and appeared in commercials for Gillette.

Our brief association with future NFL MVP quarterback and TV football commentator Rich Gannon was another memorable episode. We had convinced ourselves that, based on our Milligan experience and Kevin's NFL history, we could provide professional representation to young athletes reaching for their NFL star. (In addition to potential superstar Gannon, there were two UD grads hoping to be picked up in the draft, plus our friend and fellow Xerox salesman Dan Reeder still hoped for another shot at the NFL.) What we would find out was that, while Kevin knew football and Murray was rapidly coming up the curve on the legal aspects of being a sports agent, we were total neophytes at this game. But the college senior sought after by nearly every agent in the country bought our pitch and signed with PMI. Our honeymoon would not last long.

When Kevin Reilly and I saw Rich Gannon recently at Delaware football coach Tubby Raymond's memorial service, I joked that he might still owe us money from his short-lived contract. We had a good laugh just before he delivered a beautiful eulogy about the legendary coach.

PMI probably represented Gannon for about a month before he discarded us for International Management Group (IMG), the largest firm in the business. Our Gannon time was a rollercoaster ride, with Kevin Reilly in the front seat for most of it. Kevin, with his own NFL experience attended Gannon's workouts with NFL scouts and quickly concluded that Gannon was a thoroughbred athlete with a cocky confidence to back it up. He said Rich would push back when scouts requested that he run additional sprints because they could not believe their own stop watches. Due to his superior athleticism, the NFL began to think of him more as a defensive back prospect than a quarterback. Sure enough, when the New England Patriots drafted Gannon, they informed us they wanted him in the defensive backfield.

When you look back on Gannon's challenging early years in the NFL and see the heights he ultimately ascended (NFL Most Valuable Player in 2002), you have to credit his singular dedication out of college to pursuing his dream on his own terms. He informed our team on day one that he was only interested in being a quarterback. That point was later driven home to Murray when he spoke to Gannon's father, a Philadelphia attorney.

Based on his personal experience in the league and listening to the scouts' views on what they perceived to be Gannon's highest potential, Kevin felt Gannon might be selling himself short if he did not go for the best deal and then work on the inside to achieve his ultimate goal. Having such a limited experience with Gannon, Kevin and I decided to seek the advice of the man we thought would know him best, UD football coach Tubby Raymond. Tubby told us about his own discussions with Rich about his future, and although he felt Kevin had a point about signing the best deal today and then trying to become an NFL quarterback, he told us we would most likely be unsuccessful selling Rich on the idea. As Coach Raymond told us, "John, Kevin, some people think they are the leader of the band. Rich Gannon believes he is the whole band!"

When Gannon asked if he could be released from his contract with PMI to work with IMG, we quickly agreed to an amicable separation. It had become clear to us that if we were going to be successful in the sports agent line of work, we would have to have a higher level of dedication than any of us were willing to give this "side business."

Chapter 26

Headhunter, 1990–1994

"Prepare as best you can, but Gossage will not like anything you do."

After sixteen years with Xerox as a salesman, sales manager, district sales manager, and regional marketing manager, I began to feel like the walls were closing in. My waning interest was partly a matter of doing the same thing, day in and day out, with few career alternatives to change the picture. I also learned that corporate politics played a big role in promotion to the next level. I was never very effective applying the lessons learned in external politics to the corporate world, and in a career counseling session with our regional VP, I was told that due to a backlog of candidates it could be five years or more before I might advance. I walked out of the meeting thinking it was time to look around. (It would not surprise me if one day someone writes a book about those who went on to success after a stint with Xerox, including Starbucks' founder Howard Schultz and Michael Nutter, former mayor of Philadelphia. In the three decades since I left the company, I have crossed paths with dozens of individuals who have gone on to great careers in other fields—a testament, no doubt to the quality of the Xerox hiring and training program.)

As I was considering the lack of promotion opportunities at Xerox, I was being contacted by executive recruiters regarding other career paths. One possibility I responded to was a marketing position with the Philadelphia Flyers. When I met with the recruiter, Howard Fischer, he changed the subject to ask if I would be interested in going into the retained executive search business. I knew nothing about that world; I thought recruiters worked on a contingency basis and were paid only if a candidate was hired. Nonetheless, he gave me a book aptly titled *The Headhunters*. I found the business it described to be fascinating, and I agreed to continue discussions with Fischer.

When an offer came in from Howard to join his firm, I contacted two friends who had senior human resource manager positions with major regional companies. They conveyed some apprehension about Howard, and both suggested that if I wanted to go into the business, I should consider other firms. Another friend working as a search consultant in Chicago, urged me to negotiate at least a two-year contract because it would take that long to build a client base.

Regardless of my friends' words of caution, I moved forward with Howard. It was a "bird in the hand" situation, and I just did not want to go back to my Xerox desk another day. I also thought that, worst case, I would learn the business and could always go out on my own or join another firm. So I accepted the offer to join Howard Fischer as vice president for Delaware business.

About a month into the job, Howard came into my office and handed me a "non-compete" agreement, something we had never previously discussed. At that point, I began to realize the hazardous nature of being subject to the whim of one man or woman. There really was no process, system, or organizational structure. It was all about the owner and his perception of the world that day and in the future.

I enjoyed modest success with Howard Fischer Associates, but it was never enough. One of the challenges was the advent of the recession of 1990-91, which took hold shortly after I started in the business. With employment down, executive searches declined as well. Smaller (or what was referred to as "boutique") search firms began to cut deals by lowering the customary thirty-three percent of total first year compensation fee to capture what business was available. Anticipating the possibility of cuts, I began discussions with two other firms, but after fourteen months at Fischer, I decided it was best to strike out on my own.

In 1991, there was limited use of technology in the search business—the primary tools available were a phone and a Rolodex. Calling every business contact I had, within a few months I landed searches with Governor Castle, MBNA, the Delaware River and Bay Authority (DRBA), and Hercules. I was retained by other clients, including Mayor Frawley, Christiana Care, and Beneficial Bank for what were essentially research projects and partial searches.

I did not realize it at the time, but Mike Castle would be the first of four Delaware governors who I would work for in some capacity (Castle, Carper, Markell, and Carney—Markell in a volunteer capacity, chairing a small group of business leaders planning a state response to the crisis created by the DuPont-Dow merger). My work for Castle included searches for new directors for the pension office, the Division of Mental Health, and the new Department of Children, Youth, and Families. The work for Mayor Frawley was to determine the feasibility of attracting an experienced executive to run a possible Wilmington convention center. While this project never went forward, the need would ultimately be filled by development of the Chase Center.

MBNA was a fascinating client. With their "Affinity Card" concept, they capitalized on Delaware's favorable banking laws and the insatiable appetite of Americans for credit. The money poured into the state from around the country, fueling big salaries and impacting everything from estate homes in Greenville, luxury cars, expanded private schools, new restaurants, and millions of square feet of new office space. They began to literally dominate the philanthropic landscape, pouring vast sums into the arts, human services, and education. Also at that time, the card giant had become a public company, which required additional talent and staff to comply with SEC requirements.

I was retained to conduct a number of executive searches for MBNA, working primarily with Doug Rothwell followed by Ken Boehl. Rothwell was a talented outsider who never seemed to be comfortable with the MBNA culture. When Doug left to join Governor Castle's staff, he was replaced by Boehl. Ken had been with MBNA from the start and rose rapidly to positions of increasing responsibility. Smart, patient, kind, and extremely hard-working, Ken was everything you would want a business leader to be.

When I decided to go out on my own, I gave little thought to what it meant to be an entrepreneur. After seventeen years of working for others, including a Fortune 100 company, I suddenly found myself shopping for and paying retail prices for health care, disability, and life insurance, while paying estimated taxes and both ends of the social security payroll tax. While I had been a Republican for over a dozen years, my conservative views intensified as I began to view government waste and spending with a more critical eye.

Tom Carper was elected governor in 1992, and during his early discussions with the outgoing governor (and congressman-elect), Mike Castle, he asked him about the challenge of recruiting talent for his cabinet. Castle was kind enough to suggest that Carper give me a call, and shortly after, I was hired as a consultant to Carper's transition team. The co-chairs of the transition were a couple of Wilmington lawyers,

Steve Rothschild, a corporate lawyer with the high-powered firm of Skadden Arps, and Leo Strine, who was slotted to become Carper's legal counsel. For a period that extended from November until after Carper's inauguration, I scoured the country looking for talent while meeting weekly with Carper or the co-chairs to review candidates or update them on our progress.

My time working with Carper and his transition was one of the most intense and exciting business and political experiences I had ever had. Nothing was more important to the state's chief executive than selecting the right team. The governor-elect would not be deterred from his mission to find the very best people for his government, in spite of the fact that it had been sixteen years since a Democrat had held power and there were many politically connected people raising their hands. Adding to the frustration felt in the Democratic political ranks was the fact that Carper had retained a known Republican to help him in his quest. State Democratic leaders and legislators let Carper and his team know they were not happy.

With the added political pressure, it was imperative that every decision be able to withstand both professional and political scrutiny. Strine and Rothschild were the perfect committee co-chairs. Steve, who never cracked a smile, was bright and professional and asked all the right questions. Leo, whose sense of humor and quirky style has since become famous in the legal community, was the political guy who always ensured he had Carper's back. Towards decision time on each search, Carper became fully engaged, getting to know the candidates and taking final responsibility for the choice.

Carper had strong views about the search for his chief of economic development. He had briefly worked at the state economic development office before running for state treasurer, and he believed that the state should deemphasize the current model of recruiting companies from outside the state and move towards a model he called "grow our own." Some of the ideas being discussed had been put forth by author and futurist David Osborne in books such as *Reinventing Government* and *Laboratories of Democracy*. In a meeting with Strine and Rothschild to review our progress on the economic development position, Strine said, "I guess we can't just call up David Osborne and get his ideas."

I had learned in the search business that it really was not all that difficult to "network through" to reach people with whom you wanted to speak. Before the afternoon was out that day, I had spent a half hour on the phone with David Osborne. On the list of names Osborne gave me who fit the profile we were searching for, was a guy by the name of Bob Coy. Osborne had met Bob at a conference, and he was impressed by the things he was doing in Pennsylvania, including his work with the Ben Franklin Partnership. After I interviewed him a couple days later in Valley Forge, I recommended that Carper meet him. It turned out that Bob had an offer for a position in the new Clinton administration, but Carper liked him and persuaded him to join his team. Bob's selection would have major implications for me for years to come.

For a period of four months I had devoted nearly one hundred percent of my time to Carper's transition, so it was time to get back to developing other clients. One of the searches I completed around that time was for Hercules. I look back today on my connections with Hercules and think it must have been preordained that someday I would work for them full time. Hercules had been one of my largest corporate accounts at Xerox, and I came to know various members of the executive team through my association with the Leukemia Classic golf tournament and my friendship with Tom Ciconte, who served in several executive level positions and Bob Fraser, who was a possible future CEO.

One day Tom invited me to join him in a round of golf with chairman & CEO Tom Gossage. Before we finished, Gossage asked me if I would like to conduct a search to recruit a woman to manage executive communications. It was my first deep dive into the executive culture at Hercules. As I prepared for my initial meeting to review the search Ciconte warned me, "Prepare as best you can, but Gossage will not like anything you do."

To my surprise, the Gossage meeting went better than expected. Within the first month I had lined up three talented women, including a young presidential speech writer in the Bush White House. After completing references, the nod was given to Amy Binder, whom I had recruited from Arco Chemical. While many viewed Gossage as a rather cold-blooded leader, I had made a connection with him. Another relationship developed during the search was with Don Kirtley, the company's vice president of public affairs. I had met Don years before through Republican activities. He had worked for Senator Bill Roth in Washington and was a true Delaware political insider. He became an advisor to me when I joined Hercules years later.

Mike Harkins, my old political mentor, had served a few years as Delaware's secretary of state before Governor Mike Castle appointed him executive director of the Delaware River and Bay Authority (DRBA). While his tenure there would ultimately have a bad ending, he moved quickly to transition the agency from a sleepy political sinecure to an economic development engine for Delaware and southern New Jersey. One of the challenges Harkins had at the DRBA was to try to turn around the Cape May to Lewes ferry system, improving the service and minimizing its losses. He called me one day and said, "Riles, do you think you could find me an admiral to run the ferry system." I mention this brief experience because it led to one of the great personal relationships of my life.

To begin the "admiral" search I decided to call the U.S. Naval Academy alumni office. The lead alumni executive was a retired captain, and during the course of our discussion, he suggested I talk to Admiral "Bud" Edney. When he explained that Edney had recently retired as Supreme Allied Commander of NATO, I thought that I would have no chance of getting this guy on the phone. But he also mentioned that Edney had been chief of naval personnel and commandant of the Naval Academy, so no one would know the Navy's top leaders better than Admiral Edney. To my surprise, Bud picked up the phone when I called,

and we spoke for nearly an hour. We found out we had at least one thing in common—we were both avid golfers.

While Bud Edney referred several excellent candidates to us, the search took a turn halfway through when Harkins decided to go with another referral. But the contact with Bud started a decades-long relationship with an American hero who had flown 350 combat missions over North Vietnam and captained the carrier U.S.S. Constellation. Bud was on the same mission as John McCain when McCain was shot down.

With Admiral Edney on the Carrier Midway, 66th anniversary of the Battle of Midway

When I first met McCain and mentioned I was a friend of fellow pilot Bud Edney, the diminutive senator and presidential candidate looked up at me and said, "Son, you couldn't call me a pilot, but I can tell you that Bud Edney was a hell of a pilot."

PART IV

Delaware

Economic Development

Chapter 27

Delaware Economic Challenges, 1994–1995

"Governor, this is a real honor to have you visit us in person. We can't even get a New York City councilman to return our phone calls."

It would be difficult to overstate the challenges facing the Delaware economy in the early '90s. For nearly two hundred years, the DuPont company had dominated the state's economic landscape. It wasn't just the 24,000 jobs they accounted for in 1991, but the fact that these were high paying headquarters and research and development positions. DuPont's progeny, Hercules and Atlas (ICI), were also pillars of the local economy, along with the auto plants which were critical to the manufacturing sector. Hundreds of small businesses and thousands of families were dependent on the jobs and wealth generated by these corporate giants.

In July 1991, citing the impact of global competition, DuPont chairman and CEO Ed Woolard announced a billion-dollar cost cutting program that would eliminate thousands of jobs and signal the beginning of the end of a DuPont-dominated Delaware. Global competition had also been battering the auto industry for years, and just one month after Tom Carper was elected, General Motors announced it would close Wilmington's Boxwood Road assembly plant, signaling the loss of 3,500 critical manufacturing jobs.

Uncertain times in Delaware

Governor-elect Carper loved to refer to himself as a "glass half-full guy," but he would need more than slogans of optimism to get through the dilemma being posed by a complete reordering of the Delaware and global economy. Adding to his challenge was that many misunderstood the scope of what we were facing, including the editors of the *News Journal*. In an editorial the day after the GM closure announcement, they wrote:

> *The state's governmental and industrial leaders must begin an aggressive outreach program to replace lost manufacturing jobs. The goal, which should be as clearly articulated as the Financial Center Development Act, should be to broaden manufacturing job opportunities that take advantage of global markets.*

With the benefit of hindsight, we can see today that the challenges facing Delaware were not going to be fixed by a plan to broaden manufacturing job opportunities. This was not just a Delaware problem; it was a national issue. The United States was losing millions of manufacturing jobs due to vast productivity improvements and to overseas competition. The economy was increasingly becoming service-based. Fortunately, former governor Pete du Pont and others had the foresight to have passed and implemented the Financial Center Development Act (FCDA) in 1981, which would help to fill some of the economic void.

While Bob Coy was making progress in his first year implementing the new "grow our own" approach to economic development in Delaware, he had some political challenges because he was an outsider and many business and government leaders were of the view that economic development meant recruiting new companies. Feeling a need to increase the recruitment focus, Bob asked me to meet with him to discuss a search for a sales executive to lead a beefed-up state marketing effort. In reviewing his thoughts on the position profile, Bob paused and said, "I'm looking for someone just like you. Why don't you consider the job?"

While I liked the idea, there were some complications since I was managing several searches at the time. I said if he could allow me time to close out my accounts I would be interested. The next day I met with the governor, and I was formally offered the position.

As soon as the word got out on my appointment, protests erupted from some state Democrats. For several days I did not know where things would end up, but I learned that other Democrats weighed in support of my appointment, thus calming the waters. One of those who contacted the governor to boost my candidacy was Ed Bennett, a state representative. I had gotten to know the well-respected Bennett during a golf trip I went on each spring with others from political circles—the bipartisan affair was eventually taken over by John Burris at the Delaware State Chamber and was dubbed the "Southern Policy Conference." Ed was a great guy who died way too young.

When I accepted the position in economic development, I did so thinking I would stay two years (that is, to the end of Carper's first term), and then return to my executive search practice. I was confident the role would allow me to expand my knowledge of Delaware businesses and enhance my level of contacts. As it turned out, I would end up staying with the Carper administration for nearly six years.

During my time with the office, we implemented several strategic initiatives in response to the changing economy, as we also reacted to significant threats and opportunities along the way. The headline events over my time were saving Playtex Products in Dover, growth issues involving major banks, development of the Biotechnology Institute, and the fight over AstraZeneca, but there were other stories involving Delaware leaders and personalities along the way. The fun would begin on day one.

On that first day I reported to the Dover office to meet the staff, I was informed by Bob Coy that I needed to fill in for him the next day and join the governor on a trip to New York to meet with the CEOs of the nation's largest banks. Since my first day was filled with introductions, I would be heading off with the governor with zero preparation.

There are banks, and then there is JP Morgan. Their legacy included their founder J. Pierpont Morgan bailing out the U.S. Treasury in 1895 and helping to rescue the country from a two-year economic depression.

Upon arrival on executive row in their august Wall Street offices, you could feel the history and the stuffy high finance environment. Standing among the pin-striped Morgan leadership team sipping coffee, Carper and I looked like we had purchased our suits at Sears. After we took our seats around the board room table, chairman and CEO Douglas A. Warner III announced, "Governor, this is a real honor to have you visit us in person. We can't even get a New York City councilman to return our phone calls." Of course, the pin-striped team laughed right on cue. Warner then immediately turned his attention to me, the guy who thought he came along to carry the governor's briefcase and take notes.

"John," he said. "We are all looking forward to your presentation on why we should stay and expand in Delaware."

Fortunately for me, I had been selling recruits on moving to Delaware for several years so after shaking off the shock of Warner's announcement, I was able to plow ahead without making a complete fool out of myself.

The biggest issue in 1994 was the announced closure of the General Motors plant. It was a big blow to the state. In response, Carper established the GM Task Force to look at strategies to save the plant, reuse potential for the million square foot facility, and other ideas to recruit replacement manufacturing jobs to Delaware. Mike Hare, a business development specialist on the DEDO staff represented the office on the Task Force. (The office changed its name in 1994 from Delaware Development Office to Delaware Economic Development Office, or DEDO.) He recruited a national economic development firm, Wadley-Donovan, to study the situation and make recommendations.

The Wadley Donovan report recommended a full-scale business recruitment campaign targeting small to mid-sized manufacturers in the northeast corridor. The plan conflicted or at least changed the focus away from the Carper "grow our own" approach, so I was worried as Mike and I prepared to present it to Carper and the cabinet. As I feared, it did not go over well and the governor let us know it. He compared the strategy of providing financial incentives to companies selling cars by offering rebates. But he agreed to allow us to present the plan to the business community to see what the response was.

A few weeks later we invited the business community to the Gold Ballroom of the Hotel DuPont to hear Dennis Donavon of the Wadley-Donovan firm present the plan. An important segment of the plan was to create a "marketing council" where companies would help fund business trips and advertising campaigns to sell the benefits of locating in Delaware. While the business community reacted positively to selling Delaware and recruiting new businesses, they did not initially like the idea of paying for it. Other business organizations, such as the Chamber of Commerce, also did not like the idea of having another entity compete for limited corporate dollars.

One strategy several in the business community liked and were willing to fund was the idea of attracting a semiconductor manufacturer. Recruiting this high-tech industry was rapidly becoming the "Holy Grail" for cities and states around the country. Due to the high cost and regulatory restrictions of doing business in Silicon Valley, companies such as Intel, AMD, Texas Instruments, and various international electronics firms, were scouring the globe looking for new sites for their billion-dollar plants or "fabs." It was well known they were looking at the East Coast, so we decided to join in the game. Since a microchip plant would need lots of land, water, and energy it had appeal to developers and utilities. With this as a first line strategy we were able to raise hundreds of thousands of dollars for several years.

The view was that if we attracted one company, they would need hundreds of engineers and a thousand technicians. This would lead to other related businesses coming here and a business cluster forming. Since we did not have any experience in the industry, we were able to use the private sector funds to hire consultant Jack Barrington, who had recently retired from DuPont, where he had led a component of their business focused on selling DuPont products to the industry. Jack was the consummate professional salesman with a deep knowledge of the science.

Ultimately, several prominent companies looked at Delaware, but we were not successful in attracting a semiconductor manufacturer. However, the approach of combining the expertise and resources of the private sector to market Delaware had worked well. In 2017, this approach would be adopted for economic development by Governor John Carney, the business community, and the legislature, and I would find myself as the person tapped to get it up and running.

Chapter 28

Saving Playtex, 1994

*"All I can tell you is that when I give corporate this message,
they will say, back up the trucks, we're going to Virginia!"*

T he top story in the August 5, 1994 edition of the *News Journal* was the announcement that the sanitary protection division of Playtex Products in Dover had decided to stay in the city and build a 172,000 sq. ft. manufacturing facility. When CEO Joel Smilow made the announcement the day before, the 300 employees directly affected erupted with cheers and applause. The impact of losing Playtex in the heart of Dover may have been more serious than losing GM in New Castle County. The several months–long episode remains one of the most rewarding and emotional economic development projects I was ever involved with.

That spring, I had taken a call from Jim Cook, the general manager of Playtex in Dover. Jim told me they had to replace and expand their existing facility at an estimated cost of more than ten million dollars. He was instructed to look at other states. Virginia had made an aggressive offer of three million dollars in relocation assistance and free land with infrastructure in place, and unless Delaware could do something drastic,

Playtex will remain in Dover

Longtime ties are factor in decision

By JANE BROOKS
Staff reporter

DOVER — Playtex Products Inc. is staying in Dover and will build a $10 million addition to its Saulsbury Road plant to house its sanitary-protection division.

The news, delivered by chairman and chief executive officer Joel E. Smilow, drew cheers, whistles and a standing ovation from more than 300 employees Thursday. Their jobs are secure.

For James Cook, senior vice president of operations and man-

ager of the Dover plant, it was "the best birthday present ever."

The decision to remain in Dover was made by the company's board of directors after visiting the local facilities Thursday. The announcement at a hastily called gathering of government officials and media ended speculation on the plant's future.

In June, Sara Lee Corp., which bought Playtex Apparel in 1991, announced it would need the space leased to Playtex Products' tampon division to consolidate apparel production in 1996.

Playtex, part of the Dover economy for 57 years, began site shopping in June. Other states came courting.

Delaware economic development officials came up with a $3 million incentive package over three years to help build the 172,000-square-foot facility. City and county governments promised tax breaks.

In the end, "the decision turned on history and the concern for employees, many of whom have over 30 years of service" at the Dover plant, Smilow said.

"Preserving the more than 300 jobs and nearly $3 million in state revenues that are represented at this facility is critical to the health of the state and local economy," Gov. Carper told the gathering.

The company came to Dover in

1937 with sales of $1 million, Smilow said. Today, sales are approaching $500 million and Playtex has spawned "three home-grown companies — ILC [Dover], Reichhold Chemical and Playtex Apparel," he said.

Playtex Products is a leading manufacturer of personal care products marketed under the brand names Playtex and Ultimates tampons, Playtex disposable nursing systems for infants, Cherubs baby products, Banana Boat sun and skin-care products, Jhirmack hair products and Tek toothbrushes.

Dover is the company's largest location with 950 full-time employees and three plants.

The News Journal/GARY EMEIGH

Ressurecion Pearls and co-workers react to news their jobs are safe.

he did not see any way his corporate bosses in Connecticut would let him turn down Virginia's deal. The real kicker that never made it into the newspapers, however, was the fact that they would save at least $3.00 per hour per employee by moving, since Playtex's Dover employee base was older, more tenured, and better compensated. If they moved the sanitary protection unit, the rest of the company and up to a thousand jobs would move within a few years to the new site.

We huddled in the office to craft a response but there were disagreements over how serious the threat was. Some thought our advantages were many and the relocation disruptive and expensive for Playtex, so we should not overreact. In addition, we had no funds or funding mechanism in order to match (much less exceed) Virginia's offer, so we would have to go to the legislature for an appropriation—not impossible, but a bit messy when trying to keep negotiations confidential.

Finally, we decided to offer a $1 million loan. I was convinced by my earlier discussions with Cook that he wanted to stay in Dover, but he had little control over the final decision by corporate in Connecticut. I was also convinced my call to offer the million-dollar loan was not going to go well. After I got the words out, there was silence for a minute. Finally, Cook blurted out, "What!? Virginia will provide a $3 million in cash, plus free land, and you want to give us a small loan? All I can tell you is that when I give corporate this message, they will say, back up the trucks, we're going to Virginia!"

After Bob and I briefed the governor on the Playtex reaction, he agreed to match Virginia's offer of $3 million. We believed the money could be made available from a proposed new economic development vehicle dubbed the "Strategic Fund." Coy and the governor had proposed the $10 million fund during that session of the legislature, but it had not yet been considered. So, after leaving the governor, I headed to Legislative Hall to see Senator Nancy Cook (no relation to Playtex's Jim Cook), the powerful co-chair of the Capital Improvement (Bond) Committee.

Where state funds were concerned you had to have Nancy on your side. Since Playtex was critical to the economy of the fifteenth senatorial district, there was a good chance Nancy would try to help. I told her the time constraints we were working under and the potential consequences of a failure to act quickly. In classic Delaware bipartisan style, she took me by the hand and marched me down to a meeting room. She motioned to her Republican co-chair, Representative Bill Oberle, to join us.

Bill said, "Make it quick."

Nancy turned to me and said, "John, tell Bill why we need the money."

Standing in the hall with the door half open, I crammed the Playtex story into two minutes, finishing with the need for the $3 million. Bill listened attentively and said, "OK, I agree to the $3 million."

As he started to step back to his meeting, Nancy said, "Bill, we need agreement on the whole $10 million to cover projects in the future."

Oberle glanced back at us and said, "OK."

For twenty-four years, the Strategic Fund has continued to be the primary economic development tool for Delaware. In early 2018, as the interim CEO of the Delaware Prosperity Partnership, I had to make a brief presentation to the Council on Development Finance (CDF), the board that was set up after the Playtex project to consider economic development grants and loans. Although Nancy Cook lost her Senate seat in 2010, she continues to serve the state as a member of the council. After I spoke, Nancy with a smile on her face said, "John, tell everyone the story about how the Strategic Fund was created." Nancy was justifiably proud of her role. It not only demonstrated the power she wielded at that time, but also provided a glimpse into the bi-partisan trust that kept the state on a steady course for many years.

Several weeks after the Playtex announcement, I was in the Wilmington Trust bank branch in Dover filling out a deposit slip when two young women who had apparently not seen each other for a while were catching up. One asked the other about her job at Playtex. She responded by saying how much she loved her job and how grateful she was that the company had decided to stay.

You could sense how important this event was in that woman's life and it underlined how truly consequential the business of economic development could be. While the loss of Playtex would have had serious economic and political implications for Dover, the greatest impact would have been the human toll and the lives that would have been turned upside down. That moment in the bank did more to shape my commitment to Delaware's economic future than any other and it would play out on a larger scale when a few years later we were facing the loss of Delaware's largest pharmaceutical company, Zeneca.

Chapter 29

Scott, the Eagles, and the Riverfront, 1995–1996

"Never trust a man who wears a Nehru jacket or a pinky ring."

Not long after I joined DEDO, Jim Burke joined the staff as finance director. While I did not know Jim well, we were in the same graduating class at Salesianum, and in 1968, when I captained the UD golf team, Jim captained the UD tennis team. After leaving the Army and obtaining his MBA, Jim rose up in the ranks of the Manufacturers Hanover Bank in Manhattan and eventually moved back to Wilmington when they expanded operations here. Over the coming decade, Jim would have a significant impact on Delaware economic development. One of his early opportunities to exercise his business acumen occurred when Philadelphia-based Scott Paper was looking for a new headquarters.

In early 1995, the governor asked Tom Gossage, CEO of Hercules, to host an event at the Hercules Plaza in honor of Scott Paper CEO Al Dunlap. Attended by many Delaware business leaders, the pitch made that night along with a commitment to provide relocation assistance, resulted in a decision by Scott to move to Delaware. On May 3, 1995, Dunlap, soon nicknamed "Chainsaw Al" in the media, came to Wilmington for a press conference to announce the move. The press conference took place in the governor's conference room, with Gossage and future Hercules CEO Keith Elliott in attendance.

Generally regarded as a corporate turnaround specialist, Dunlap had already attracted scrutiny by the Philadelphia and national business press. To our surprise, many reporters showed up with cameras, mics, and questions. While there were a few softball questions at first, the

Philadelphia press started asking him about the corporate cuts he was making and about previous positions. If Dunlap did not like the question, he would answer, "That's a red herring. Next question." Soon, that was his answer to every question, and he finally said, "That's enough for today," and ended the press conference. Based on the look on the governor's face, he was probably thinking, *what have we just gotten ourselves into?*

Tom Gossage had his own reputation as a hard-nosed CEO, but even he was taken back by Dunlop's handling of the press. Speaking after the meeting, Gossage said to Elliott and me, "I wouldn't want to work for that guy." Then after a short pause he added, "But then again, I wouldn't want to work for me either."

We eventually negotiated a $1 million grant to help offset the cost of renovations to the Delaware Corporate Center in Talleyville and assist with the relocation of three hundred corporate headquarters personnel. In drawing up the grant agreement, Jim Burke included a standard recapture provision that would be exercised in the event Scott did not meet their obligations under the terms of the deal. Then, while finalizing the grant, Jim received word from one of his banking contacts that Dunlop was selling the company.

With concern that the jobs might not last long enough to achieve a payback on the state's investment and that Dunlap would ignore the recapture provision, Jim informed Bob Coy and the governor that he was going to stall sending the check. Soon, the Scott CFO was calling Burke and Dunlap was calling the governor. Finally, the news broke that they were selling the company to Kimberly Clark. With that, the jobs were almost certain to either not materialize or move soon after they were established. The suspicions about Dunlap were well founded, as he would later be barred from serving as an officer in any publicly traded company. Delaware never sent the check, and we benefited from the Scott upgrades at the Corporate Center and even taxed the employees' severance pay.

Jim Burke soon gained a reputation as our office's "Dr. No." He was particularly merciless on politically savvy businessmen who used their connections to come back for state support on a regular basis and he had a knack for sniffing out phonies and bad deals. A year later, when the Philadelphia Eagles let it be known they were in the market for a new training facility and willing to move out of Pennsylvania, Jim and I went to Veterans Stadium to meet with Eagles' president Joe Banner.

We were a bit skeptical that the Eagles were just trying to leverage Pennsylvania for funding for a new stadium and financial incentives for a new training center. Banner, strangely attired in a Nehru jacket, tilted back in his chair taking calls at regular intervals while we spoke. As we headed down the corridor after the meeting past the photos of Eagles' legends, Burke summarized his view of a possible Philadelphia Eagles' deal. "Riles," he said. "Never trust a man who wears a Nehru jacket or a pinky ring."

The Eagles, of course, built their new training center in Pennsylvania and pulled in $188 million from Philadelphia and the state towards construction of Lincoln Financial Field.

A couple of months before the Scott Paper announcement, I attended a meeting in Wilmington at which former Maryland governor William Donald Schaefer endorsed the idea of developing the wasteland along the Christina into a local and regional attraction in the same way he had led the effort to revitalize the Inner Harbor of Baltimore. The Wilmington riverfront concept was the vision of former Delaware governor Russ Peterson and others, and it would soon be fully embraced by Governor Carper. Not too long after the Schaefer meeting, the McKinsey consulting firm came to Delaware to review a study they had made of the state's attractiveness to business. Overall, McKinsey felt our body of favorable business laws and tax profile was competitive with most other states, and they did not have any new programs or legislation to suggest. They did have one major criticism—Delaware was boring and needed more excitement to attract young people. Carper looked at all of us and said, "That's why we need to build the Riverfront."

The Riverfront board was formed later than year, and funds were appropriated by the state legislature. The most important issue the new board faced was the question of who would lead the organization. Our office had no direct involvement in the Riverfront, but one Saturday morning in February 1996, I received a call from Mike Purzycki, who asked if I could join him for lunch at Gallucio's on Lovering Avenue. Over lunch, Mike told me how excited he was about the Riverfront project and why he thought he was well qualified to lead the effort. He mentioned that he was throwing his hat in the ring late and was concerned the board might be close to choosing another candidate before he had a chance to make his case. He wanted to know if I would contact the governor on his behalf.

I was immediately convinced that if anyone could turn this long-shot dream into a success it was Mike Purzycki, but going directly to the governor was a bit of a challenge for me. I had already had a couple run-ins with Carper chief of staff Jeff Bullock over what he correctly perceived to be end runs around him to Carper. I said yes to Mike, but I worried the whole thing might backfire. If I went to Jeff first, I was not sure what he would do with it, and if I went straight to Carper, Jeff would rightfully be angry and might scuttle Mike's chances, particularly if he favored another candidate.

After thinking about it all day Sunday, I decided to try to reach Governor Carper at home that night. In addition to the desire to help Purzycki, I was convinced that this was the best move the governor could make to ensure the future success of the Riverfront. He listened quietly as I listed all the reasons why I thought Purzycki would be perfect for the job. When I finished, the governor thanked me and said I had made some good points. He did not tip his hand as to what he might do.

I held my breath over the next several days, worried I might see a reaction from the chief of staff. Fortunately, within a few weeks Mike was named the executive director of the Riverfront Development Corporation (RDC). On March 12, 1996 the *News Journal* editorial page praised the decision to hire Purzycki. They wrote:

> *Mike Purzycki is a first-class choice to pilot development. If he pulls it off, he will go down in local annals as one of the men most instrumental in saving the city of Wilmington …*

After twenty years at the helm of the RDC, some came to suggest that only Mike Purzycki could turn around a city recently labeled "Murdertown" in a national publication. In a September 2016 hotly contested primary, Wilmington voters selected Purzycki as their new mayor.

Joining with Mayor Purzycki and WWII veteran Raymond Firmani following Memorial Day address about Wilmington POW James J. Connell.
Photo courtesy of Christy Fleming

Chapter 30

Behind the Scenes with DuPont
and MBNA, 1994–1995

*"John, while it may sound like a good plan, the
fact is that we hate MBNA …"*

In late September 1994, I received a call from John Snyder, who at the time was vice president of DuPont's global facilities, inviting Bob Coy and I to lunch at the Hotel DuPont Green Room. Snyder was joined by Bill Sullivan, who ran DuPont's hospitality assets, including the hotel and country clubs. Huddled at the corner "power table," Snyder gave us a glimpse into the challenges faced by "the Company" as he consumed a large bowl of fresh blueberries.

Part of the plan to meet those challenges, he said was to sell off nonessential assets. With the extraordinary growth of MBNA, they felt the credit card giant was a logical candidate to acquire the DuPont properties. The problem was that DuPont and MBNA did not talk to each other, so they wanted to enlist our help to pull it off. The specific request was for me to approach MBNA executive Lance Weaver and sell him on the idea of acquiring the Louviers complex. Louviers consisted of 637,00 square feet of offices near Newark, with an adjacent eighteen-hole golf course and country club.

Although I had spent a lot of time with the human resource executives and other department heads at the bank, I did not really know Lance Weaver. I was not even sure he would take my call, but he gave me an appointment for seven o'clock the next morning. At that point in MBNA's rapid rise, their Westgate complex in Ogletown stretched for blocks. Green awnings adorned the outside of the buildings and inside, above the doorways was displayed the ubiquitous slogan, "Think of Yourself as a Customer." Seated on a couch in Weaver's massive office, I made a pitch for DuPont, detailing the potential benefits of the Louviers acquisition, including the recreation options for their employees by acquiring the country club as a part of the package. Weaver listened but appeared unimpressed. When I finished, he shared a little bit about MBNA's preferred expansion approach and closed by saying they were not interested.

A couple of days after my meeting with Weaver, I joined a delegation from Delaware on a trade mission to South Africa. Nelson Mandela had come to power only five months prior, and the State Department had urged all the states to send an economic development delegation to the country to provide a boost to the new regime and develop business ties. The day after my arrival, I called the office to retrieve my messages. One of them was a call with DuPont's Bill Sullivan and MBNA's Lance Weaver together on the line. In obvious good spirits, they wanted to let me know that they would be announcing the next day that MBNA had acquired the entire Louviers complex, golf course and all. Clearly, Weaver must have been more impressed with the potential of Louviers than he let on during our meeting.

The trip to South Africa was a unique experience in many respects, beginning with the name of our in-country consultant, Ken Tuckey. Ken had a "soldier of fortune" quality about him; seemed to know everyone of importance or at least how to gain access to them; and could speak English, Afrikaans, and Bantu. After introducing us to various fruit and wine exporters in Cape Town, he headed out on other business. Our director of international trade John Pastor and I boarded a South African Airways 747 back to Johannesburg. About an hour into the two-hour flight, right after four hundred meals had been distributed to the passengers, the pilot, in a thick South African accent, asked for our attention. He then announced, "A flight attendant has found a note left on a tray indicating that a bomb has been placed on the plane."

As you can imagine, a gasp arose from the packed airliner as the pilot continued with instructions to the flight crew to pick up all the trays and prepare for an emergency landing. He then put the 747 into a steep and rapid descent bordering on a nosedive as the plane shook and passengers prayed, John and I included. Before long, we touched down at Jan Smuts International Airport (now Nelson Mandela Airport). As the giant jet pulled to a stop, perhaps a mile from the terminal, we were surrounded by fire trucks, security details, and buses. We were offloaded, placed on the buses and taken to a hangar where we were all questioned individually before being released. John and I scanned the papers the next day but found no mention of the incident.

The following May a headline appeared in the *News Journal* that MBNA had agreed to sponsor both the June and September NASCAR races at Dover Downs. Raceway president Dennis McGlynn referred to the development as "the final building block for 1995." What happened behind the scenes was classic Delaware corporate politics.

In early May 1995, I returned a call from Dennis McGlynn who expressed his concern over the loss of his top sponsors for their two Winston Series NASCAR races. But McGlynn had an idea and he wanted to see if I could help him execute it. The thought was to recruit DuPont, who sponsored champion driver Jeff Gordon on the circuit and MBNA, who recently entered the business by sponsoring a car driven by Randy LaJoie, to become co-sponsors of the spring and fall races.

The idea wasn't hatched completely by McGlynn. It was as much the brainchild of two MBNA card executives, Dave Elgena and Joe Purzycki, the former Delaware State and James Madison head football coach who had recently joined the bank. They wanted MBNA to sponsor the race but could not get CEO Charlie Cawley to agree. They thought that if they split the cost, they could repackage the deal and gain Charlie's approval. Despite the recent Louviers deal, relationships were not good between DuPont and MBNA, so they hoped I could help bridge the divide by packaging it as something that would be good for Delaware.

To help me make the pitch to DuPont I asked Delaware State Chamber of Commerce president John Burris to join me. I contacted DuPont general counsel and external affairs executive Stacey Mobley who agreed to meet with us. He would be joined by Jamie Murray, the head of DuPont public relations. Prepped by both McGlynn and the MBNA executives, I walked the DuPont team through the benefits of joining with the credit card company as a sponsor. After listening patiently with very few questions, Stacey responded: "John, while it may sound like a good plan, the fact is that we hate MBNA and would never do anything like that with them."

He went on to explain a grievance that was related to the Tour DuPont bike race and then finished by saying that if they did anything with the race, they would sponsor both of them on their own.

I am not sure how serious Stacey was with his threat to take over both races, but what happened next clearly demonstrated the power and nimbleness of the rising credit card company compared to the slow and lumbering chemical giant. I called Elgena and Purzycki and told them DuPont had no interest in partnering with MBNA but would probably purchase the sponsorship of both races. Within twenty-four hours I received a call back from them, along with an ecstatic Dennis McGlynn telling me that MBNA had just purchased both races. Elgena and Purzycki had gone to Cawley with the news of DuPont's position, and he made an immediate decision to take over sponsorship of NASCAR in Delaware.

No one in Delaware knew the banking world better than my friend and co-worker at DEDO, Jim Burke. With a network of Delaware and New York banking contacts, Jim would always be plugged into the latest trends and developments in the business. He would feed the information to Governor Carper and others and schedule regular visits, or customer calls on the local bank leaders and CEOs in New York and other cities.

About once a month, as we surveyed the latest MBNA job numbers, Burke would utter the words, "Riles, if MBNA ever catches a cold, Delaware will develop pneumonia!" One problem with credit card jobs was that, unlike manufacturing or research and development jobs tied to chemicals and pharmaceuticals or jobs focused on the local market, they were easy to relocate. Basically, bank employees only needed a computer and a phone to operate.

In June 2005, Bank of America announced it was acquiring MBNA. Jim Burke's concern about MBNA catching a cold was about to play out, and it would develop into a case of pneumonia for many employees (the bank announced it would cut 6,000 jobs), local businesses, and non-profits. On the other hand, MBNA generated a significant amount of wealth in Delaware, and many of employees and executives of the company remained in the area and are leaders in philanthropy and other community endeavors. Some have started successful businesses or have lent their talents to various financial operations and start-ups.

On a personal note, my venture into the stock backfired. While I thought my investment was a conservative play to enjoy a highly valued stock with a strong dividend during my retirement years, I would be abused of that notion with the advent of the financial crisis. Bank of America's shares cratered (largely due to the government's forced sale of mortgage giant Countrywide to the bank) and the dividend was basically wiped out. To add insult to injury, the federal and state governments, including Delaware, went after the bank, levying huge penalties and inflicting more pain on the shareholders.

Chapter 31

The RL&F Book, 1995–1996

"John, the governor said no one is getting fired over this."

I n early 1995, I was asked to join a meeting with director Bob Coy, our communications lead, Christine Watson, and lawyers from Richards, Layton, and Finger (RL&F). While generally considered a "Republican" firm, they had also represented Gannett when I sued the newspaper. I had never met the lawyer from the firm who visited that day, Julian "Hank" Bauman, and I did not know his political affiliation, if any. Bauman laid out an idea they had of a "doing business in Delaware" book that they would use as a free promotional give-away by the firm. He wanted to know if DEDO would be interested in supporting the

book by including an introductory letter from the governor. If so, the firm would provide copies of the book at no charge to our office for its own marketing and distribution needs. Everyone thought it was a great idea, and Bob asked me to work with Christine in support of the project. It turned out that there was nothing for me to do but to occasionally answer a minor technical question from Christine.

I thought I had pretty good political instincts, but I never even suspected that a political firestorm was about to erupt over the RL&F book. The day it was published, word shot through the legal community and firms generally identified as "Democrat" firms, and lawyers who

The one I did not see coming!

raised funds for Carper's campaign for governor started calling his office to complain. As the Republican in the DEDO office, they decided I had to be the culprit. Before long, my phone rang, and it was the governor's legal counsel, Leo Strine.

"John," Leo said. "What's the story behind this RL&F book?"

I explained as he listened patiently on the other end of the line. He replied, "Well, that sounds reasonable. I'll talk to the governor and get back to you."

When Leo called back, he said, "John, we need your help putting out this fire. We would like you to call Tom Capano, Dave Swayze, and Frank Biondi and see if you can explain what happened and smooth things over."

Being the small, connected world that is Delaware, I knew all three lawyers, but I had never worked directly with any of them. Although Capano and I would say hello to each other and we had many mutual acquaintances, he was a mystery to me. Swayze and I would chat at political and social functions but did not know each other well. I had the most experience and interaction with Biondi. On the occasion of Mike Harkins' fiftieth birthday, Frank and I were two of three "roasters" at the celebration—the other was Joe Biden.

I was concerned about calling Capano because I knew him the least. Perhaps I was naïve to think the others would not be a problem. To my surprise, Capano did not seem angry or concerned. I tried to apologize, although I was not sure what I should be apologizing for. When I finished, Capano basically said don't worry about it, it wasn't a big deal. He went on to say there were no hard feelings and he hoped to see me around town.

Although I have no record of the date of my call to Capano, it turned out to be in close proximity to the disappearance of Anne Marie Fahey, the governor's appointments' secretary. As the world now knows, Capano would be convicted of her murder in what for our little state was the "trial of the century."

My call to Dave Swayze did not go quite as smoothly, but we got through it and remained on friendly terms.

As I was working through these "mea culpas," I continued to feel the whole thing was blown out of proportion. I believed the reaction I was experiencing was simply due to the residual effects of being a Republican in a Democratic administration. The RL&F book was a modest creative marketing effort that their firm thought up and pursued.

We would have done the same thing for any other firm, but they didn't think of it and didn't ask. Now they wanted to teach someone a lesson. Clearly, they were not about to go after the governor, the man who approved and signed the "Dear Business Leader" cover letter, so I was the vulnerable target.

O. Francis Biondi was a legend in the Delaware legal and political community. He was the "top gun" among the Delaware banking lawyers because he was the attorney who wrote the law that brought the banks to Delaware—a fact he mentioned often and was justifiably proud of. My relationship with Frank had always been positive, plus he had a close personal and business relationship with my early political mentor, Mike Harkins. Harkins referred to him as the "Godfather." Furthermore, Christine Watson, who managed the RL&F project for our office, was Harkins' oldest daughter. It seemed highly unlikely to me that my talk with Biondi would be anything but cordial and that he would probably ask for similar support for his firm such as had been provided to RL&F. No doubt, I would quickly agree to that.

A face to face meeting with Biondi was quickly arranged. When I arrived at the prestigious offices of Morris, Nichols, Arsht, & Tunnell, he said he wanted attorney Mike Houghton to join the meeting. Houghton, who is well known in legal and political circles today, seemed to be more of an understudy to Biondi at that time.

From the start, Biondi peppered me with questions in a prosecutorial fashion. He seemed to want to get me to admit that I had conspired with Republicans to gain a business advantage over his firm and other Democrats. I tried to explain that there was never any such consideration; that my role was minor; Bob Coy approved the project; the governor had signed off; and Christine Watson had managed the entire project.

At that point Biondi switched gears and accused me of blaming others, particularly Harkins' daughter. My eyes glanced back and forth between Biondi and Houghton. I did not understand why Houghton was even in the room. Quickly resenting that I was being attacked, I fired back. I don't remember much of what I said, but I did announce that the meeting was over and slammed the office door on the way out.

I began to sort things out in my head as I drove to Dover. I thought to myself, *This is an unmitigated disaster. Biondi and others will be calling for my scalp, so I might as well head them off.* Within minutes after reaching the office I had Leo, the future chief justice of the Delaware Supreme Court, on the phone. I told him the meeting did not go well and that I had walked out; the governor could have my resignation if he wished. Strine asked me a few more questions and we ended the call.

As I thought about what I was going to do after my stint in government, the phone rang. My assistant Bonnie yelled out that Leo was back on the phone. As close as I can recall Leo's words were: "John, the governor said no one is getting fired over this."

And then he added, "Tom said that spending twenty minutes with Biondi was punishment enough!"

I wasn't ever sure whether Carper actually said that about the legal and political rainmaker, or if it was just Leo being Leo.

Chapter 32

International, 1994–1998

"And we will fight, fight, fight for Delaware, fight for the Blue and Gold …"

One of the responsibilities of my DEDO position was to manage the Office of International Trade and the state's attempts to land foreign direct investment. The three-person trade operation was run by John Pastor, a real character with a "can-do" attitude. John had contacts across the globe. If you wanted to get something done in any country, John would figure out a way to do it. He was supported by David Mathe and Anna White. David spoke Spanish and had extensive experience in Latin America.

A recommendation of the Wadley-Donovan report was to increase our overseas effort and specifically suggested attendance at the Hanover Germany Trade Fair, one of the largest focused on manufacturing in the world. Pastor and Mathe planned to set up a Delaware booth at the fair, handing out literature about the state and attending various receptions and seminars looking for prospects who might be willing to build a manufacturing facility in Delaware. Bob Coy and I decided to go to help with the booth and to better understand the value of this approach. What became clear attending Hanover was that it was difficult for little Delaware to get noticed. Other states made huge investments at these events and they dwarfed anything we were able to do.

After Hanover, Bob Coy and I took a side trip to Berlin. We were invited to tour a new technology park being developed at a one-time Luftwaffe base in what was once the East Berlin sector. It had only been a few years since the end of the Cold War and the fall of the Berlin Wall. Traveling to the site, we could see remnants of the Wall covered with graffiti and quickly noticed a significant drop-off in the appearance and economic vitality of the city. After a short tour and briefing on the plans for the park, our host asked us if we would like to go up to the next floor to visit Hermann Goering's former office. It was eerie standing near the desk of one of the monsters of the Third Reich; no one said a word. Then, as we headed outside to a waiting car, our host who had lived under the East German regime stopped us, and with emotion in his voice said, "We want to thank your country and President Reagan for ending the madness for us, you have our eternal gratitude." It gave us both a chill and a feeling of pride in our country as we headed through the streets of Berlin back to our hotel.

In Japan, Delaware had a long-standing relationship with Miyagi Prefecture, and our office had responsibility for concluding a "sister state" agreement with them. These agreements are made between cities and states to foster cultural and commercial relationships. Governor Castle's administration had begun the connection with Miyagi a couple of years before. Larry Windley, who later would manage special projects, including economic development for Senator Carper, was at that time working to finalize the agreement. The next step was a meeting in Japan with Miyagi officials to sign what amounted to a letter of intent. A couple of days before departing, Larry had to pull out of the trip, and he asked if I would travel with Bob Coy to the country.

I had never been to Asia, and I was completely new to this form of diplomacy and economic development. Not knowing what I was in for, I changed my schedule to accompany Bob to the Japan. We flew into Tokyo, met our Japan consultant, Yukio Nakajima, and then took the famous Shinkansen (or "bullet train") to Sendai, the capital of Miyagi Prefecture. I was not a sushi or tofu eater and soon discovered that was about the only thing on the menu. By the time we had our first official dinner engagement, I was hungry, as well as jet lagged.

The Japanese are known for their traditions and protocols, and our government hosts scheduled an official welcome dinner for our small delegation at one of Japan's most famous natural wonders, the Matsushima Islands. We were handed pajama-like Japanese garments called *yukatas* to wear to dinner—mine was particularly short. We sat on the floor, and before long, we were engaged in one sake *kampai* (i.e., toast) after another. After dinner, the senior Miyagi cabinet minister, Matsuki-san, got up and belted out a beautiful Japanese folk song. Everyone cheered him heartily, and then he looked at Bob Coy and requested that he sing a "traditional Delaware folk song."

As this request was being translated by Nakajima-san, Coy turned to me and said, "John, you have to bail me out here; I'm not from Delaware and don't know a single song." Then Bob immediately announced that I would pinch hit for him. Everyone applauded loudly as I got up, holding my yukata together and trying to think of something to sing. For the life of me in my jet-lagged state, I couldn't remember a full line of "Delaware, Oh Delaware"—and then it dawned on me. Except for the translator, the Japanese present did not know a word of English, except the word "Delaware." So I could sing anything I want with Delaware in it, and they would not know the difference.

The first thing that hit me was the University of Delaware fight song, which I had sung along to dozens of times at Delaware football games. Since Matsuki-san had put so much emotion and flair into his song, I figured I better make it look good. I made up half the words but ran through multiple choruses of "we will fight, fight, fight for Delaware." When I finished, the well inebriated Miyagi cabinet gave me a standing ovation as Coy fell over backwards laughing. I guess I had passed Japanese diplomacy 101.

I would return to Japan again in February 1998 with Jack Barrington, our electronics industry business recruiter, to meet with the site teams of the major electronics firms such as Matsushita (Panasonic), Toshiba, Sony, Hitachi, and Fujitsu, among others. In the 1990s, these firms were globally dominant players, making significant investments overseas and we wanted them to know all the reasons why they should be considering Delaware. The February 1998 trip happened to coincide with the Nagano Olympics.

As I was leaving for Japan my daughter Amy asked me if I could bring her an Olympic sweatshirt. I said yes, believing Tokyo shops, airports, and train stations would be fully stocked with Olympic sportswear and souvenirs. As it turned out, I could find nothing, but I then realized we would have a down day for a Japanese national holiday and decided to make a side trip to Nagano, 150 miles west of Tokyo. Traveling alone for the first time in Japan, I found just deciphering the train schedules and getting to the right track unnerving.

Arriving at the train station in Nagano was even more disorienting. The first problem was the temperature was below freezing, it was beginning to snow, and I was not dressed for it. Determined, I set out on my quest on foot looking for a sweatshirt. At an information center, a volunteer told me I might be able to find something at the hockey arena, a good half mile away. By the time I reached the vicinity of the arena, it was dark out, the snow had accelerated, and the streets were nearly empty. With my head down to protect against the blowing snow I barely noticed a pedestrian passing by. Suddenly I heard the voice yell back to me, "Hey, buddy, are you from Delaware?"

I walked back, trying to make out the face in the blowing snow. The guy looked familiar.

"Hello," I said. "I'm John Riley, and yes I'm from Delaware. How did you figure that out?"

"The Blue Hen on your jacket gave you away. I'm Kevin Tresolini from the *News Journal*," he answered.

We chatted for a minute, and he told me I would need credentials or a ticket to get into the hockey arena, so that was not going to be an option to find a shirt. I soon found a taxi for the trip back to the station and on to Tokyo. Amused by the chance encounter with a Delawarean on the other side of the world, I did not think about the downside.

The next day in his "Report from the Olympics," Tresolini told how he ran into a Delawarean, John Riley, at the Olympics in Nagano. Checking out the sports section that morning, Governor Carper was not thrilled to read about my adventures. He left a message for Bob Coy seeking an explanation, and Coy left a message for me. My Olympic excursion was easily explained, but it did cause me to think back to my encounter years before with star reporter Curtis Wilke, when he commented that nothing "was off the record." In the end, I never did find that sweatshirt.

My Olympic snowstorm experience was not the only encounter with mother nature on that trip. One morning in Tokyo, as we began our pitch to a room full of executives at Hitachi, alarms went off and we found ourselves out on the street as part of an earthquake drill. Our next stop was a meeting with Japan's electronics industry association, and as we sat down in the conference room, everything started to shake. We evacuated again. Later that afternoon, back on the fortieth floor of the ANA Hotel, the entire building began to sway, and alarms and sirens blared as we walked down forty flights. I knew that Japan was famous for seismic activity (as many as 1,500 earthquakes a year according to the website "Live Science"), but this was getting ridiculous.

"Hey buddy, are you from Delaware?"

Chapter 33

End of an Era, 1998

"This will be my last valve job. I will take this one to the grave."

In the spring of 1998, Bob Coy resigned to accept a position with a Washington, DC–based advocacy organization. I was named the interim director and would continue in that role for the next three months. While I did aspire to the cabinet-level position and enjoyed strong backing from the business community, I knew my Republican profile would be an issue. Carper had already dealt with several eruptions from Democratic Party leaders during my tenure, and I was not sure if he had the stomach for more. After a couple of months of silence from the "twelfth floor," I sat down with the governor to discuss the position. In an awkward meeting, Carper said that he did not believe I would be confirmed by the Democratically-controlled Senate.

Soon after our meeting, the governor announced he would move Darrell Minott from his position as secretary of labor to be the new DEDO director. He also announced the appointment of his staff assistant, Lisa Blunt Bradley (Rochester) to replace Minott as labor secretary.

While disappointed to miss the chance for a cabinet position, I was not surprised. The experience served to heighten my focus on my next career move, but I had plenty to keep me occupied in the interim, including the work we were doing to develop a biotechnology institute for the state. Darrell Minott soon joined the office, and we worked well together over my last eighteen months at DEDO. He ultimately moved on to a lobbyist position with Bank of America. Lisa Blunt Rochester would be elected to Delaware's at-large seat in the U.S. Congress in 2016. Bob Coy made a couple moves in the venture capital world and today serves as CEO of "16 Tech," an innovation district being developed in Indianapolis. We have stayed in touch over the years, and he was briefly retained as a consultant by the committee established to plan the Delaware Prosperity Partnership.

With the funds we raised through the Marketing Council, we expanded our marketing efforts. Part of the effort was directed at the corporate real estate executives of Fortune 500 companies and the site selection consultants they often retained on major projects. These real estate leaders gathered twice a year for a convention known as the Industrial Development Research Council (IDRC). Basically, each state tried to one-up the other for the attention of the real estate leaders in attendance. Larger states, such as Texas, appeared to spend more on entertainment at these events than our office spent on marketing for an entire year.

Since we couldn't compete with Texas, Virginia, New York, and other larger, more aggressive states, we decided to create a niche event that our target audience would find appealing. We settled on the idea of hosting a small dinner at the convention featuring local entertainment or a celebrity speaker. If he was available, we tried to get the governor to attend, thus providing additional gravitas compared to the bigger states. As in previous years, our 1998 event planning was handled by staff assistant Bonnie Ingram. Since we were in Baltimore that spring, she lined up baseball Hall of Fame third baseman Brooks Robinson to sign baseballs and speak at the dinner. Carper also flew in on a state police helicopter.

In the middle of the governor's dinner remarks, a waiter slipped me a note asking me to call my sister. When I reached Bernadette, she was with my mother at St. Francis Hospital in Wilmington. She said Mom had some sort of a seizure and it did not look good. Could I come right away? I started to head for the exit, but then decided to wait for the governor to finish his remarks to see if I could hitch a ride with him on the helicopter back to Wilmington. When I told Carper, he said, "Let's go." Minutes later, we were on the roof of a downtown Baltimore skyscraper buckling up for lift-off. I had experienced numerous chopper rides in my time but never one like that—we dropped several stories between the buildings before we began to level out towards the harbor.

By the time I arrived at the hospital, a St. Francis resident physician had attempted to perform a spinal tap, and my mother lost all feeling and movement below her waist; she was left paralyzed by the procedure. Another resident doctor, obviously disturbed by what had happened, recommended that we take my mother to the neurosurgical center at

Thomas Jefferson Hospital in Philadelphia. She approved the transfer, and my mother was placed in an ambulance helicopter and flown to Philly. Over several hours, the Jefferson team prepared for surgery to see if they could relieve the pressure on Mom's spine. Then, just before the surgery hour, they determined that due to my mother's other health issues, the procedure would be too risky and called it off.

Mom had undergone open heart surgery at the University of Pennsylvania Hospital in 1975. It was the early days of this type of surgery and they told her the new aortic valve, made of plastic and cowhide would probably have to be replaced in ten to fifteen years. Her surgery and the recovery were extremely difficult and she announced to everyone, "This will be my last valve job; I will take this one to the grave." As it turned out the valve had lasted twenty-three years, but her weak heart was seeing its final days. Mom hung on for about two more months, finally dying of heart failure on June 24, 1998. Sadly, she never walked again following the bungled spinal tap at St. Francis, the hospital where she gave birth to nine Riley babies.

To this day, brothers, sisters, cousins, and friends, marvel at what Bernadette Riley accomplished raising nine kids, managing life with my father, and making ends meet in so many creative ways. Totally "old school," she never received or asked for help outside the immediate family. With all she endured one would think she deserved a break in her later years, but my brother Denis' suicide in 1987 crushed her. Her pain would be compounded soon after when my sister Patricia, her first child and mother of five, was diagnosed with ovarian cancer.

My lifelong support system

Tricia's often experimental treatments resulted in intense suffering and she died three years later at age fifty.

Two years before Mom passed away in 1998, we all chipped in to move her out of the Pine Street home to a house in north Wilmington. For a brief period of time, the little home seemed to put some spark back in her life. Rarely does a day go by that does not trigger a memory of our mother. On August 19, 2018, twenty years after her passing, several of my brothers and sisters and our spouses gathered at the place she loved the most—the beach—to toast her hundredth birthday. We all still realize we won the lottery of life being born into her world.

Chapter 34

The Delaware Biotechnology Institute, 1998–1999

"Not even the Queen of England can get in to see Dolly."

With the presence of DuPont Agricultural Products, DuPont Pharmaceuticals, and Zeneca, Delaware had a toe-hold in an industry that was beginning to undergo a revolution. The sequencing of the gene in 1995 and the cloning of a sheep in 1996 generated headlines, while life science companies began to look towards biotechnology as a platform for future growth. In the spring of 1998, after Bob Coy departed Delaware and I was serving as interim director, Mike Bowman, director of the Delaware technology Park, introduced me to a former DuPont colleague, David Weir. Weir, like Bowman, would come to have a significant impact on the direction of the state's economy.

Dr. David Weir, who held a PhD in chemical physics, had recently retired from DuPont as vice president of research and development. The charismatic Weir had played a key role in advancing DuPont's growth in plant science and biotechnology, and he believed Delaware could capture some of this opportunity by developing a biotechnology institute based at the University of Delaware. Dr. Weir knew a lot about business and science but little about government and politics. We formed a close working relationship and set out on a course to sell Weir's idea to the governor's office.

The "institute" that Weir envisioned would be an interdisciplinary program focused on both research and education. The plan could proceed on two possible tracks: the preferred but more expensive route would include a state-of the art facility complete with labs, while the other would be "virtual" in that it would be supported by existing university labs and facilities of corporate partners. Due to a projected price tag for a building of an estimated $10 million, we settled on the virtual approach and an initial request of $5 million. Dr. Weir worked for months refining the concept and preparing a presentation to the governor and his cabinet. Darrell Minott, who had recently replaced Bob Coy, secured a spot on the cabinet calendar.

The meeting could not have gone better. A native of Scotland, who had taught at St. Andrews, Weir mesmerized the cabinet with his knowledge of the science and his vision for the future. Following the presentation, cabinet officials asked many questions and the meeting ran a full hour over. One of the questions came from State Budget Director, Pete Ross, who asked Weir if he was certain $5 million was all the funding he would require. David said yes, but the tone of Ross' question seemed to have opened a door to another opportunity—one that had been a part of Weir's thinking from the beginning. We left the room with a $5 million commitment to start the institute, but the Scotsman was clearly intrigue with the thought that more funds might be available.

Around seven o'clock the next morning I was getting dressed for work when the phone rang. Worried to get a call so early, I picked it up immediately and on the other end was the familiar Scottish brogue, "John," David said. "I couldn't sleep all night. I sensed the administration might be willing to do more. What would you think if we went back and asked the state for another $10 million to build a state-of the art biotech facility?"

"Well," I replied. "It probably would have been easier had we addressed it yesterday, but Carper seems to love this idea, so we should probably strike while the iron is hot. Can you go to Dover today? We better start with the budget director. The worst they can do is say no."

Recently, the state had experienced a windfall of more than $200 million from a lawsuit against New York over unclaimed property, and Carper had set up a "21st Century Fund" to make certain investments in the state's future. Naturally, nearly everyone in the state, especially legislators, had ideas on how the money should be spent. Somewhat tongue in cheek, Carper would sometimes be heard to say, "God, I hate that damn surplus!"

A few hours later, we made the pitch to Pete Ross in Dover. While developing the original concept, Weir had looked carefully at the "bricks and mortar" approach, so he was able to fill in some of the details that had not been presented in the cabinet meeting. I was surprised by how receptive Ross was. After asking all the right questions, he said he would discuss it with the governor. Just the fact that he was willing to present it to Carper meant that the funds were available, and that at least he believed the biotech institute had more potential for the state than other requests on his desk.

Later that week, we received word that Carper had approved the added $10 million. The building would be located at the Delaware Technology Park and be completed within two years. With the commitment of state funds, other support began to fall rapidly into place, including corporate commitments from DuPont and Hercules. The University of Delaware allocated funds to support fourteen faculty members and four endowed chairs.

The development of the Delaware Biotech Institute (DBI) would prove timely for Delaware in another respect. It added an element of credibility in our battle in early 1999 to land the U.S. headquarters of the newly formed AstraZeneca. (That battle will be covered in a later chapter.) Upon completion of the deal, David Weir proposed that we visit the major R&D sites for both companies in Europe to tell them about Delaware's commitment to the company and the industry and to see if we might recruit them to become a sponsor of the institute. The trip to Sweden, Germany, Scotland, and England would prove to be a memorable one.

David Weir and I left for Sweden the day after my daughter Amy's wedding in September 1999. With the help of Zeneca business and R&D leaders in Wilmington, we scheduled meetings in Stockholm and Gothenburg; London and Manchester, England; and Edinburgh, Scotland. Before leaving the continent, we stopped in Aachen, Germany to meet with the leaders of the Fraunhofer Institute. We had an existing Fraunhofer center at the University of Delaware focused on composites and Weir wanted to assess their biotechnology capability.

While in Aachen (the first German city captured by U.S. forces during WWII), I had to visit a spa for therapy on my back, which I had wrenched as we were leaving for the trip. Dave Weir had been carrying my bag for three days. Weir would later embellish this story, telling anyone who would listen that he had carried my "golf clubs" across Europe.

Our fifth city on the biotech tour was Edinburgh, Scotland, home of the world famous Roslin Institute—and a very famous sheep named Dolly. Joining us for a tour of Roslin would be Dr. Robin Morgan, soon to become dean of the College of Agriculture and Natural Sciences—and later provost—of the University of Delaware. Following a briefing on the scope of the research being conducted at Roslin, including their cloning experiments, Dave Weir popped the critical question: "Would it be possible to meet Dolly?"

The director looked at us and said, "Not even the Queen can get in to see Dolly."

As we broke for lunch and headed down the corridor, Weir turned to me and said, "I don't know about you, but I'm not leaving here without seeing that damn sheep!" His passion caused me to wonder exactly what Weir had in mind to force the issue.

Perhaps the Roslin leaders were exaggerating the sheep security to some extent, because an hour later we found ourselves escorted to the sheep pen. I have little experience with sheep pens, but this one I would describe as upscale. And as we approached, one wool covered creature broke away from the flock and trotted up to us. The Roslin team explained, Dolly, the cloned sheep, had quickly figured out she was a celebrity and would always come out ahead of the others to meet her admirers.

Twenty years later, the Delaware Biotechnology Institute continues to deliver benefits for the university and the state. In addition to cutting edge research and job creation, the Institute catalyzed the formation of the Delaware Bioscience Association. Internationally prominent faculty have joined the Institute staff, including Dr. Cathy Wu, who later formed the Delaware Data Science Institute and Dr. Kelvin Lee who was awarded a $250 million National Institute of Standards and Technology (NIST) grant to form a biopharmaceutical center at UD's new Science, Technology, and Advanced Research Campus (STAR).

The Biotech Institute Team
Photo courtesy of the University of Delaware

Chapter 35

Vietnam, 1998

"Do you believe this? Can you believe we are sitting here in Hanoi with the United States ambassador?"

I guess a couple stanzas of the Blue Hen "Fight Song" was not enough to discourage the Miyagi government from pursuing a "sister state" agreement with us, so a signing ceremony was planned in Japan for September 1998. As John Pastor and I began to develop a trip itinerary, we decided to focus on advancing our appeal to major Japanese and Taiwanese semiconductor manufacturers. Tom Carper had been recently elected chairman of the National Governors Association, and with such a national profile, Asian leaders wanted to meet him and discuss various trade and policy matters.

After months of planning, we set an itinerary that would include stops in Sendai, Tokyo, and Osaka in Japan; Taipei in Taiwan; and Hanoi and Ho Chi Minh City in Vietnam. Japan and Taiwan were home to some of the largest chip manufacturers in the world and having Carper along would open doors at the chairman of the board level. In Tokyo, Tom Jordan, former president of DuPont Asia, had contacted me to see if Carper would speak at their annual dinner. A prestigious event, a recent speaker had been Bill Gates. Vietnam was of interest to Carper, as his friend Pete Peterson had recently been named ambassador when diplomatic relations were reestablished the previous year.

In addition to Delaware's first lady, Martha Carper, and John Pastor, we were joined by Jack Barrington and Joe Hickey with the Department of Labor. We had invited a representative from the Delaware business community and the Chamber of Commerce recruited Mike Ratchford, who at that time had responsibility for government relations at Delmarva

Power. Others joined for part of the trip, including representatives from the Division of Incorporations.

I did not exactly get off on the right foot for the trade mission. The plan was to arrive a day early to get acclimated before the governor landed and before we headed to the embassy for our first meeting. When I arrived in northern Virginia with John Pastor and Jack Barrington for a direct flight to Tokyo from Dulles Airport, I realized that I had forgotten my passport. Missing the flight, the only way to beat Carper to Japan was to drive to JFK Airport in New York and fly out the next day. Fortunately, I was able to get a seat. I would arrive in Tokyo just in time to join Carper to head to the embassy. The main reason for the meeting at the embassy was to prep for a recently added discussion with the Japanese Prime Minister, Keizo Obuchi.

All went well in Sendai. Governor Asano and Carper hit it off well, including taking a run around the city early the morning of our departure. This addition and calls from Delaware, including the sad word that state senator Phil Cloutier had died of cancer, would take us up to the last minute before we had to catch the train that would get us to Tokyo in time for the meeting with the prime minister. We became so pressed for time that Carper asked me if I could talk to someone about holding the Shinkansen for five minutes. It is a point of national pride in Japan that those trains always run on time. I promised Carper I would look into it, but confess I simply told Pastor how ridiculous the idea was and then went back to the governor to tell him it could not be done. We had to catch the next train or miss the prime minister.

By the time we bolted from the hotel, we only had minutes to make it several blocks to the Sendai train station. Being in the middle of the morning rush hour, the streets were jammed. I handed a wad of yen to our driver and asked our interpreter to communicate our plight. The next thing I know the driver pulled up onto the sidewalk and pedestrians were scattering. Within seconds, we were running through the station and made it with two seconds to spare. (The Shinkansen has a large digital clock on the platform that counts down the seconds before the doors automatically close.)

The most fascinating part of the meeting with Japan's prime minister was the reception in front of the Japanese Diet. As we pulled to a stop in front of the building, a scrum of at least twenty-five members of the Japanese press corps descended on the car and started shoving cameras and mics into Carper's face. They surrounded us as we tried to get into the building. Fortunately, the U.S. Embassy's charge' d'affaires, Chris LaFleur, met us and somehow managed to tame the press until we were able to get through the door to meet the prime minister.

That afternoon we told the Delaware story to the leadership of Toshiba and NEC, and Carper ended the day that had begun in Sendai with the speech at the American Chamber dinner. The next morning, we were on the train to Osaka where we would meet with the eighty-five-year-old chairman of Matsushita (Panasonic), Masaharu Matsushita, before catching a flight to Taiwan. In Taipei, we would be meeting with Taiwan's president, Lee Teng-hui, whom the People's Republic of China considered a hardline leader. As a result, tensions were high in the region at the time of our visit.

While Governor Carper certainly read the briefing material provided to him, he still had some questions about handling things with President Lee. After we landed in Taipei, Carper, appearing a bit bewildered by overseas dialing with his cell phone, handed me Joe Biden's number and asked me to reach him. A minute later Jill Biden answered the home phone. The message from the ranking member of the Senate Foreign Relations Committee was generally to push back on Lee to let him know that his American ally did not want matters to escalate.

We had arrived in Taipei in the early evening to be met by what I would describe as a SWAT team for dignitaries. They formed us up, putting the governor and Martha Carper into a limo with the rest of the delegation behind. Police escort vehicles took positions in the front, back, and sides of the caravan. As we pulled away from the airport you could see that the highways of this city of nearly three million were jammed with rush hour traffic. Suddenly, the SWAT team pulled out lighted batons that looked like something from *Star Wars* and leaned out of their windows, beating back cars and forcing them out of our way. This scene would continue all the way to the Taipei Grand Hotel.

I think it would be safe to say that no one had ever seen anything quite like the Taipei police performance. When we exited the cars in front of the hotel, the SWAT team had

The only way to travel
through Taipei traffic

already lined up and were clearly proud of their performance. The governor thanked them, and we all posed for photos. I thought to myself that if someone ever tried that back in the states, they would surely have gotten hurt.

With the meeting with President Lee scheduled for late morning, we planned to have breakfast with the team from the American Institute in Taipei (sort of a "surrogate embassy" for the United States in Taiwan due to the absence of an official American embassy given our diplomatic relations with mainland China). I was up several hours before breakfast sitting in the hotel lobby when a friend who worked for Hercules, John Montgomery, approached me. When we both recovered from the fact that we had run into each other a half a world away, Montgomery said, "John, I saw you and the governor on television in Hong Kong yesterday meeting with Prime Minister Obuchi." Now that is what you call a small world!

The meeting with President Lee went about as expected. He was clearly agitated over the actions of the People's Republic of China, which included recent missile firings over the island. Carper listened patiently and reiterated the U.S. policy of maintaining the status quo in the region while still emphasizing our economic ties. There was even a pitch for Taiwan to purchase more "Delmarvelous chicken!" As for me, I sat there mostly reflecting on the fact that I was even in the room—a kid from Pine Street in the middle of discussions with a man who was driving Jiang Zemin of the PRC to the point of distraction.

That afternoon, Jack Barrington had arranged a visit to a Taiwan Semiconductor (TSCM) factory so the governor, bedecked in "clean room" garb, could gain a deeper understanding of the technology and the employment opportunities. We would follow up that visit by having dinner with the company chairman, Morris Chang. Chang had become one of the leading businessmen in Asia by building a company that made microchips for the entire electronics industry. Born in Ningbo in mainland China, Chang was known as the founder of the semiconductor industry in Taiwan.

Reputed to be one of the wealthiest businessmen in Asia, Chang was accompanied by a serious looking gentleman, who quietly waited for the chipmaker outside the private room he reserved for the dinner. Part of the focus of conversation was the impact of the scandal involving President Clinton and Monica Lewinsky which was then dominating the news. The Asian tabloids were running front page photos of Clinton and Lewinsky every day of our trip and there were rumors of a possible Clinton resignation or impeachment.

As the conversation shifted to business, Chang discussed the current state of the semiconductor business. He was very frank about the challenges, particularly the heavy capital investment and the cyclical nature of the market. He caught us a bit by surprise when he asked why we were pursuing the industry, since he felt that it was becoming commoditized and that the growth opportunities had probably peaked. A bit taken back that the founder of the Taiwanese semiconductor industry would downplay his own business, Carper asked what he would be targeting if he were in the governor's shoes. Without hesitation Chang said, "I would be looking at the Internet and the opportunities it will bring."

We would later discuss Chang's viewpoint, but we kept coming back to the fact that we were looking for manufacturing jobs—replacement jobs for the shrinking auto assembly and chemical industry positions. In addition, the talent for the "Dot.com" world was centered in Silicon Valley and other tech hubs. In late 1998, we just did not see the fit, and the frenzy around Internet stocks was beginning to look like "Tulipmania," the speculative bubble that hit Holland back in the seventeenth century.

The pace and intensity of the Japan and Taiwan schedule was such that I had given little thought to what lay ahead. The next morning, we would be on a flight "back to the future!"

As we boarded Vietnam Airlines for the 1,016-mile trip to Hanoi, I felt what I could only describe as a haunting feeling. The very word *Vietnam* and all it implied had dominated my young life. It was more than the name of a country, more than a war that took 58,000 young American lives. It was a time and a place that had penetrated every corner of America for more than a decade. Historians would say we lost the war, but more than that, we lost part of the American soul. The war had nearly torn the country apart.

No doubt some of what I felt was guilt, driven by the fact that I had never served in combat. Many, perhaps most, of more than two-and-half million soldiers who made the trip in the 1960s and early '70s did so with fear and apprehension, a state of mind I never had to experience. Those Americans were on my mind as our flight descended through the clouds to the former French colonial city. Another thought weighing on me was how we would be received by the people of a country we had dropped more bombs on than were deployed in all of World War II.

Hanoi's airport in 1998 was still "third world." We picked up our luggage amid a chaotic scene of hundreds of Vietnamese darting in every direction. Throughout the terminal, people pressed against us and nearly everyone was offering us a ride or trying to sell us a bootleg copy of Graham Green's *The Quiet American.* As we broke through the clogged doors into the blazing hot sun, we could see a man about fifty yards away waving to us. He was standing on the running board of a large SUV with two American flags on the front. It was Carper's friend, U.S. Ambassador to Vietnam Pete Peterson—a man who had spent six years in Vietnam as a POW. Carper and Peterson had served in Congress together and had traveled to Vietnam years before on a mission to recover the remains or determine the status of Americans who were still missing in action (MIA).

We fought our way through the sea of humanity and jumped into the two embassy vehicles for the trip to Hanoi. Although this was the first time I set foot in this exotic country, it all looked very familiar. The landscape was full of rice paddies and water buffalo with peasants wearing "Non La" conical hats. They seemed unfazed by the SUVs with the American flags kicking up dust on the poor roads.

About forty-five minutes later, we arrived at the Daewoo Hotel. When dropping us off, Peterson told us we were invited to the ambassador's residence that evening for dinner. Checking into the hotel, something strange grabbed my attention—a replica of the Statue of Liberty dominated the lobby. My first thought was that it might be there for our benefit. We were one of the first delegations to the country since diplomatic relations had been established, so perhaps they just wanted us to feel at home. It would turn out that the display was a promotion for the hotel's "American Foods Week." When I looked at the menu, the feature for that day was "the hamburger"—cooked by Vietnamese chefs in a Korean hotel. The landscape had certainly changed over the previous twenty-five years.

The trip had taken on a diplomatic slant. So, just as in Japan and Taiwan, we were scheduled to pay a courtesy visit on Vietnam's leaders. We headed downtown amid the hundreds of motorbikes and bicycles and thousands of pedestrians. At the time, Hanoi had no traffic lights, so basically everyone would converge on intersections and traffic circles and just sort themselves out. We soon arrived at the Presidential Palace, a mustard-colored French Colonial structure where official meetings were held.

Governor Carper, Martha Carper, John Pastor, Mike Ratchford, Joe Hickey, and I were escorted into a conference room with a large beautiful table. We were informed that this was where Ho Chi Minh met with

General Giap, First Secretary Le Duan, and others to run the war. Soon, into the room came Vietnam's deputy prime minister and foreign minister. We had what I would characterize as a guarded exchange. Perhaps that was all we should have expected in a communist country skeptical of the intentions of their former capitalist enemy.

Governor Carper pitching Delaware to communist leaders

That evening we made the short trip to the ambassador's residence, where we met Peterson's Vietnamese wife, Vi Le, who had a day job representing the Australian government. In the years I had known Tom Carper, I had never seen him have an alcoholic beverage except during a toast. But when asked what we wanted to drink, Carper said he wanted a "Tiger Beer," a popular choice amongst our troops for many years in Southeast Asia. To my surprise the Governor downed a couple of Tiger's. Clearly feeling it a bit, the former naval flight officer leaned over to me during dinner and said, "Do you believe this? Can you believe we are sitting here in Hanoi with the United States ambassador?"

It was fascinating to be in a position to observe the two worlds of Vietnam. On the one hand, it was a tightly-run dictatorship; on the other, it had a bustling capitalist system. One Vietnamese business consultant John Pastor had lined up to assist us was the nephew of the famous General Giap. You had to suspect that this young entrepreneur might have some double-agent in him, but since we were not there on a mission of national security, everyone got along fine.

While we made connections to establish future business relationships and possible cultural exchanges as we enjoyed with Taiwan and Japan, we also took some side trips to Vietnam landmarks, including a visit to the mausoleum where Ho Chi Minh's remains are preserved below ground for all to view. Another compelling stop for us was the Hoa Lo prison, better known to Americans as the "Hanoi Hilton." The first thing that struck me as we entered the forbidding structure was the presence of a guillotine, a dark reminder of French Colonial times. In addition, there were guys dressed in prison garb. They were filming a movie about the American POWs.

After two days in Hanoi we were back on Vietnam Airlines for the two-hour flight down the long skinny country to Ho Chi Minh City, formerly Saigon. While Hanoi is a beautiful and somewhat quiet capital, Ho Chi Minh City is a bustling chaotic city of ten million. The thousands of cars, taxis, motorbikes, bicycles, and pedestrians dwarfed what we

Is that a Xerox ad?

had seen in Hanoi. One of the most exotic sights were the women in their "ao dai" dresses riding sidesaddle on the backs of motorbikes. Again, while we hosted several business events and met with exporters, we found some time to visit several Saigon landmarks: the Notre Dame church where a couple of us went to Sunday Mass, the Independence Palace (renamed the "Reunification Hall" after the fall of Saigon) and the former U.S. Embassy, symbols of the fall of Saigon. We also made it to the Caravel Hotel, famous as the international press hangout during the war. But my personal favorite stop was a trip to the *Apocalypse Now* bar, complete with a poster featuring Marlon Brando on the wall.

Any concern about how we would be received by the Vietnamese was put to rest quickly. Aside from the communist leaders in Hanoi, everywhere we went we were welcomed with open arms. From a distance kids would shout, "Americans, Americans" and come running. Typically, they were begging or selling more Graham Greene books. Teenagers and young adults would tell us of their dream to go to America and "make money." As I left the country, I was reminded again of the distant war: We departed via Ton Son Nhut airport, the same entry and exit point for hundreds of thousands of troops decades before.

Americans...Americans!

Chapter 36

AstraZeneca, 1999

"CG, that's a lot of spice!"

L ate one December afternoon, I picked up a call from the governor's executive assistant, Carrie Casey. "John," she said. "The governor would like you and Darrell to come up here at 5:30 to join him for a meeting with Keith Willard from Zeneca and an executive from London, Sir Alan Pink. And he wants to know if you have any idea why they would want to meet with him," she asked.

"No," I said. "But there are lots of mergers and acquisitions going on in the industry."

Zeneca was one of Delaware's largest employers, with approximately 2,400 employees at their Fairfax headquarters campus near the intersection of Rt. 202 and Murphy Road. They also employed several hundred at their manufacturing operation off I-95 near Newark. Although a British company, Zeneca had a long Delaware lineage reaching back to 1912, when the United States government broke up the DuPont Powder Company as part of an anti-trust settlement. Both Hercules and Atlas would be formed as a result, and Atlas would be purchased by London-based Imperial Chemicals Industries PLC (ICI) in 1972. Atlas had previously entered the pharmaceutical business through the purchase of drugmaker Stuart. Further portfolio changes would result in a "de-merger," where ICI would spin off its industrial chemicals and form a new company named Zeneca, consisting of their drug and agricultural products businesses. In 2000, the ag products division would spin off and become Syngenta.

The governor, Darrell Minott, and I listened intently to Willard and Pink as they explained that Zeneca was merging with Astra AB, a Swedish company that had operations in Chesterbrook, Pennsylvania, twenty-seven miles north of the Zeneca Wilmington campus. Astra owed much of its success to a blockbuster heartburn medication called Losec (sold under the brand name Prilosec in the U.S.), but they would soon be facing a patent expiration and therefore needed to find ways to bolster their product pipeline. Zeneca was strong in oncology and cardiovascular drugs, with central nervous system drugs (CNS) in their pipeline. Their research and development labs on the Fairfax campus were focused on CNS drugs, and this became their "center of excellence" under the combined company. Whatever the existing products and pipelines, it became clear during the conversation that the new company would move quickly to consolidate the Pennsylvania and Delaware operations, raising the specter that Delaware was at risk of losing thousands of high paying jobs and squashing any hope of building an industry cluster in life sciences.

Willard and Pink made no requests during the meeting, but in a matter of minutes they had delivered the merger message and set up an impending Delaware–Pennsylvania "border war" for the combined company's operations. As we wrapped up, and in what seemed like an ominous sign, most of the power went out on the twelfth floor of the Carvel State Office Building. With the elevators shut down, Carper tried to make light of the moment and guided the corporate executives down the staircase behind the offices.

A short time later, Carper, Darrell, and I sat in the dark discussing the risk and opportunities of this development and decide on our next steps. We would want to do all in our power to save the 2,400 existing jobs and convince the combined company they should locate their full operation in Delaware. If they expanded at the present site, it would mean adding up to a million square feet, which would have a major impact on traffic and other infrastructure. Based on my experience on county council and service within the Brandywine Hundred civic organizations, I was immediately concerned we could face community opposition to such an expansion. The governor's reaction was, "I don't see that as an issue. I just can't believe anyone will object to this."

While Tom Carper was certainly not naïve regarding the growing role of civic organizations, he had not yet had to fight a major battle of this nature before. Having watched local activists build political careers by opposing any increase in traffic in the area, I was not so sure most civic leaders and the politicians who listened to them, would automatically agree to a major expansion at Route 202 and Murphy Road.

In an effort to build support and mitigate any opposition, we concluded it would make sense to inform a broad base of state and county leadership about the risk we were facing and what we felt we needed to do to land the entire combined company. Sharing details like this would be contrary to the normal course of most economic development projects, where everything is kept highly confidential by restricting the news to only those who needed to know. We also discussed a strategy where we would look at the pent-up demand for traffic relief, open space and parks, to see how we might package the deal to enhance the appeal to possible opponents.

The day after the meeting with Willard and Pink I went up to Zeneca to meet with their head of government relations, Jerry Quinn. As we tried to imagine where the combined company might build up to a million square feet of office space, we decided to cross Murphy Road in front of their building to see what the land looked like behind the wall of trees on the other side. It was not long before we were blocked by dense undergrowth and rugged terrain, but based on our quick perusal, it appeared that this parcel of land, referred to as "the Triangle" had potential for a major project.

With mud on our shoes and burrs clinging to our business suits, we returned to Jerry's desk. There we sketched out a possible expansion scenario that included a widening of Murphy Road with a pedestrian and vehicular overpass reaching to the extended campus on the other side of the highway. This back-of-the-envelope drawing ended up looking close to the appearance of the site today. Jerry thought the land was owned by the Nemours Foundation, but unfortunately it would prove to be more complicated than that. The land, as well as adjacent parcels totaling 156 acres, were owned by Nemours, but developers had options on the parcels, and any significant road expansion would elevate the value of their holdings.

Although we considered other site possibilities, Delaware's best option was to offer the adjacent land so the new company would not have to move existing offices and labs and could expand right where they were. To make such a proposal however, we needed to be in control of the land. So I called Mark Chura, with the Department of Natural Resources and Environmental Control (DNREC). Mark was the staff person responsible for working with the State Open Space Council on land acquisition. I had collaborated with Mark previously on land acquisition connected to a potential W.L. Gore project in Newark and knew that he understood the ins and outs of having the state acquire properties. When he answered his phone, I asked, "Mark, how long would it take you to do all you need to do to acquire a 156-acre parcel of land?"

"John," he said. "It depends on certain factors, but typically it takes a couple of years."

I said, "Mark, what if it was absolutely critical to the state and you had the governor and everyone supporting and pushing it?"

"Well, in that case," he answered. "We might be able to get it done within a year."

"Mark," I said. "You have to get this one done in ninety days."

After the site decision announcement was made at the end of April 1999, the Sunday *News Journal* ran a front-page story providing an inside look at how the process played out during the four-month "border war" with Pennsylvania. Under the Freedom of Information Act (FOIA), reporter Trif Alatzas pieced the story together by gaining access to emails and other documents, as well as conducting interviews with the key players. He described the state's response as unprecedented and creative.

"Since Delaware had never gone after such a big economic fish, its plans to attract AstraZeneca had to be novel."

Alatzas went on to describe the meeting that we held in early January in the governor's office. He highlighted how the meeting set the tone for the rest of the process. But what Alatzas was not able to fully capture was how the meeting served to head off the possibility of opposition from the usual suspects. It was not that we expected outright opposition; the fear was that if controversy erupted over details around changes to roads and traffic flow, it would only serve to diminish Delaware's appeal and the welcoming image we hoped to establish. In addition, we knew we would have to gain New Castle County approval for all development plans, and we could not risk any part of the process being stalled. Delay during the normal county land use approval process was about as certain as the sun coming up tomorrow.

The January meeting in the governor's Wilmington conference room was standing room only. We had spoken to several respected leaders in advance to request that they provide a vigorous endorsement for the effort, creating the sense in the room that there was strong consensus for the plan. Congressman and former Governor Mike Castle, who as governor had experienced serious opposition to Hewlett Packard's (Agilent Technologies) move to Delaware from Pennsylvania, was particularly effective in making the case. (Much of the HP opposition was focused on the state sale of land near the Ferris School.) The questions that were eventually raised, such as the need for improved roads and open space preservation had all been anticipated, so we were able to quickly provide most of the answers.

Understanding that the site acquisition would be a complicated process, we decided to bring on additional support to work through everything. I suggested we retain real estate consultant Andy Lubin to assist with the land acquisition and county regulatory process. For legal support we retained Mike Parkowski, a Dover lawyer with extensive environmental experience. Mike would take the lead in negotiations with the option holders. In order to motivate the developers to settle at reasonable prices, Mike was effective at using the specter of eminent domain in his negotiations.

If there were ever a time when Delaware demonstrated the advantage of being small and nimble, it was by clearing out the ownership and contractual issues on the Nemours property. With the help of former Delaware Trust president and Nemours board member Jack Porter, the Foundation agreed to sell the land to the state. At that point, developer Tony Fusco sued to stop the sale. The case was quickly scheduled and resolved in favor of Nemours, but we still had to settle on a value to Fusco and a couple other option holders.

Mike Parkowski proposed bringing all parties together in the DEDO Wilmington conference room for a negotiating session. Mike began with the admonition to them that over the next several hours they would all have to reach a deal or risk getting even less for their rights than we would offer that day. With the county attorney and a representative from the state attorney general's office in the room, he let it be known that he had the full backing of the state and the county—and that if anyone chose to hold out, they risked killing the AZ deal, resulting in a devaluation of the property as well as lasting enmity from state leadership. Over the next several hours, while attorneys darted from one room to another, things became tense and emotional at times. Eventually, Mike gave each party the state's final offer, and we reached a deal.

Shortly after this meeting of state leaders, I was contacted by Tony Felicia of Zeneca. He introduced himself and informed me that he had been named as the lead for site selection. (Tony would later explain to me that he was in a meeting at a Zeneca site in England when he received a call from Zeneca president Bob Black telling him to drop everything he was doing and catch the next plane to the U.S.) I had never met Tony, but I would get to know him quickly as we would spend a great deal of time together over the next four months. While it was Tony's job to help the newly merged company make an unbiased, fact-based decision, I sensed that he hoped the facts would prove Delaware to be the right choice. On the Astra side, the Pennsylvania-based corporate real estate manager Chuck Manula was a key member of the site team, and there was no doubt about his bias—he had a look in his eyes bordering on contempt whenever I saw him.

While the engineers reviewed the suitability of the Triangle parcel of land, Astra and Pennsylvania officials led an effort to find an appropriate location in Chester County. Pennsylvania had more options to choose from, but each site had its own complications. When word leaked out about one site in Chester County, local citizens turned out to protest. This was exactly the reaction we hoped for and worked hard to avoid in Delaware.

Internally, we developed a core team consisting of the governor, Darrell Minott, Jim Burke, and myself who communicated on a daily basis. But it was all hands-on deck for our small office. Externally, we were in constant communication with Mark Chura and Chas Salkin at DNREC and Anne Canby's team at DELDOT. After some initial tension with New Castle County officials, things smoothed out as they sensed the community was behind the effort.

In addition to support from the political leadership, numerous business executives offered their services. DuPont COO Kurt Landgraf, the former CEO of DuPont-Merck, was particularly helpful in providing insight into the thinking of the pharmaceutical industry.

Always trying to ensure that no stone was left unturned, we learned to anticipate a call most mornings between 7:30 and 8:00 from the governor. "John, Darrell," he would ask. "What can I do today to ensure we are successful?"

Our first critical deadline was February 1, 1999, when we were to deliver the state proposal and incentive package. Our DEDO team spent Super Bowl Sunday on the tenth floor of the Carvel State Office finalizing the details. We worked all the way up until kick-off, fielding a periodic check-in call from the governor. He sometimes ended the call with one of his favorite lines, saying, "Guys, as long as we don't worry about who gets credit, we will be successful."

After the call, we laughed and said, "Sure, as long as the governor gets the credit."

The centerpiece of the proposal was the incentive package, including the eighty-six-acres of land. (We had not yet closed on the Triangle but had cleared the major hurdles.) We valued this land at $13.8 Million. In addition, we offered $3 million in relocation assistance and tax credits valued at $21.9 million, credits that were available by statute and based on the jobs and investment numbers. Another key component was the promise of improvements to area roads to ensure current traffic levels of service were maintained (estimated at $70 million, including implementation of long-planned upgrades). Zeneca president Bob Black would later call the forty-six-page proposal the "best business proposal he had ever seen."

There was one last angle we hoped to use to our advantage—the Swedish–Delaware connection. There was a growing sense that the Swedish company, Astra, was the senior partner in what had been originally described as a merger of equals. Swedish settlers had arrived in Delaware in 1638 aboard the Kalmar Nyckel, and the ship had been recently reconstructed and launched by the Kalmar Nyckel Foundation. As we were completing our spiral bound proposal submission, communications manager Jennifer Powell proposed adorning the document with a photo of the Kalmar to emphasize the historical connection between Delaware and Sweden. It would definitely catch the attention of the Astra staff, especially the Swedish CEO, C.G. Johansson.

The next morning, right on time, I handed the proposal to Tony Felicia in the lobby of the Zeneca headquarters on Murphy Road. He said they had not yet heard from Pennsylvania. I would soon learn we received a big break—PA apparently had no one on point for the project and missed the deadline. When the company contacted them, they quickly put together a three-page proposal and faxed it in. Later, after the decision had been announced, Astra real estate executive Chuck Manula was quoted in the Sunday *News Journal* saying, "When you looked at the two proposals side by side, it was hard to make a comparison."

Shortly after the proposal submission, we made our pitch to the entire AZ site selection team. AstraZeneca officials let us know they were not interested in hearing from the governor at this point, indicating there would be a future opportunity for him to meet with the CEO. In addition to Felicia and Manula, the conference table was surrounded with executives from legal, finance, HR, and engineering. After Darrell gave opening remarks, I ran through dozens of slides before turning it over to Burke to review the incentives.

It happened that a few days prior to the presentation, Bob Dayton of our staff went to the bank and secured a roll of just-released Delaware quarters. To my surprise, Jim Burke, the conservative former New

York banker, decided he would use the quarters as props during his presentation. He turned his portion of the presentation into sort of game show with new Delaware quarters as rewards for correct answers from the AZ site selection team. I was very uncomfortable with the idea, but most of the AZ executives received it in good humor.

After AZ "Jeopardy," we moved to the Q&A. Unsurprisingly, we learned that the AZ team's major objection to Delaware was education. Fully anticipating the concern, we had prepared a detailed description of ongoing programs to improve the schools. Someone from the Astra side made a crack, "Based on the detail in this proposal, it looks like you have something to hide." It sent a chill up my spine.

While we were always nervous about Pennsylvania's massive size advantage and ability to provide an incentive package we could never match, we took some comfort in our site advantage. A Delaware decision meant they would only have to move half the employees. The current Astra location in Chesterbook offered no room for expansion, so if they choose Pennsylvania they would have to move everyone. We also pinned some hopes on a belief that the new CEO or chief operating officer would come from Zeneca. There is a general view that when companies are in a relocation situation, they tend to land where the CEO and senior leadership want to live. Then, as we approached decision time, I received a call from project leader Tony Felicia.

"John," he said. "I'm afraid I have bad news."

He explained that Zeneca president Bob Black, whom we all hoped would be the new company CEO, was out completely; he would retire when the merger was completed. Astra CEO C.G. Johansson would become the head of the combined enterprise, and David Brennan of Astra would be #2 and heir apparent. We had never met either gentleman and they lived in Pennsylvania, well north of the Zeneca Wilmington campus. Even Governor Carper, the man who always looked at the glass as "half-full," was worried.

Just as we had gotten our hopes up over our initial proposal advantage, our spirits sank with this latest news. The school situation was a distinct disadvantage, and we now assumed the leadership had a clear Pennsylvania bias. I was concerned our situation was impossible—that these disadvantages could not be overcome. That evening I turned on television and a documentary about the construction of the Hoover Dam caught my attention. When I saw what the dam builders had overcome to complete that project, my mood changed. I joked with some of the staff the next morning saying, "If they could build the Hoover Dam, we surely can land the AZ headquarters."

Weeks went by as the company continued their due diligence. Whatever Tony Felicia said they needed, we turned around in hours. We knew we had one distinct advantage over Pennsylvania —we couldn't afford to lose. The loss of 1,800 jobs for Pennsylvania would certainly have an impact, but based on their lower personal income tax rate and education advantage, Pennsylvania-based employees were unlikely to move. Even future hires might choose to live in Chester County since it was so close to Zeneca. We played up the idea that Delaware really wanted the company—AZ would be a big fish in a small pound, surrounded by a supportive community and responsive government.

Finally, as April rolled around, we received word that Johansson wanted to meet with the respective governors to review the offering and confirm the final incentive offer. It was going to be a high stakes moment, so we recommended to the governor to have all the key cabinet secretaries around the table, so answers could be provided immediately. Everyone was front and center when Johansson and the team entered the governor's Wilmington twelfth floor conference room.

With English as his second language, C.G. Johansson was stiff and deliberate delivering remarks. Being difficult to make "small talk," he jumped right to the point. He said he appreciated Delaware's responsiveness and the generous incentive offer, but then added, "Governor, in Sweden, we have an expression called spice the pudding, and we would like you to spice the pudding with another $15 million."

You could hear a pin drop as everyone present winced a little and fixed their eyes on Carper. We had expected that the company might ask us to double the $3 million relocation grant, but no one anticipated anything on a $15 million order of magnitude. The seconds ticked away as Carper appeared to be almost stunned and searching for a response. Finally, he leaned forward, stretching his arms out towards Johansson and shouted out, "C.G., that's a lot of spice!"

The whole table, state officials, and the AZ team broke out laughing. It seemed to give pause to the proceedings, and Carper recovered, telling Johansson that our team would reconvene and get back to them. After they left, we regrouped and sized up the problem. At least one cabinet official urged us to give Johansson what he asked for. That would have raised our relocation assistance offer to a total of $18 million.

While Carper played "head coach" and counseled us constantly to assume we were behind, following the dark days after the AZ leadership announcement I began to pick up vibrations from Felicia and other Zeneca executives that we were inching into the lead. In addition, there was evidence, including their unprofessional proposal submission, that Pennsylvania was taking victory for granted. In discussing how far we should go to meet CG Johansson's "pudding" request, I thought it would be safe to respond conservatively. We eventually settled on an additional $5 million, raising the relocation grant to a total of $8 million, well below the additional $15 million requested.

Early on the morning of April 29, I received a call from Tony Felicia alerting me to the fact that a decision was coming down and I should expect a call from the company's PR office. When I picked up the call a short time later, the AZ representative suggested that we should prepare a statement for both a losing and winning scenario. I guess the tension that had been building for months was getting to me, so I did not handle the call particularly well. I shot back that we would not plan a "sorry we lost and congrats to Pennsylvania" statement but would instead recommend to the governor that we mount an all-out effort to change the decision, including traveling to London to make the case to the board. It was "white knuckle" time.

Later that day, Johansson tracked down the governor in Washington where he was testifying at a hearing and gave him the news we all hoped for—AstraZeneca chose Delaware! The news flashed through the office and the state. Darrell suggested we organize an "official" toast to the big win, and we immediately made plans to convene with the media and numerous state leaders at the Triangle site the next day.

ASTRAZENECA PICKS DELAWARE screamed the headline of the *News Journal* on Friday morning, April 30, 1999. The sub-headline read: **VICTORY MEANS THOUSANDS OF JOBS. MILLIONS IN TAX REVENUE.** Filling most of the front page as well as pages six and seven, it was nearly all good news. In a column on page seven, entitled "Winners," was a photo of Governor Carper—a couple lines down the Delaware Economic Development Office was listed.

Further down the page were listed "Losers" featuring a photo of Pennsylvania Governor Tom Ridge. Never missing a chance to crusade on the subject of traffic, the *Journal* added "U.S. 202" motorists as losers.

With calls out to dozens of state leaders to come to the celebration, we ran into a roadblock. The only place to park near the open field was the parking lot of a building owned by Fusco Enterprises, but we received word that they refused to allow us to use the lot. I called Fusco's attorney Peter Gordon, and he said he would discuss the request with Fusco and get back to me. When Gordon called me back, he said the company would open up the parking if Mr. Fusco could join in the celebration. So there, smiling and celebrating with the rest of us was Tony Fusco.

Soon after the announcement, it came time to finalize the grant agreement between Delaware and AstraZeneca. Like every economic development deal, the company had to commit to reaching certain employment and investment targets. Additionally, Jim Burke, Mike Parkowski, and John "Chip" McDaniel from the state attorney general's office drafted "recapture" or "clawback" provisions to protect the taxpayer funds in the event the company did not live up to the terms. The meeting to review the terms of the agreement was like no other I observed during my six years with the office and it resulted in at least one humorous exchange.

Celebrating after the announcement with Darrell Minott and Tony Felicia

AstraZeneca arrived at the DEDO office with so many lawyers, there were not enough seats in our conference room. In addition to state, county and company attorneys, led by general counsel Glenn Engelmann, there were outside lawyers such as Wendie Stabler from Saul Ewing and Frank Biondi from Morris, Nichols, Arsht, & Tunnell. Shortly after the meeting started and introductions were made, Bob Milkovics, AZ's vice president of business operations and the overall project implementation manager arrived to view the proceedings and squeezed in next to me. As lawyers from around the table began to chime in, Milkovics leaned over to me and said, "Who is that talking?"

I said, "Bob, that's your lawyer."

When the next lawyer spoke up, Bob said, "John, who is that guy?"

Again, I answered, "Bob, he's your lawyer."

When the next lawyer spoke up, he said, "I guess you are going to tell me that's my lawyer, too!

It was.

The Legacy of the AstraZeneca Deal

During the ensuing years, AstraZeneca grew in Delaware as predicted but continued to face challenges in the marketplace and with their drug development pipeline. Based on their employment growth and capital investment, the company generated a strong return for the state, well exceeding what was required under the agreement. But as the company's business fortunes declined and incentive deals for other projects ran into trouble, AZ ended up as a focal point of criticism from the media and others.

In January of 2017, I authored an op-ed in the *News Journal* defending the AZ deal and the use of financial incentives to attract and retain jobs. While I am certainly one who finds providing cash incentives to companies less than desirable, I also believe it would be a mistake for Delaware to unilaterally disarm and hope for the best. In the case of AZ, I found much of the criticism to be particularly off target since it seemed to value the highway investment dollars as an exclusive AZ incentive while disregarding the parks, open space acquisition and development and historic preservation. Some politicians and media critics would also virtually ignore the fact that JP Morgan Chase added 3,000 jobs to the site after AZ jobs declined. And, of course, there is never a mention of the extraordinary toll the loss of 2,400 high paying AZ jobs would have had on the community and the state treasury had we fallen short in 1999.

Part V

The *Decline* and *Fall* of *Hercules*

In 2008, one of Delaware's most iconic companies was swallowed up by Ashland, a former Midwestern refining company on a mission to transform itself into a specialty chemical company. This event was at least eight years in the making, following an announcement by Interim CEO Tom Gossage, who had returned to the company in 2000 after having led it from 1991 to 1996. He rapidly concluded that Hercules was too small to survive on its own and needed to put itself up for sale. Ironically, Gossage had led the effort to shrink the size of Hercules by selling off its significant aerospace business. Instead of investing those proceeds in another acquisition, he used the funds to buy back Hercules shares in his drive to enhance "shareholder value."

So, why did an independent Hercules fade into history after nearly a century of adapting successfully to market conditions, including two World Wars, major economic downturns, and the significant pressures of globalization? While I do not expect to fully answer that question in this book, I will take the reader behind the scenes to see what these often-chaotic final years at Hercules looked like. I had made another career change in 2000, excited to have secured a role I coveted—head of government relations for one of Delaware's most important companies. But almost overnight, I found myself with a view from the highest levels of a global corporation in serious distress. The coming years would be an intense, wild ride.

Chapter 37

The Spiral Down, 2000

If the press calls, you tell them the dividend is safe!
Do you understand me, the dividend is safe!

The Hercules Powder Company was born in Wilmington's DuPont Building in 1912 as a result of a suit filed against explosives maker DuPont by the U.S. government under the Sherman Antitrust Act. According to the dense but excellent history of the company *Labors of a Modern Hercules* by authors Davis Dyer and David Sicilia, the newly formed company would operate out of DuPont's headquarters for the first nine years of its existence. As Dyer and Sicilia write,

Hercules Plaza

> *On June 13, 1912, the district court had decreed the general terms under which DuPont, by far the largest explosives-maker in the United States, would be broken up. The court ordered that roughly half of DuPont's capacity to make explosives be divided between two new companies (Hercules and Atlas) and specified how the new companies would be financed, the properties each would own, and the general terms under which they would compete.*[3]

By the turn of the twenty-first century, Hercules had become a global specialty chemical company operating out of a beautiful building along

---

3   Davis Dyer and David B. Sicilia, *Labors of a Modern Hercules: Evolution of a Chemical Company* (New York: McGraw Hill, 1990), 28.

the Brandywine Creek known as the Hercules Plaza. Although existing in the shadow of its historic parent, DuPont, the company had its own legacy as it approached its ninetieth birthday. According to the company's 1999 SEC 10K filing, Hercules had 11,347 employees worldwide and $3.25 billion in revenues.

Some time after the AstraZeneca announcement, as I began to wonder what to do with the rest of my life, an opportunity emerged. And it came from a lifelong friend, my old high school and college golf teammate, Tom Ciconte. Over the years Tom had become a top financial executive at Hercules and then was named vice president, public affairs, which included government relations. He told me he was not enjoying his new public affairs role. "John," he said, "I'm like a duck out of water in this position. Why don't you come over and replace me."

"Are you serious?" I asked.

"Yes, I may take a package and retire."

I had joined the Carper Administration in 1994, believing I would stay two years and return to the executive recruiting business in a better position to grow a client base in Delaware and the region. I had continued to cultivate a few contacts in the business and had an opportunity to interview with top firms like Korn Ferry and Heidrick and Struggles, but nothing materialized. So, as we approached the final year of Carper's term, I began to consider more options. My "dream job" at that point would have been to manage government relations for a major Delaware company, but since these positions were few and far between, I tried not to get my hopes up.

The surprise alert by Ciconte about his position more than piqued my interest, but unfortunately it turned out to not be as simple as Tom recommending me to the company. When I later interviewed with human resources executive June Barry, she as much as said, "Don't call us, we'll call you." Ciconte soon retired, and I thought the opportunity had passed. A few months after my disappointing interview with Barry, Hercules' director of government relations, Jack Pounds, visited the DEDO office. As he was leaving, he asked if I might be interested in his position at Hercules. (Pounds, who had come to Hercules through the BetzDearborn acquisition, told me later that he was unhappy with Hercules management and had decided to take a position leading the Ohio chemical industry council.) He was not aware I had already interviewed with the company without advancing.

With the departure of then CEO Keith Elliot and the continuing integration of the recent acquisition of BetzDearborn, much change was going on at the top of the company. Ciconte had been replaced by an experienced PR executive, Neil Stalter, who had recently joined Hercules from Campbell's Soup. Neil had grown up in Delaware and attended Archmere Academy with Joe Biden. The senator and soon to be U.S. vice president had even dated Neil's sister in high school. Neil had moved away from the area after graduating from Notre Dame. (He was so dedicated to ND that he pointed out his cemetery plot on the campus to us when we attended a Fighting Irish–Michigan State football game with him a few years later. Also joining us on that trip were MSU graduate and Hercules CEO Craig Rogerson and my old friend John DiEleuterio, who was then serving as Joe Biden's state director.)

Jack Pounds lined up a dinner with Stalter, and it seemed like an evening with an old friend. We hit it off immediately. Neal scheduled me to meet with the new Hercules CEO, Vince Corbo, and members of his leadership team and coached me on what to say. Almost immediately, they asked me when I could start. When I returned to the DEDO office that day and told my friend and associate Jim Burke, he quickly went to the latest Hercules SEC 10K filing and remarked, "Riles, are you sure you want to go there? They have a lot of debt on the balance sheet."

"Jim," I said. "I really don't care. Head of government relations for a global public company is something I have aspired to for a long time. I'm not about to pass up this opportunity."

My start date was the Monday after the beginning of the new millennium. At that point, I assumed the only thing that could go wrong was if the world started to unravel due to the Y2K bug. But before I had an opportunity to tell the governor I would be leaving, Vince Corbo saw Carper at a Delaware Business Roundtable breakfast and broke the news ahead of me. Clearly taken back, Carper immediately asked Corbo to delay my start date so I would be available to assist with some of the complications that had arisen with the AstraZeneca project. Unaware of this development, I received a call from Carrie Casey, Carper's executive assistant, who said the governor had heard that I was leaving. He wanted to see me in an hour.

Concerned that I had not been the one to inform the governor, I felt uncomfortable in the meeting. Having had little inkling about what kind of person Tom Carper was when I started with him six years prior, I had over time developed a deep respect for the career politician—he was no longer just a boss but had become a good friend. He was one of the hardest working people I had ever met; he refused to give up even when the cause seemed beyond reach; and, as much as possible, governed in a non-partisan manner. While I was flattered that he wanted me to stay on longer , I knew it was time to go. I agreed to remain for a one-month transition, with a promise that I would help on a volunteer basis if called.

Towards the end of January 2000, friends and associates put together a farewell event in my honor at the state conference center at Buena Vista, the beautiful and historic estate built by former U.S. Secretary of State John M. Clayton. Several speakers roasted me, including Mike Harkins, director of the Delaware River and Bay Authority. During his remarks, Harkins referred to me several times as the only Republican in the Carper Administration. Speaking last, the governor looked at me and said, "John, I didn't know you were a Republican!"

Soon on the job, I began to understand better the implications of my friend Jim Burke's warning about Hercules' debt load. Anxiety was building among employees and investors. The core complaint was that the CEO at the time of the BetzDearborn acquisition, Keith Elliott, vastly overpaid to buy the water treatment company, spending $2.4 billion and assuming $700 million in Betz debt ($72 per share). What made everyone even more bitter about the deal was that the board paid out a multi-million-dollar bonus to Elliott for completing the transaction. When the deal was announced, the *Wall Street Journal* stated, "The purchase price is an amazing 100% over BetzDearborn's current stock price of $35.875 a share." Later, Hercules CEO Craig Rogerson would be quoted in a *Delaware Today* article remarking, "We [meaning Elliott and the Hercules board] actually got emotional over the deal, bid against ourselves, and overpaid for Betz by 100%."

Another factor that was killing company morale was that the deal required $100 million in spending cuts to successfully integrate the two companies. People who had worked at Hercules for decades were about to lose their jobs to pay for Elliott's folly—and his bonus.

Although I did not have communications responsibility at the time, my boss Neil Stalter thought I could use some "face time" with Vince Corbo, so he assigned me to fly down on the company plane with him to the R&D center in Jacksonville, Florida. This complex was previously part of the Betz operations. While employees at the Hercules Plaza were voicing anxiety and resentment at every turn, the response of the former Betz employees in Jacksonville was even less encouraging. Relaxing over a beer on the way back, Corbo expressed his own anger and frustration with Elliott's deal and the bind he put the company in.

A couple days before the trip, I went into Corbo's office to review the presentation slides with him. When I walked in, he yelled, "Who's buying the stock, who's buying the stock?" On the screen behind his desk, I could see the stock volume intraday chart spiking upward towards ten million shares traded—ten percent of the company's value. This would automatically trigger the "poison pill" provision that had been adopted by the Hercules board. Not having a clue as to what was happening, I responded to him, "I don't know. Maybe a corporate raider?"

A lucky guess on my part—or perhaps not so lucky. As it turned out, the buyer of the company's shares was the one and only Sam Heyman, the infamous '80s corporate raider, who was covered by Connie Bruck in her book *The Predator's Ball.* Also covered in that book was Nelson Peltz, another raider who would go on to have a significant Delaware chemical business connection.

Under continuing pressure, including from Heyman, Corbo began to take further steps to sell businesses and cut jobs, but it was not putting a big dent in the huge interest payments on the debt. A concern was also developing about the dividend payment to shareholders—a significant obligation of up to $100 million per year. A reduction or suspension of the dividend seemed to be inevitable. However, we knew such decision would be another harbinger that the company was in trouble and would cause more shareholders to dump their stake.

Meanwhile, Governor Carper had invited Sharon and me along with the Corbos to join a black tie business leaders' dinner at the governor's mansion in Dover. With the cocktail hour ending, the Corbos had not yet arrived. Finally, as we were being seated, they came rushing into the reception area. The bearded Corbo seemed distressed and quickly took me by the arm, pulling me over to the side of the room. With his face only inches from mine he said, "If the press calls, you tell them the dividend is safe. Do you understand me? The dividend is safe!"

Within weeks, the dividend was slashed—and it would be gone entirely by the end of the year.

Looking back, what was about to happen was entirely predictable. But I had no experience at this level of the corporate world in 2000, so I did not realize that something significant was in the making when Stalter entered my office on the afternoon of October 17. He told me my presence was needed at a private room on the second floor of the Hotel

DuPont. I quickly covered the two blocks to the Delaware landmark where Hercules was born in 1912.

When I knocked on the door, who would answer but former chairman & CEO Tom Gossage. I knew Gossage from my executive recruiting days, and he welcomed me like we were old friends. He introduced me to the three others in the room: Dick Dahlen, Ed Carrington, and Larry Rankin. He then gave me some rather stunning news saying, "John, Vince has resigned, and I am the new Hercules chairman and CEO."

I remember thinking, *Wow, I'm in the middle of a coup d'état.*

Gossage then explained that Dahlen would be the new general counsel and Carrington would be the new head of human resources (referred to by veteran employees as "Fast Eddie," Carrington bore an uncanny resemblance to Jack Nicholson in *The Shining*). Carrington would be at the helm for all the coming job cuts. Larry Rankin was sort of the odd man out in this gathering, as I believe he was also meeting Gossage for the first time. He was there in his role as the senior executive at BetzDearborn (in Trevose, PA) and would leave the company shortly after.

Gossage began, "John, I would like you to prepare a press release announcing my appointment, as well as the new leadership team." He followed this by saying, "By the way, have you gotten rid of that country club yet?" (Gossage was referring to the company country club that had come under criticism from investors.)

A few days later, I found myself sitting in on a meeting with Gossage and others as he reviewed the balance sheet and business plans and discussed the state of the business. I was included because we were getting calls from members of the congressional delegation about the state of the company and he wanted to discuss it. The last topic was the financial picture, including interest payments and debt covenants—things I knew little about. As the meeting was ending, Gossage turned to me and said, "John, what the hell was Keith thinking?!" (He was, of course, referring to former CEO Keith Elliott and the debt engendered by the Betz acquisition.)

On November 28, 2000, Gossage announced that Hercules was for sale. The headline in the *News Journal* on November 29th stated, "Corporate move may have huge impact on city, state."

As the expression goes, I had been "drinking out of the firehose" since I arrived at Hercules. Part of the challenge was trying to figure out what the hell everyone was talking about. Each day I was either talking to chemical engineers about products or financial professionals about balance sheets and earning statements. While I did my best to fake it and not sound like a complete fool, it certainly made me wish I had paid better attention during high school chemistry. One chemical compound I heard a lot about my first year was nitrocellulose, an explosive material that was once a moneymaker for the company.

The only remaining nitrocellulose manufacturing site in the U.S. in 2000 was our Parlin, New Jersey plant. Just south of Staten Island, Parlin was an old industrial community located within the borough of Sayreville, New Jersey. In keeping with its roots, the Hercules plant operated adjacent to a former DuPont explosives plant. The town had a rich Polish heritage. Trenton lobbyist and director of the New Jersey Chemistry Council Hal Bozarth used to joke that if you walked into bar in Sayreville and shouted "Stan," everyone at the bar would turn around. A prominent figure in town was local New Jersey assemblyman John Wisniewski. "The Wiz," as Bozarth referred to him, would lead the charge against Governor Chris Christie during the "Bridgegate" scandal. Wiz would lose the nomination for governor in 2017 to Phil Murphy, after achieving some notoriety among New Jersey Democrats by endorsing Bernie Sanders over Hillary Clinton in the 2016 presidential primary.

At that point, nitrocellulose was no longer profitable due in part to changes in military procurement. The other product made at the Parlin plant was hydoxyethylcellulose (HEC), one of Hercules' most profitable products. The plant was basically divided in two, something I would see in other Hercules locations. A former Hercules employee believed he could find support to sell the explosive material to the Pentagon, so he formed a company called Greentree and purchased the business. The employees who worked at the plant would have been eligible for severance when the business shut down, but when Greentree decided to take it over and hire most of the workers at lower wages, the new Hercules executive team decided that the company would not honor the severance.

When the workers heard about the severance decision, protests erupted at the site. Assemblyman Wisniewski attacked the company in a newspaper op-ed accusing Hercules of reneging on an earned benefit. I then received a call from the plant manager asking what to do as the workers were now marching on the plant demanding Hercules pay up. Since things were happening so quickly and it would take at least two hours to drive to the plant, I called Hal Bozarth. Hal was at a meeting on the other end of the state, but he dispatched a member of his staff who monitored the protest and reported back to me. Ultimately, we settled with the workers, but the Greentree military contract never materialized, so that portion of the plant was completely shut down and the workers laid off again.

The Parlin–Greentree eruption was the first of many interesting New Jersey encounters during my Hercules/Ashland years. It was difficult to figure out the alliances and political infighting in the state, so I relied heavily on the chain-smoking Bozarth, perhaps the most respected man in Trenton. Standing over 6' 5" with a ready smile and booming voice, the former teacher and basketball star stood out in the New Jersey corridors of power. But Hal had no illusions about what it took be successful in Trenton—money, money, and more money! He ran numerous fundraisers for all the important players, while at the same time being a cynic when it came to the state's reputation for corruption. When I complained about the request for donations from every politician we encountered, he would quip, "Welcome to my world!" I quickly became convinced that New Jersey had figured out a way to legalize corruption.

Only weeks after Gossage took over, Neal Stalter walked into my office and told me he was leaving. He also said that Sue Towers, the director of corporate communications, was leaving as well. (Sue had been business editor at the *News Journal* and had started the same day as I did.) "You're in charge," he said. "You are the new head of public affairs [which included government relations, corporate communications, community relations, and corporate philanthropy]. You will be reporting to Allen Spizzo, VP of investor relations."

Public Affairs was a vice presidential-level position, but since we were in the middle of a company meltdown, I did not think it was a good time to discuss title or pay. My first orders were to let a couple of staff members go, close the Washington office, and terminate the contract of the long-time Hercules' lobbyist. With a recently penned three-year contract, that would prove easier said than done.

Putting Hercules up for sale was not enough to satisfy Heyman, so he filed a slate of four proposed directors to the Hercules' board. It was assumed that the reason Heyman pursued Hercules with such zeal was to capture and integrate our Aqualon division into his International Specialty Products company (ISP). While the largest component of Aqualon was the industrial side (water soluble polymers sold for use in paints, grout and other applications), the highly profitable "personal care" side (ingredients that went into toothpaste, shampoos, pharmaceuticals, etc.) was believed to have the greatest growth potential. And the base of raw materials used by Aqualon (cellulose derived from cotton linters, and other natural sources) would enable ISP to diversify their hydrocarbon-based chemistry.

I was pulled into the battle as corporate spokesperson and as a member of our proxy team, a far cry from the government relations role for which I had been hired. The primary tactic deployed in the proxy fight consisted of firing letters off to shareholders and blasting the dissidents after Heyman and his proxy solicitor would level attacks on Gossage and the Hercules board. The "fight letters" were often accompanied by a press release with me as the spokesperson, so after Gossage, I became the face and name associated with the proxy fight. (I always thought it would be exciting to be quoted in the *New York Times* and *Wall Street Journal*, but this was not what I had in mind.)

It was a bad sign that current management appeared to be losing the "hearts and minds" of the Hercules' employees. While I don't believe they trusted Heyman to protect their interests, they were bitter at Gossage and Keith Elliott and wanted to file their protest in some meaningful way. In a move that to some appeared self-defeating, those that crossed over would help elect Heyman and friends to the board and launch what became a multi-year struggle between Hercules and Heyman. There would be more millions wasted on lost executive time, "New York" legal fees, and proxy solicitors in the battles ahead.

Shortly after Gossage returned to Hercules, business reporter Seth Agulnick of the *News Journal* penned an article with the headline, "Is the fat lady ready to sing yet?" He quoted Gossage speaking before analysts on Wall Street:

> *"I used to come before you dealing with Mozart, the light operas and how good things were. I've been thinking more lately about Wagner,"* Gossage told the analysts.
> *"The Flying Dutchman,"* he said, *"has provided clarity for me as to where I think this is all going to end up and what the end game will be."* The comment started a mad scramble among shareholders, Wall Street analysts and company employees to learn more about Wagner and "The Flying Dutchman."

Gossage had gained a reputation as a patron of the arts and lover of opera during his first tour at Hercules. This was not the last I would see or hear about Gossage's affinity for the form of theater reaching back to the sixteenth century. Before the annual shareholder's meeting and the culmination of the proxy war, he hosted a retirement dinner for Hercules' director Robert G. Jahn at the Delaware Art Museum. Much to the delight of the late Princeton aerospace scientist and other executives and board members present, Gossage recruited a couple of opera singers in full costume to serenade the professor over a catered dinner with fine wines. As we were hurtling towards the annual meeting and the showdown with Heyman, the evening at the opera had a certain Louis XVI air about it. (As the reader may remember, King Louis and his famous bride, Marie Antoinette, renowned for their extravagant lifestyle, were guillotined during the French Revolution. I hoped we wouldn't suffer a similar fate.)

Gossage quickly announced the company would sell the Hercules Country Club, as well as the company jet, and the company guesthouse. Ed Carrington led the effort to dispose of the club with a sense of urgency that reflected his "Fast Eddie" persona. Over the coming weeks we listened to a pitch by several bidders for the property, and settled on a deal offered by R.J. Palumbo and Associates of Media, PA. While the new owners and the company professed interest in maintaining the property as a country club, there was a development brewing in county government that all but insured that would not be the case.

One day while the country club sale discussions were proceeding, I received a call from Rich Abbott, a county councilman. He asked, "John, are you aware that all of Hercules' lands on Route 48 are set to be rezoned this Thursday night? It is being 'proactively rezoned' to residential by Tom and Sherry." (Tom was Tom Gordon, the county executive, and Sherry was Sherry Freebery, chief administrative officer.) While serving on county council, I had never seen a "proactive rezoning." Rezoning requests were typically brought forth by a land owner or developer.

What motivated the county administration's intrusion into Hercules' affairs remains a mystery to me. Neither Gordon, Freebery, nor the Land Use Department attempted to contact our company to explain what seemed at the time to be an unprecedented action. (They later claimed that they had mailed us a letter that we did not receive.) Their administration had staked out a strong position in support of civic groups who opposed growth and development, but we had no plans to develop the site so there was no known opposition. Furthermore, if the site remained under the existing office zoning, there was little chance it would be developed in the foreseeable future—even if we were taken over by a larger enterprise.

However, with the demand for new homes, it was almost certain to be developed under the proposed residential zoning.

Based on what Abbott told me, it seemed clear that the "skids had been greased" to push this unusual ordinance through council. It looked like the only way to prevent passage was to have the vote delayed. Chris Coons had just begun his term as president of the county council, so I called and asked him to table the request. (I had worked closely with Coons while in economic development on a project to have W.L Gore expand in Delaware.) He agreed to do it, but he warned me that he could probably only hold it until the next meeting in two weeks.

When I arrived at council that Thursday night to ensure there were no last-minute glitches, members seemed familiar with the proposal and ready to support it. One councilman told me he would vote for the measure "to prevent Hercules from stabbing the community in the back." He did not bother to explain what his hyperbole meant, but it seemed clear there had been anti-Hercules guidance provided to county council with no opportunity provided to us to respond.

While my reaction was that this was an outrageous assault on the company at a vulnerable time, events were about to take a surprising, 180-degree turn. After getting council to table the rezoning, Ed Carrington informed me that the country club buyer and the bank loaning them the money preferred that the residential zoning pass. Suddenly, all the major players had determined "residential" was the correct zoning. What the benefit was to the county and the surrounding communities continues to escape me, but it was a good move for the company because Hercules could close the deal and get paid; the buyers now had a more valuable and more liquid asset; and the bank was able to make the loan. On the other hand, it made it almost certain that the new owners would flip the property for housing and the members would lose their golf club. It did not take long for that to materialize.

Meanwhile, our annual meeting had to be postponed into May because the company was unable to file the annual report in time, further

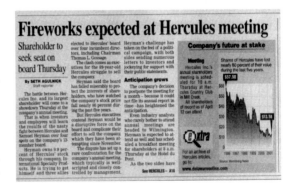

raising everyone's doubts about the company's future. On the big day, the Hercules Country Club was jammed with press, analysts, and hundreds of shareholders, mostly retirees living in the area. When the club ballroom filled up, we expanded to an adjacent room where we set up audio so attendees could follow the proceedings. As I stood at the far end of the room discussing logistics with country club staff, I noticed a tall figure making a beeline directly towards me. I was about to meet Sam Heyman, just minutes before it was announced he had been elected to the board.

"You, you're the one saying all those lousy things about me," Heyman shouted as he pointed a finger in my face.

Completely taken back, I stammered out, "Mr. Heyman, I'm just doing my job."

Sam no sooner headed towards the other side of the room, when a short, older gentleman approached me with a half grin on his face, a grin I would be seeing a lot of over the next couple of years.

"Hello, John," he said, "I'm Bill Joyce. I'm your new chairman and CEO."

Joyce had been recruited by the board from Dow, where he was vice-chairman. He had previously served as chairman and CEO of Union Carbide. He would remain in the background, playing no role in the meeting.

Soon Gossage got up to speak and he did not disappoint the media present, since he rambled on about the opera, Wagner and the "Flying Dutchman," while most of the room wondered what the hell he was talking about. Gossage then announced the results of the election: Heyman had elected all four of his directors. No doubt he might have replaced the entire board at that time had Hercules not prevented the move by the adoption years prior of staggered terms for board members, another takeover prevention device.

All present soon witnessed another almost surreal moment when Heyman came forward bearing an authentic native American peace pipe. The message seemed to be that the opposing sides should smoke the pipe and work on the future of Hercules together. Unfortunately, there would be no peace in the years ahead.

Tom Gossage had failed to stop Heyman. He walked off the stage of the shareholder meeting and headed back into retirement. The battle for control of Hercules would be quickly rejoined with Bill Joyce at the helm.

Chapter 38

Asbestos and Other Battles, 2001–2002

"Thanks for softening him up for us, John!"

The executive offices on the eighth floor were referred to by Hercules Plaza employees as "behind the glass doors." If you went to visit the top dozen officers of the company, you had to enter a code to gain access to the fortress-like inner sanctum. The hallways were wide and lined with great works of art from N.C. Wyeth, Norman Rockwell, Arthur Davenport Fuller, and others. Many of the artworks were from calendars issued by Hercules Powder Company in the first half of the twentieth century. Most of the offices opened to the east with beautiful views of the Delaware Memorial Bridge in the distance.

Bill Joyce did not waste any time de-populating the executive wing. Every time I went behind the glass doors, another office was empty. Like a plague of locusts, consultants arrived from New York and other locations and lined up in the reception area to sign in. They called the turnaround strategy "Work Process Redesign" and poured over the books and conducted interviews with managers basically counting the heads they could cut. What amounted to a Hercules D-Day—the day employees would be informed how deep the cuts would be was scheduled for September 11, 2001.

The employee meetings would take place in two sessions, a morning session at the Hercules Country Club for approximately five hundred research center employees, and an afternoon session at the Plaza for another seven hundred Herculites. We had an audio visual contractor who completed all the communication arrangements in order to broadcast Joyce's comments to Hercules remote locations. I stayed back to complete arrangements at the Plaza, as we did not have a facility to accommodate such a large gathering. We ended up renting hundreds of fold-out chairs and lining them up on one of several empty floors in the building. The country club staff organized the first session.

After checking on the logistics that morning, I headed up to the Computer Aid, Inc. (CAI) office at 9th and Market to meet with Ernie Dianastasis and Skip Pennella to discuss plans for an upcoming fundraiser. As I was leaving the meeting, Ernie's assistant Patti Pfarrer told me an airplane had just flown into the World Trade Center in New York. We speculated for a minute as to what it might be and then I went on my way. Troubled by what I just heard, I decided to detour through the DuPont Building to see if I might learn anything about what was going on. As I approached the area around the Green Room, I noticed the lobby bar was open and people were standing around looking at the TV screen behind the bar. I walked up to see one of the towers on fire. Suddenly, a bolt shot from the right of the screen and the second tower exploded. I starred at the screen trying to absorb the additional news that a plane had hit the Pentagon, and another was reported to have crashed in Pennsylvania.

As I walked down the hill from the DuPont building to the Plaza, I began to sort out in my head the implications of this extraordinary event. I had family that worked in Washington and in New York, so my first thought was to try to find out if everyone was safe. Like so many others, I discovered that the cell phone network had failed; it would be hours before I received a family all-clear signal. (My niece Katie's husband worked in building six at the World Trade Center, and it would be late afternoon before it was determined he was safe.)

Soon, my attention turned to the employee meeting. Bill Joyce's message would be difficult for Plaza employees under any circumstances (headquarters was destined to be the target of most of the coming cuts), but now it would be taking place as the dark cloud of the 9/11 attacks was settling in across the country. I quickly concluded that we should postpone the meeting and allow employees to take off if they needed time to verify the safety of family members. Everyone I checked with reinforced my thinking, so I waited for Bill at his office.

In the months I had worked with Joyce, I came to realize he had a singular focus on his goals. Generally, his goals were to "right-size" the company and prepare it for sale and to fend off the effort of Sam Heyman to take Hercules over. The town hall meetings were planned to inform employees about what to expect from his agenda and the process that was about to unfold. Having watched his driven personality for months, I fully expected him to resist any attempt to postpone the meeting, so I prepared arguments in my head in the event my premonition proved correct. The emotions of 9/11 had already overwhelmed me, so the thought that I might be on his wrong side meant little. I planned to stand my ground, believing I was saving Joyce from himself. The anger and resentment people already felt towards the man would only be compounded if he went through with the meeting.

When he arrived, I said, "Bill, I'm sure you heard about the attacks in New York and Washington. I am recommending we postpone this afternoon's meeting."

Just as I feared, he pushed back. "I'm not postponing the meeting. We will go on as scheduled."

I repeated my concern, but he would not budge and was growing frustrated with my insistence. His executive assistant, Linda Rudnick, was watching the situation unfold when the phone rang. Bill turned away and headed to his desk to pick it up. When he disappeared behind the door I turned to Linda and said, "Do you think he is going to fire me?"

Linda looked at me and said, "I don't know."

Within seconds, Joyce returned to Linda's desk and appeared puzzled that I was still there. I was convinced the totally focused CEO had just not absorbed the trauma of what was occurring. "Bill," I said. "I must emphasize again that holding this meeting is a mistake and I think you will regret it." I then added, "The situation is so serious that the governor has declared a state of emergency."

Raising his voice, Joyce responded, "The governor is overreacting!"

Just then the phone rang at Linda's desk. Linda said it was one of our senior executives, Monica Reise-Martin. Bill grabbed the phone and in an angry voice told Reise-Martin that John Riley wanted him to call off the employee meeting.

As he listened to her response, which Linda and I could not hear, his face grew redder. A second later he slammed down the phone and as he turned back toward his office, he shouted back at me, "OK, cancel the damn meeting."

I never spoke to Reise-Martin about her comments to Joyce, but suspected she endorsed my recommendation to cancel the meeting.

From my standpoint, the terrorist attacks on 9/11 were every bit as traumatic as the assassination of President Kennedy back in 1963. The national reaction was very similar in the sense that the attacks, and the aftermath dominated the news coverage for weeks and you could still feel the emotion several years after. The son of one of our friends from the golf world, Davis "Deeg" Sezna, had just started his new job in the World Trade Center south tower. We would all attend a memorial service in Deeg's honor days later.

Also, at the time my wife Sharon was working at insurance giant AIG in Wilmington and was asked to go to New York immediately after the attacks and assist with claims at the Pier 94 Family Assistance Center. She described a dramatic scene of thousands of people in a state of shock over lost loved ones trying to put their lives back together. It was a world full of sadness, but also full of many acts of caring and kindness.

I always wondered if Bill Joyce had second thoughts about his reaction on 9/11. He was not one to talk about such things, but approximately six months later we were on a train together returning from New York when he directed my attention towards southern Manhattan. Rising into the sky was the "Tribute in Lights," a memorial to the heroism of 9/11. He didn't say anything, but I sensed that he wanted me to know it had made an impression.

In the weeks and months after 9/11, I found myself spending more time with Joyce, often sitting with him deep into the evenings, listening to his plans and strategy. But he was not much interested in my opinion or that of many others. I concluded that he was basically "rehearsing" those nights because I soon observed that what he would say to me in the evening, would become talking points days later. Every so often, I would make a suggestion, often about employee issues. On just about every occasion, he would look at me and say, "Here's why I'm not going to do that."

While I did not attend the board meetings during the proxy battle, I would hear from Joyce and others about what a disruptive force Sam Heyman had become. He was relentless in pursuit of Hercules, but he had run into the Bill Joyce wall. The Hercules chairman and CEO would not give an inch.

With responsibility for media and corporate communications I continued to serve on the proxy team. We all took direction from two primary sources, our proxy solicitor, Dan Burch of MacKenzie Partners and David Katz, a one-person Hercules legal brain trust from New York-based Wachtell, Lipton, Rosen, & Katz (WLR&K).

In the bestselling book *The Outliers*, published five years after the Hercules–Heyman wars, author Malcolm Gladwell described WLR&K

as "generally regarded as the finest in the world." The book examines how the hyper-successful in life were influenced by various factors including birth months and years. In the case of several great New York law firms, such as WLR&K, it started by being Jewish and being blocked out of opportunities with the closed world of the Ivy League dominated "white-shoe" firms. These firms had avoided the "hostile takeover" world and referred it to lawyers like Herbert Wachtell, and they became experts in a field that would soon explode with opportunity for the profession. Regarding fees, Gladwell stated: "Unlike every one of its competitors, WLR&K does not bill by the hour. It simply names a fee. Once while defending Kmart against a takeover, the firm billed $20 million for two weeks' work."

The proxy team would convene in the executive conference room for hours reviewing "fight letters" that were to be sent to thousands of shareholders defending our board and attacking Heyman. Sometimes, we would agonize at length over a single word or phrase before we agreed, only to be overturned hours later after further review by Katz.

Dan Burch was a technocrat in a very narrow field—proxy solicitation. Although bedecked in a pin-striped suit, he presented a rather rumpled appearance. His blunt speaking style seemed to get under Bill Joyce's skin, but he was clearly respected by David Katz and others on Wall Street. I worked more often with his deputy, Jeannie Carr, a smart, patient professional who understood my lack of experience but took the time to counsel me on the reasons behind their strategy and tactics. After preparing at length for proxy fight number two with Heyman in 2002, Sam suddenly withdrew his slate. We learned he had cancer and would be undergoing treatment. The big showdown was postponed until 2003.

One area of agreement with Heyman was regarding asbestos. Heyman battled America's trial lawyers at his company, GAF, while Hercules was also fighting off their relentless attacks. Hercules was not an asbestos company; we simply had the misfortune of once owning a company that encapsulated asbestos into heavy tanks and pipes that were used in the bowels of industrial plants and as piping at chemical plants and refineries. At the time, asbestos was "state of the art" for fireproofing.

When all the asbestos companies went bankrupt, the country's trial lawyers sought out any company that had ever used the product and began to sue them as well. They became very creative in their quest for multimillion-dollar payoffs. A typical strategy involved naming as many as a hundred companies as defendants in lawsuits with multiple clients.

While there no doubt were some legitimate injuries (mesothelioma or lung cancer), the problem for companies was defending against an ocean of dubious claims. Companies were placed in a bind since juries in plaintiff friendly jurisdictions around the country such as Madison County, Illinois might award huge judgements based on a single individual. (In 2003, a single plaintiff in Madison County case was awarded $250 million in a case against U.S. Steel.) In an article for the American Enterprise Institute in 2006, author Ted Frank wrote:

> *Although asbestos use all but ceased by the early 1970s—and although asbestosis was called a "disappearing disease" in 1988—trial lawyers have filed hundreds of thousands of new claims in the last decade. As Lester Brickman, a professor at Cardozo Law School at Yeshiva University, has documented, the majority of these plaintiffs have suffered no impairment; the majority of the defendants they sued did not produce products to which they had substantial exposure. According to a study by the RAND Institute there have been dozens of asbestos-related bankruptcies, the majority of which have taken place in the last five years; another study identifies tens of thousands of lost jobs. As the original manufacturers of asbestos went bankrupt, plaintiffs' attorneys have greatly expanded the penumbra of liability to include companies that happened to have asbestos present in the workplace or manufactured asbestos-containing products. Over 8,000 companies in over 90 percent of American industries have been sued for asbestos-related claims.*

With the asbestos pressure and job losses mounting, the National Association of Manufacturers (NAM) was leading an effort to garner sixty votes in the Senate for something called the Fairness in Asbestos Injury Resolution Act (the FAIR Act). While Bill Joyce was worried about the rising number of times Hercules was being named in asbestos suits, he was skeptical that politicians in Washington could solve the problem. I managed to convince him that we should at least discuss the matter with Senator Carper.

Democrats in Washington were a reliable ally to the trial lawyers, who fought all efforts to reform the legal system that was costing business billions every year. Along with the labor and government employee unions, the trial bar constituted one of the largest funding sources for the party. In the same 2006 AEI article discussed above, Ted Frank discussed the power of Fred Baron, the famed asbestos lawyer from Texas:

Fred Baron, who in 2002 promised a "jihad" against politicians who supported liability reform, went on to be the finance chair of John Edwards's presidential campaign and co-chair of the Kerry Victory '04 Committee.

When the FAIR Act hearings kicked-off in the Judicial Committee in the Russell Senate Office Building, I watched as four men made a grand entrance into the chamber just before the hearings began and four paid "seat savers" immediately jumped up from the first row and left. I asked an industry lobbyist sitting nearby who they were. "That's the famous Fred Baron," he answered. I wondered if they were there to watch the proceedings or to send a message to the Judiciary committee members.

As a U.S. senator, Tom Carper often referred to himself as a "recovering governor." Running a state was a lot like running a business, which meant solving problems and paying attention to your customers and your financial health. Carper understood that Delaware needed companies like Hercules to stay healthy to protect high quality jobs and help generate the taxes that kept the state going. As a Democrat, Carper was under significant pressure to stay in line with the party on what was generally referred to as "tort reform," but when I called and told him Hercules was perhaps in greater danger from asbestos than corporate debt, he agreed to sit down to listen.

And listen he did.

I joined Bill Joyce, general counsel, Dick Dahlen, deputy general counsel, Michael Rettig, and members of Carper's staff for what I would describe as a two-hour seminar on Hercules and asbestos. In a very persuasive presentation, Dahlen and Rettig told the story of Hercules' misfortune and the corruption permeating the legal system, particularly in jurisdictions labeled by business organizations as "judicial hellholes." The most famous of these venues at that time was Madison County, Illinois, but Texas, Mississippi, and other locations with elected judges were also favorites of the trial lawyers. (In Mississippi, famous trial lawyer Dickie Scruggs would go to prison for bribing two state court judges.)

Although Carper did not sit on the Judiciary Committee where the asbestos law would be considered, he clearly understood the threat to the company and the hundreds of jobs in Wilmington. Over the coming months he would lead an effort to garner the support of several Democrats and help to give the bill a chance. When he was leaving that day, he pulled me aside and asked me what I had done to secure the support of

Delaware's senior senator and judiciary committee member, Joe Biden. I told him I had spoken to his staff, but they told me Joe would not support our efforts. Carper insisted that I should bring our story to Joe and make the case. That would prove to be another interesting experience with Delaware's most famous citizen.

Vice president stops for a photo with a Republican and his daughter Carie

A short time after calling Claire DeMatteis, Biden's state director, Joyce, Dahlen, Rettig, and I were ushered into the senator's Wilmington Tower office, only a block from Hercules Plaza. Bill and the lawyers had never met Senator Biden. I thought I knew Joe fairly well and had briefed everyone on what to expect—which was generally that Joe would do most of the talking and that he was unlikely to see things our way. Joe led off with his famous charm and said some nice things about me. All seemed well as Dahlen started into his presentation about the Hercules asbestos nightmare. But he had not even finished his opening remarks when Joe cut loose with the full force of the other side of the Biden personality. Raising his voice, Joe pointed his finger at Dahlen and said, "No, you listen to me!"

And listen we did—for the next forty-five minutes.

Well into Biden's monologue, I looked over at Joyce, and he had the half grin on his face I had seen many times before. Dahlen was ashen. Joe focused most of his attention on examples of stricken workers and how corporations were not fulfilling their responsibilities, never allowing us an opportunity to explain the inherent unfairness of the Hercules situation. I tried to interject some comments to see if we could shift things back on track, but Biden would not be diverted. Mercifully, Claire finally walked in and informed the senator that he had to move on to his next appointment (ironically, a campaign finance committee organizing meeting, which I had been asked to attend). We gathered up our papers and bid our good-bye without ever been given the courtesy of telling our story.

As soon as we cleared Biden's office and the elevator doors closed, Joyce looked at me and said, "Well, John, thanks for softening him up for us!"

When I got back to my desk at Hercules, I called Claire and told her about Bill Joyce's comment. She said, "But John, you did … you did soften him up."

As it turned out, the fun was not over because it was time to head up to the Hotel DuPont. I had been asked to join the finance committee by longtime Biden aid and now fundraiser, Dennis Toner (I had served with Dennis' father on the county council). Toner had hoped that I might have been able to draw in support from Hercules executives for the Senator's re-election campaign. As we were beginning to take our seats, Joe made his grand entrance and when he caught sight of me out of the corner of his eye, with a sly smile he yelled, "Hey, John, still have your job?" I did not bother to explain to Dennis our chances of securing contributions for Biden's campaign had greatly diminished that morning.

While you would have never guessed it at the time, Joe Biden would come to play a positive role in the battle over the FAIR Act. The senator's judiciary staff lead, Jon Meyer, had listened to the full story and must have received Joe's approval to work with us. (In a later meeting in Biden's office on Capitol Hill with Joyce's successor, Craig Rogerson, and company chairman, John Wulff, Joe told them I had helped him "see the light" on the issue. Joe was so gracious with his comments that day, I was certain he was "making up" for the earlier beating in Wilmington.)

The concept of the FAIR Act was to establish a trust fund, not unlike the fund set up to cover injuries from Black Lung disease, that would pay a set amount to individuals proven to have an asbestos related illness. The pay-outs would vary based on several factors, with the most severe cases of mesothelioma receiving more than a million dollars each. The initial draft of the bill represented a serious challenge for Hercules. The major corporations designed it so that every company contributed at the same level. Companies many times the size of Hercules, such as the auto companies or General Electric, would contribute the same as Hercules.

Efforts to influence the bill during committee meetings at the NAM proved futile, so we turned our attention to the idea of submitting an amendment that would break companies down by size and limit our exposure. The amount we would pay would be top-stopped at $15 million a year. While we felt any amount was an injustice since we were not an asbestos company, at least the amount we paid each year would be predictable and forty percent of the expense that was going to trial lawyers would be eliminated as well.

The only chance to get our amendment introduced was to go back to Biden through Jon Meyer. Fresh off the Wilmington meeting debacle, I was concerned Jon might laugh me out of the Russell Senate Office Building, but to my surprise he said he would take it up with the boss—then he added, "As long as you understand we will not be for the final bill."

As a bill makes its way through committee and heads to the floor for a vote, it goes through what is referred to as "mark-up," where members have the opportunity to submit amendments. Mark-up for the FAIR Act occurred on a night I had joined a couple of our executives for dinner at Sullivan's in north Wilmington. My Blackberry suddenly went off as we were talking. I saw Jon Meyer's name in the screen, jumped up and dashed outside so I could hear.

"John," Meyer said. "Joe wants to know if you still want him to offer your amendment and push it through."

'Absolutely," I answered.

"Ok, but he wants you to understand he will not be voting for the final bill," Jon replied.

The amendment passed, leaving staff at NAM and other companies a bit bewildered. No one saw it coming and the newly adopted funding arrangement changed the calculation for all the big companies, increasing their potential exposure. Before long, the amendment was labeled either the "Biden Amendment" or the "Hercules Amendment." In the final analysis, though, it was all for naught as the bill failed when it only received fifty-eight cloture votes, with Carper voting for and Biden against. Joe giveth, and he taketh away!

Chapter 39

The Final Showdown, 2002–2003

"So, Dan, who will win tomorrow?"

You know your company is in big trouble when they are selling the art off the walls, the country club, and the jet. Gossage seemed to have great enthusiasm for getting rid of the club, but the jet was his ride home to Georgia every Friday. I surmised that stuck between commercial travel or the G-3, he was in no hurry to complete the sale. As with the job cuts, though, Joyce moved forward quickly. He closed a deal for the plane and commuted by car every weekend back to Connecticut. Another area Joyce zeroed in on were corporate contributions.

Hercules and Betz had a history of giving generously to various community causes and I was told to turn off the spigot for of all of them. Joyce said his view was that public companies had no right to give away the shareholder's money. As someone who was active in the community and familiar with many of the organizations, including their leadership and boards, I found it an unpleasant task. Some of these grants were multi-year commitments reaching into six figure territory. While organizations were deeply disappointed by the news, most seemed to understand that Hercules had to focus on saving itself first, but a few pushed back hard. I received calls from lawyers insisting that we had a legal requirement to make the grants. One Pennsylvania college threatened to sue, and we finally settled with them for less than half of the original commitment. Joyce made one exception to the corporate philanthropy dictate. He agreed to meet the commitment of matching fifty cents on the dollar for employee United Way contributions.

From Gossage's return in 2000 until the proxy war with Heyman concluded in 2003, bad news about Hercules made headlines on an almost weekly basis. While some such as Senator Carper reacted to the news by trying to come up with ways to help, the State of Delaware sent in a firm to conduct an audit over "unclaimed property." I was generally aware of Delaware's use of these audits and the state's reliance on the revenue raised in this manner, but mostly in the context of securities that had gone unclaimed. By the time Hercules' vice president of tax Bruce Jester brought the issue to my attention, we were staring at a bill for $5.5 million—more than the value of the guest house, the artwork, and charitable grants combined. While reforms have been put in place in recent years, the process used by Delaware's finance department in the early 2000s was described by some in the business community as a "shakedown."

The auditors used by the state were an outside firm that received a percentage of what they collected. So they were motivated to dig into Hercules records going back fifteen years, finding such things as returned checks for payment to a vendor or contractor that had never been cashed. While the company believed that this was probably a case where the check could have been issued for the wrong amount and later reissued, due to poor record-keeping they could not prove it. The auditors then basically multiplied whatever they found in one year by fifteen, adding in years of interest and penalties.

With Jester in my office, I called the secretary of finance, Dave Singleton, and told him how outrageous I found their methods and informed him that we would have to lay off more than fifty employees to pay the bill. I added that the company was already struggling to survive and that we would put out a press release blaming the state for the layoffs. Singleton, who lived on the same block with us in suburban Wilmington told me to relax—the $5.5 million was basically a starting point in negotiations.

Shortly after the exchange with Singleton, I received a call from state economic development director, John Wick. He told me he wanted to bring Governor Minner in to meet Bill Joyce and learn what they could do to assist Hercules. Joyce seemed to have little interest in meeting the governor, but he acceded to the request.

The first problem with the meeting was that John Wick had apparently confused the time, and the governor arrived alone. It also seemed that she may not have read her briefing materials or had planned to rely on Wick to guide the conversation. Minner did not mention the "unclaimed property" issue, and at one point stated how pleased she was to have Hercules as a Delaware corporate citizen.

Joyce had not said a word up to that point, but this was his cue. "Well, Governor, if you are pleased to have us here, you sure have a funny way of showing it," he answered. He then handed Minner the letter from the state demanding a payment of $5.5 million. Minner appeared surprised by the letter.

At about that point, the economic development director arrived. Being unaware of what had already transpired, Wick began to make his Delaware pitch. It was an awkward moment, to say the least. The meeting wrapped up quickly, and they took the bill and promised to look into it. Hercules eventually settled for an amount well below $1 million.

The proxy mud-slinging pressed forward unabated into the summer of 2003. Much of the effort was directed at a few major shareholders like hedge fund manager Lee Cooperman of Omega Advisors and Mario Gabelli, of Gabelli Asset Management. At one point, the colorful and flamboyant Gabelli scheduled a Wall Street debate between Joyce and Heyman, but Joyce balked. He agreed after Gabelli threatened to vote against anyone who did not show up. Despite the hype, the debate basically fizzled. I traveled to New York with Joyce and watched from the sidelines as he went through his normal set of talking points.

With just over a week to go before the showdown at the annual shareholder meeting, the *News Journal* ran a detailed account of what was at stake and a review of the charges being leveled by both sides. One of Heyman's favorite targets was Joyce's compensation. Quoting from a recent Heyman fight letter, reporter Fred Biddle wrote:

> *"Many remaining employees have had their salaries frozen or capped while Joyce and senior executives receive huge salaries, bonuses, stock grants and golden parachutes"* [he cited the $10 million payment that would be awarded to Joyce should the company change control after the proxy contest].

An ironic twist to the charges by Heyman was that he was now attacking the recently completed sale of BetzDearborn. With debt crushing the company (Hercules was paying approximately $300 million a year in interest payments), Joyce and the board had accepted an offer of $1.8 billion for the water treatment business. Heyman was quoted as saying: "[Joyce] sold the best business at the worst possible time."

Late the evening before the meeting, I joined proxy solicitors Dan Burch and Jeannie Carr for dinner at the Deep Blue restaurant near the Plaza. Dan continued to trade calls with staff in New York and various large shareholders. Heyman had won the first round in 2001 and success the next day would give him control of the company. "Dan," I said. "Who is going to win tomorrow?"

"John, I really don't know," he replied.

He went on to explain some of the dynamics we were dealing with, which was that basically Heyman was a master dealmaker, and that even though it looked like we had the edge, Sam would be working the phones all the way up to the meeting itself. Dan said there was still a possibility he could cut a deal and flip enough votes to pull it out. Knowing I might be one of Heyman's first targets if he prevailed, I did not sleep well that night.

We planned the July 25th shareholders meeting to be held at the Chase Center at the Riverfront (then known as Bank One Center). I worked with our planning staff consisting of Mike Hassman, Bill Mahon, Susan Cavanaugh, and

Showdown over Hercules' future comes today

Dissident director Heyman makes last-ditch effort to gain control of company or he'll step aside

By FRED BIDDLE
Staff reporter

In the latest twist in the battle for Hercules Inc., dissident director Samuel J. Heyman said Thursday he would step aside before the company's annual meeting today unless its largest shareholder changes the terms of an endorsement that would keep Chairman and Chief Executive William H. Joyce in control of the board of directors.

Gabelli Asset Management Inc., which owns nearly 10 percent of Hercules shares, said in a Thursday filing with the U.S. Securities and Exchange Commission that it would vote for two of Heyman's director candidates and one of Joyce's.

Should other shareholders vote with Gabelli today, Heyman would lead five others on the 13-member board - insufficient for his goal of ousting Joyce. A spokesman for Gabelli said Chairman and CEO Mario J. Gabelli wouldn't comment further on his endorsement before the meeting.

For months, Joyce and Heyman have attacked each other verbally over how the specialty chemical company has been run since 2001, when

Joyce took over and Heyman, already the company's second-biggest shareholder, became a director. Today's scheduled vote has been a rematch of the 2001 proxy fight, when Heyman won four seats, including his own.

No matter who runs Hercules after today's meeting at the Center on the Riverfront, however, the company will remain up for sale and in debt with an uncertain future. Hercules employs 5,100 worldwide, including 700 in Delaware, and pays retirement benefits to thousands more. Among the challenges it faces:

■ Surviving a likely sale. In recent interviews, Joyce said Hercules' rebound from the brink of bankruptcy under his watch has made selling the company unnecessary. But last Thursday, he told institutional investors in New York that "whether it's merged with another company of the same size or with a strategic buyer, there's a large synergy to be had."

At the same meeting, Heyman said he would take the company off the market. Yet in a letter to shareholders Tuesday, he wrote, "We are in favor of a sale of the company

See HERCULES — A13

Kathleen McDonough of Potter, Anderson, & Corroon, who provided legal guidance. We had planned for up to five hundred attendees since we were close to that mark in 2001, but only half that number attended.

The atmosphere was tense as Bill Joyce began his chairman's remarks. As he spoke, Sam Heyman rose up from the audience and began to walk towards the podium. When Joyce noticed him coming, he stopped and addressed him directly. "Sam, please sit down. You will have your turn to speak," he said.

Heyman didn't stop, and for a second no one knew what to do. I was looking around for Mahon, worried we might have a security situation developing. Heyman continued his interruption and began to address Joyce and the shareholders present. To everyone's surprise, he announced he was withdrawing his slate and resigning from the board.

No one really saw that end coming. Heyman, in the *News Journal* the next day said, "We do this without the slightest rancor but rather because we believe this is the right thing to do."

Joyce thanked Heyman for his "gracious speech," and he went on to say, "As much as I hate to admit it, you did do a lot of things that made us more shareholder friendly."

So, after years of only rancor, Heyman suffered what he said was his first proxy defeat. You sensed that he had developed a begrudging respect for Joyce, who was relentless in opposition. With the fight behind the company, attention quickly shifted towards concern about what would happen to the $11.00 share price when Heyman dumped his stock, shares he originally purchased for $14.00 a share. He would lose millions.

A few hours later, Joyce was standing at my office door. He was complimentary about the meeting and then told me that if I was interested, he thought I would make a good head of investor relations. This visit by Joyce was a bit surprising because it was the first time he had come to my office in his two-and-a-half-year tenure as CEO and one of the few times I ever saw a CEO venture out from behind the "glass doors." In addition, compliments by any executives were virtually non-existent. The atmosphere was so negative, you simply got used to it. It was a dark corporate culture where people did not trust each other, driven in part no doubt by the fact that we were constantly in survival mode and most feared for their jobs.

While I turned down the opportunity to move to the investor relations position, I thought it was finally time to bring up the fact that I had been doing the work previously done by vice presidents. The company had stabilized, we had turned back the challenge from Heyman and our public affairs team had performed consistently well through the challenging times. I decided to only mention my pay—that I had not been upgraded since I started, and I was being paid well below my peers in the industry. Joyce looked at me with that familiar half smile and said, "John, if you want to earn more money, get a job in the pharmaceutical industry!"

The *News Journal* headline on October 7, 2003 read: *"CEO Who Saved Hercules Quits."* While the seemingly cold, impersonal Joyce was widely disliked by employees, he did accomplish the mission of rescuing the company from bankruptcy and fending off a takeover. I heard him say on more than one occasion that he had to make the cuts to save the company and thereby save the majority of the jobs.

Much of the bitterness towards Joyce was focused on his compensation and the sense that he was financially benefiting from the disaster. When a brave employee directly criticized him for his pay package at a town hall meeting, he simply dismissed it by saying not to waste time worrying about his pay. This issue had caused some employees to favor a Heyman takeover, but I am not so sure the "corporate raider" would have saved any more jobs than Joyce. Joyce certainly did not come to Hercules to make friends, and he did not need the money. My own assessment was that he just relished the challenge.

Chapter 40

Craig Rogerson and the Sale of Hercules, 2003–2008

"Get to the airport—your family is the most important thing!"

With the proxy contest over, it was no surprise that Bill Joyce was looking for his next opportunity. By October, he was gone, having accepted an offer to become CEO of Nalco, a water treatment company. He was replaced as chairman by John K. Wulff, who also served as interim CEO. A former chief financial officer of Union Carbide, John Wulff had been recruited to the Hercules board by Joyce, but their styles could not have been more different. The tall, patrician-looking Wulff was an outsider with limited knowledge of the company, but he was an engaging listener. Together with the board, he launched a search for a new CEO and, to my surprise, he sought my input.

In an extended conversation, I told Wulff that I thought it would be a mistake to bring in another outsider and gave Wulff my impression of the internal candidates, urging him to look carefully at Craig Rogerson. Reservations about the young-looking Rogerson focused primarily on his limited experience with Wall Street and major investors. My own bias towards Craig was that he was a good communicator and that he had a sales and business orientation. In my opinion, our senior executives had neglected the business and our customers for years, as they focused almost exclusively on financial and governance issues. Also, Craig was one of the few Hercules' executives I had encountered who had a human touch—he cared about people. With all the trauma the employees had been through, another cold, hard, bean counter, focused exclusively on cost reductions to prep the company for sale, would only further sink morale.

Just over two months after Joyce's departure, Craig Rogerson was announced as the new CEO of Hercules. The change in leadership style was dramatic from what I had seen with Gossage and Joyce. Rogerson projected little ego and was an attentive listener. He made several reporting changes and shifted me from reporting to our CFO Allen Spizzo to working directly for him. Whereas several on the leadership team kept you continuously off balance by not sharing information, Rogerson was clear, direct and decisive. He never kept more than one piece of paper on his desk—quite different from some of our executives, who were buried behind mountains of files and papers and often took several minutes to locate important documents. In addition to enhancing employee communications, he began to re-engage Hercules with the community, albeit at a more modest level than the pre-crisis version of the company.

Rogerson was so different that sometimes you were left questioning what just happened. I struggled at first with making my own decisions on important policy matters, believing they required buy-in by the CEO. But he would push back and tell me to make the decision. Other times I would bring something to him that I was certain required his involvement and he would ask my recommendation. When I gave it to him, he would say, "Do it!"

Two stories I have told many times over the years illustrate both Craig's decisiveness and his humanity. When we were working with the Delaware State Chamber, DuPont and Chrysler on an initiative to persuade the Delaware courts to change the way they were managing a sudden influx of asbestos cases, I was discussing the arrangement with the DuPont representative. I asked how long it would take to get a commitment from DuPont to move forward. He proceeded to explain that a decision of this nature would involve a team that would follow a "Six Sigma" process and that it would take weeks to then move up the ladder. He thought I was kidding when I said I would take it to the CEO and have a decision that day—and we did.

While Craig had the ability to assess a problem and make a hard business decision, he also had a human touch. He took time to understand your interests and learn about your family. In 2007, I worked with Craig and our China president, John Montgomery, to plan a series of meetings with Chinese officials in the communities where we had plants and employment centers in the country. This would be my second trip to the People's Republic. About six months prior, I had traveled to our Shanghai headquarters and our plant sites to provide media and crisis management training. One meeting was more than I bargained for.

When I finished our training session at the plant located in Zhangjiagang, between Shanghai and Nanjing, John Montgomery informed me that we had been invited by the mayor of the city of 1.2 million to a dinner. This was my first trip to China, but I had enough experience in other Asian countries to understand that these people take dinner very seriously. Exhausted and jet-lagged, I immediately questioned John about what to expect. Perhaps sensing my rising anxiety, he insisted that it would be a "low key" affair. I later learned that to attract a high-level participation by regional communist party officials, our joint venture partner had embellished my resume a bit and this dinner would be anything but low key.

After crawling through the streets of the crowded city, we pulled up in front of a hotel and were greeted by a couple representatives of the mayor who pushed us through the lobby and into an elevator. John looked at me before the door of the elevator opened and said, "Are you ready?"

Before I could answer I was blinded by television lights and dozens of media and staff from the local and regional government. We were quickly ushered into a large room with perhaps forty seats, with only three vacant—one for me, the mayor, and the regional commissar. The press poured into the center of the room with cameras running and it was finally starting to dawn on me that I was the target of this press conference. I could not even feel my lips and tongue to formulate a sentence assuming I could have thought of one. As my brain searched for a coherent thought, Montgomery leaned over from a couple seats away and with a grin on his face said, "John, want me to take this one for you?"

I have little recollection of what I said, let alone what the Chinese were saying. Montgomery later told me that I did OK, but I had my doubts. My only thought had been to avoid an international incident and not commit the company to anything.

In the week before Craig and I were to depart for Shanghai, my son Tim was hospitalized with complications related to ulcerative colitis, a chronic condition he had battled for more than a decade. He seemed to be responding to antibiotics, so the hospital released him the day before we were scheduled to depart.

Due to a glitch in our airline ticketing, Craig had to take a later flight than me from our Tokyo layover, and we agreed to meet the next morning for breakfast at the hotel. As I was crossing the Huangpu River peering through the Sunday evening Shanghai smog, my cell phone rang. I saw the call was from Sharon—it was seven o'clock on Sunday morning back in Delaware. Sharon explained that Tim had been readmitted to Christiana Care hospital Saturday with a blood clot in his arm and had an unidentified secondary infection that was not responding to antibiotics. "I'm afraid of where this is headed. I wonder if you should think about returning home," she said nervously.

I hesitated for a minute, struggling to absorb that my son was in a life threatening situation. Were we overreacting? Did I need to wait for further updates? Although worried about my responsibility to Craig and the company, I immediately contacted our travel department to see when the next flight was leaving for the U.S. There was one through Tokyo heading to Portland, Oregon early the next morning. I expected Craig to arrive at our hotel before midnight Shanghai time, so I camped out in the lobby waiting for him to get there. When he came through the door, he recognized something was wrong. I began to explain the call from Sharon and Tim's condition, but he immediately cut me off. "You don't have to explain any further. Go home."

I started to bring up our schedule and the father of three interrupted me again. "Get to the airport—your family is the most important thing!"

Thanks to some great detective work by our family physician, Dr. James Loughran, hematologist, Dr. Phil Blatt, Christiana Care hospital, analysis of bloodwork by the Mayo Clinic, and multiple visits to the hospital chapel by his mom and dad, Tim finally turned the corner and the fever broke. The dangerous sequence of events involved an original misdiagnoses of salmonella poisoning, followed by a blood clot and a c-diff infection (an infection caused by antibiotics). It was a truly grim trifecta.

While I believe Craig Rogerson was the right leader at the right time for Hercules, he had no shortage of challenges ahead of him. In addition to thousands of asbestos claims and continuing debt and pension problems, we faced other legacy concerns, lawsuits and expensive site remediation issues related to a banned pesticide, the defoliant Agent Orange, and a former munitions site dating back to World War II. We even held our breath when Julia Roberts hit the big screen playing the role of Erin Brockovich.

Authors Note: On the next four pages I will provide some background on these "Labors of Hercules" and discuss how they played out during my tenure.

Toxaphene

My first week on the job at Hercules, I traveled to our Brunswick, Georgia plant. The plant was the last vestige of the hundred-year-old industry once known as Naval Stores. Aged pine tree stumps were harvested for their rosin, and after processing the finished rosin would be shipped out in tank cars to be turned into products such as Pine-sol cleaner, adhesives, and as a "weighing agent" in fruit flavored drinks like orange soda.

But the primary reason I was traveling to Brunswick was to learn about Toxaphene. At one time a successful product, Toxaphene had been credited with saving the U.S. cotton crop in the 1960's and 70's, and it had been manufactured at Brunswick. Recognizing certain health risks, including being labeled a "probable human carcinogen," most uses of the product were prohibited in the U.S. in 1982. Residue from the manufacturing and disposal of product waste existed at the sprawling plant, various dumping sites in the area, and at the "outfall" that drained into Terry Creek, adjacent to the plant. I would spend many days over the next eight years working with plant personnel, politicians, community leaders, and consultants helping to defend the plant and the company from what at times seemed like a siege by environmentalists, particularly the Glynn Environmental Coalition (GEC).

While the overall Brunswick community seemed unperturbed by the issue, activists demanded more aggressive steps to remove any trace of Toxaphene from the area, including a school property adjacent to the plant. At one point, Hercules, under a consent decree, had removed the soil from the yards of adjacent homes or settled with the owners on a dollar amount. Being a low-income area, and perhaps believing the risk was not great, many of the residents (some of whom worked at the plant), accepted the cash settlement in lieu of the soil removal. Locals were known to have used Toxaphene on their dogs to kill fleas since it had been so effective against the boll weevil.

We ultimately sold the Brunswick business, which had been renamed Pinova to a private equity firm, who then sold it to Symrise AG, who in turn sold to a French company in 2016. Clearly value still remains, and with more than two hundred employees, the plant is one of Brunswick's largest employers. One could argue that Pinova has been an example of innovative capitalism at work.

Kenvil and other New Jersey sites

As Hercules evolved over the decades, it shut down various sites. While the sites no longer generated income for the company, they did generate expense and liability. Several of these sites were in New Jersey, and the granddaddy of them all was Kenvil, located in Morris County. Kenvil had a fascinating history dating back to 1871. During both World Wars, the plant was a key armaments supplier for the Allies. Several explosions resulting in a loss of life occurred over the years, with the most devastating taking place on September 12, 1940. Fifty-one workers lost their lives and another two hundred were wounded in the largest munitions plant explosion in U.S. history. While sabotage by German spies was a distinct possibility, the true cause was never determined.

As far as what was in the ground, the stories told by site manager Jim Bevis were fascinating to hear. One area where he urged caution to avoid what was referred to as "energetics," was the former nitroglycerine section. During World War I, this portion of the plant was considered so dangerous it was only worked by Chinese immigrants—indicating that management apparently deemed their lives to be expendable. Due to the potential to end up in the hereafter, the term "angel buggy walk" was the moniker given to a wooden bridge traversed by workers pushing wheelbarrows full of nitroglycerine in that location.

I was asked to work with both state and township officials in hopes of eventually offering the thousand-acre property for redevelopment. Sitting on Interstate 80 with rail access, it was believed to have significant value far above the remediation costs. The project ran into two major roadblocks: a fear of what was in the ground and a resistance to growth that surpassed anything I had seen in New Castle County, Delaware. Driving much of the growth opposition was a New Jersey court decision and subsequent law requiring a component of affordable housing in an area designated a growth area. There was fear that development at Kenvil would add both low income housing to the community and result in a need for more schools to be built, which would of course impact the community's already high property taxes.

Every New Jersey township has significant autonomy over land use and engaging with each government is a little like meeting a new sheriff in an old wild west town. Meetings with township officials in Roxbury were simply mysterious as you tried to determine any path towards receiving development approvals. Meetings with the mayor of Sayreville, Kennedy O'Brien, were bizarre events. On one occasion, when our real estate manager asked for an appointment with "his honor," he received a follow up call from the chief of police asking questions about why he wanted to meet with the mayor. At another closed plant site, we sought a demolition permit to raze an abandoned building that was often vandalized. Officials of the town demanded we escrow funds with the township before processing an application, and they informed us that any work performed on our company property must be done with union labor. Amazingly, politicians in Trenton would wonder why New Jersey continued to hemorrhage manufacturing jobs and needed to offer millions in incentives to attract new business.

Governor Christie – all smiles just days before "Bridgegate"

Allegany Ballistics Lab

Soon after Craig Rogerson became CEO, we were informed by the U.S. Justice Department, on behalf of the U.S. Navy, that Hercules was liable for more than $70 million in clean-up costs for a former munitions plant, Allegany Ballistics Lab (ABL) in West Virginia. This demand was made at the same time litigation on our former Agent Orange manufacturing site in Arkansas (Vertac) was advancing towards a conclusion. That judgement would ultimately come in at $119 million. If the company was to survive, we had to have a favorable result on one of these issues. Although at ABL, the Navy worked closely with Hercules and routinely inspected and approved the maintenance, they were standing fast on the clean-up bill and not engaging in serious discussions.

I contacted Senators Carper and Biden to see if they could help us encourage the Navy to negotiate. When I met with Biden's staff, they indicated support, agreeing that at a minimum there should be shared responsibility for the clean-up. Then, only days later, they called back and said they could not help, without offering a reason why, and recommended I contact Senator Robert C. Byrd of West Virginia. I reached Byrd's chief of staff who listened patiently to the story. When I finished, he said, "What state is Hercules located in?"

Not realizing where this was headed, I said, "Delaware."

"Well, then call Joe Biden," he said. Then he hung up.

As he had with asbestos, Carper jumped in to help. He immediately called the top naval facilities contact at the Pentagon and got him to agree to meet with us. Along with our outside counsel, Peter Gray, Hercules attorney Rich Williams, and Tom Strang, vice president of safety, health, environment, and regulatory (SHERA), I made my first trip to the Pentagon, nearly forty years after joining the Army. The meeting was friendly and productive, and we soon had an offer for a settlement from the Navy. They started high, we countered low and when we finished, we had an offer of $13 million on the table. Having just been badly burned on the Vertac verdict, Craig Rogerson took the last offer.

Agent Orange and Vertac

One of the most emotional and controversial issues of the Vietnam War was the use of the defoliant Agent Orange. Some twenty million gallons of the herbicide were sprayed on the jungles of Vietnam in order to deny cover to the enemy and protect American troops. As with asbestos, an argument could be made that Hercules was more victim than perpetrator.

Hercules acquired the herbicide manufacturing plant of Reasor-Hill Corporation in 1961. Soon after, the U.S. government required Hercules to produce a mixture of two herbicides at their specifications in order to produce Agent Orange. Hercules complied, and in the process lost its domestic business, while making little from the government contract. As one Hercules lawyer told me, "The government literally commandeered our product, and in the process enmeshed Hercules into decades of expensive and risky litigation involving personal injury lawsuits." Thirty years after a settlement was reached with the manufacturers of Agent Orange, and fifteen years after the government took some responsibility for veterans through passage of the Agent Orange Act, the issue still filled an entire page of company's 10k filing.

Ultimately, the "government contractor" defense would protect Hercules from further liability but that would not help the company on the issue of the clean-up of the Agent Orange manufacturing site in Jacksonville, Arkansas. (Hercules had ceased operations at the site in 1970, and it was taken over by Vertac Chemical. Vertac was placed into receivership after abandoning the site in 1987.) Although the government required Hercules to make the product to their specifications and regularly inspected the plant, they sued Hercules for $119 million in remediation costs. The company went all out, hiring renowned lawyer Lawrence Tribe for its appeal to the U.S. Supreme Court. The Harvard law professor had represented Al Gore in the 2000 Florida presidential vote recount. Unfortunately, the high court refused to hear Hercules' appeal. After thirty-seven years and tens of millions in clean-up costs and legal fees, the final bill came due on Craig Rogerson's watch. While a dramatic blow to the company's fortunes, we received good news via a settlement with the IRS that offset the cost associated with the final Vertac decision.

Erin Brockovich

You could say that the BetzDearborn acquisition was the gift that kept on giving. Betz had been a supplier to Pacific Gas & Electric (PG&E) of Dianodic, a hexavalent chromium containing anti-corrosive used in cooling towers. After use, PG&E disposed the remains into unlined ponds resulting in ground water contamination. While Betz was not a defendant in the original cases that were the focus of the movie starring Julia Roberts, the company was ultimately sued over four thousand new ones. PG&E asserted a cross-claim for the $333 million it paid out in the earlier cases. Ultimately, we were able to settle these cases.

The Hercules Plaza

Many were surprised to learn that Hercules never owned the Plaza, only the ground it sat on. Back in the early '80s, using a creative financing arrangement, former chairman & CEO Al Giacco had structured a deal to build the Plaza that allowed the company to enjoy a very low rent during his tenure. Hercules then moved approximately 1,200 employees into the building. Based on the terms of the thirty-year lease, the rent escalated significantly after the first fifteen years. No doubt there were opportunities to restructure the Plaza deal over the years, but a series of CEOs kicked the can down the road, and it landed in Craig Rogerson's lap decades later.

When Rogerson became CEO, only about three hundred employees worked in the Plaza, and the company occupied less than a third of the building. We offset a portion of our costs by subleasing several floors, but with low occupancy and high costs, the Plaza was another anchor around the company's neck. Fortunately, the McConnell Companies, owners of the neighboring 1201 Market Street building, were looking to expand their portfolio on that end of town, and we were able to structure a deal and rent back from McConnell. Despite expensive renovations and a stronger marketing effort, the new landlords have struggled to fill the building and the value has continued to decline.

After years of turmoil and crisis, the atmosphere inside the company settled somewhat into a state of normalcy—one where we worried more about the price of natural gas than the latest lawsuit or board member eruption. Conversations about the possible sale of the company were subdued and on a "need to know" basis. But the incentives for executives at the top of the company for a deal were significant, especially the restricted shares and "golden parachutes" that had been allocated by the board to those who came out of retirement to join Gossage, plus a handful of others who were looking forward to an early retirement.

Celebrating 75 years on the New York Stock Exchange left to right: Fred Annonsen, NYSE Official, John Wulff, Craig Rogerson, Stu Fornoff, Stuart Shears and me
Photo courtesy of NYSE

On the morning of July 11, 2008, I received a call from Craig Rogerson's executive assistant, Linda Rudnick. She sounded anxious as she told me Craig wanted to see me right away. When I walked into his office, he looked at me and said, "We sold the company."

He could clearly see the shock on my face and followed with, "You didn't know?"

When I said that I was completely surprised, he replied, "Good. I wasn't sure how successful we were keeping it under wraps, but if you didn't know, we did a pretty good job."

I then learned our new owner was Kentucky-based Ashland, a Midwest refiner. Ashland's acquisition of Hercules was part of an overall strategic plan to reinvent itself. In 2005, Ashland had sold its position in the refining business to its former partner, Marathon Oil. The Hercules deal was the initial step on the road to becoming a specialty chemical company. (Specialty chemicals are functional products directed at more narrow applications such as cosmetics or paints as compared to commodity chemicals, where there is little product differentiation.) There would be many more transactions in the years ahead.

I had always hoped that if or when this day came, whether buyer or merger partner, Craig Rogerson would end up at the helm. He informed me that was not the case but gave no hint of what came next for him. By the time I got back to my office, I began to think about my own situation. *Would I still have a job when things shook out?* I wondered.

In December 2008, Craig Rogerson was named chairman & CEO of Chemtura, another troubled chemical company formed through a merger of Great Lakes Chemical and Crompton Corporation. Unfortunately, tragedy also struck in Craig's life at that time when his wife Cari, who had just completed her master's degree in nursing from Villanova University was diagnosed with pancreatic cancer. After her death in 2009, the family established The Carina Joy Rogerson Endowed Memorial Graduate Nursing Scholarship at Villanova. Today, Craig Rogerson serves as chairman & CEO of Ohio-based Hexion, Inc.

Chapter 41

Takeover, 2008–2010

"Around here, when John Riley calls, we clear the decks!"

The weeks following the announced sale of Hercules to Ashland were filled with trepidation and uncertainty. When mergers or acquisitions occur, there is of course a duplication of corporate positions. The most likely outcome is that executives and their support staff in the acquiring company assume the position in the new company. But the Hercules situation was compounded by the 2008 financial crisis. Ashland had taken on significant debt at high interest rates to purchase Hercules, and it would greatly increase the pressure to bring costs down. Not only would lay-offs be accelerated, pay frozen, and bonuses cancelled, the company would soon take the dramatic step of cutting work hours and pay. Ashland shares dropped seventeen percent the day the deal was announced to $40.29 and then tumbled to below $4 a share that December. The question was not only will you keep your job, it was, will the company survive another month. Wall Street didn't seem to think so.

As director of public affairs at Hercules, I had responsibility for corporate communications, community relations, and government relations. I was also the corporate spokesperson, when the media called. Each of these functions were well covered at the vastly larger Ashland (then more than four times the size of Hercules). In fact, their corporate communications function had nearly forty employees. My only option at Ashland would be in the government relations role, except they already had an experienced executive in Mike Toohey. Mike was based in Washington. The good news initially was that I was told to continue to cover Hercules businesses and issues and that Mike would cover

Ashland business. But as the cost cutting pressure built, it looked like this arrangement would have a short life.

Heading into the final days of 2008, more and more "Herculites" were getting the word their services would no longer be needed. Ominously, my new boss, general counsel David Hausrath, told me they preferred I be "outsourced" and work for Ashland as a contractor. They did not feel coverage of Hercules required a full-time person with benefits. That sounded like the first step out the door for yours truly.

The week before Christmas, I received a call from Mike Toohey, whom I had not yet met. "John, do you think you could get Jim O'Brien [Ashland's chairman & CEO] a meeting with Senator Carper," he asked. "It's a serious situation, and he would like to meet with him to discuss it this week." As Mike spoke and began to explain the problem, I thought to myself, *If I can't get Jim O'Brien a meeting with Tom Carper, they have absolutely no use for me at Ashland.*

The issue was a complicated one, with no obvious solution, but O'Brien and Toohey thought the best place to start was with a member of the Senate Banking Committee. In the months before the financial crisis, Ashland had invested $275 million in cash into a financial instrument known as Student Loan Auction Rate Securities (SLARS). In their creative wisdom, the investment banks had organized buckets of federally guaranteed student loans into securities that they marketed to customers. The broker-dealers sold the treasury officers of hundreds of companies on the idea that they could get a better return on their short-term cash knowing the funds were secure due to the federal guarantee. One small problem: When the financial crisis hit, the SLARS market became illiquid, and no one could get their money out without taking significant losses. (According to Ashland's 2009 10K, the company recorded a $32 million loss on the portfolio that year.) One major insurer had parked $3 billion in SLARS.

The SLARS problem was particularly painful for Ashland due to coinciding with the purchase of Hercules. Already borrowing millions to close the deal, both Standard & Poor's and Moody's downgraded the company's credit rating, increasing our interest expense. The banks were squeezing us both ways.

As soon as I hung up from speaking with Mike, I called Bonnie Wu, Senator Carper's New Castle County director, to request the meeting. Bonnie explained that the senator was booked solid until Christmas break and then was departing on a vacation with the family. The first available meeting was the end of the first week of January. "Bonnie," I pleaded. "This meeting is extremely important to me personally. I'm asking for a big favor. Please find a way to fit us in." Bonnie promised to get back to me after discussing with the scheduler. She soon called back and gave us a meeting for that Friday in the Wilmington office.

Thursday, the day before the meeting I got a call from Jim O'Brien's assistant Pam. "John," she said in her thick Kentucky accent. "Jim has a conflict tomorrow and wants you to reschedule the meeting with Senator Carper for next week."

I couldn't believe what I was hearing. "Pam," I replied. "I'm afraid that's impossible. The senator is leaving town next week and won't be back until after the holidays." In pushing back, I was trying to make the point that whatever business issue had come up for the CEO it would just have to wait.

She replied, "Well, John, the problem is that Jim forgot it's their annual Christmas party at home. If he goes to Wilmington, he won't make it back in time and Katie [Jim's wife] will not be happy if Jim is not there. He can come on Monday or Tuesday, and he would like you to change it."

I thought to myself, *How could this be such a critical issue that one minute the CEO wants to drop everything to fly to Wilmington to meet with the senator and the next minute he can't come due to a Christmas party.* On this end, I only knew Carper was leaving with the family before Christmas, which meant by Wednesday that coming week.

I decided to call Larry Windley, Carper's state director. Larry and I had worked together in economic development, and I felt he was my best chance to work this out. When I reached Larry, I told him "something critical" had come up in Kentucky for our CEO and was there any way to find a new time for the next day's meeting. Larry said he understood but wasn't sure about Carper's travel plans.

Soon I got a call back offering ten o'clock Tuesday morning, and that was the last and only time available before the Carpers left for the airport. Jim flew into the Wilmington airport on "Ashland Air" (the company had multiple planes, all soon to be sold) Tuesday morning where Mike and I met him. We drove into the city and made our way to Carper's Wilmington office at 4th and Walnut Street.

When we arrived at the office, Bonnie, Larry, and a couple members of the Wilmington staff joined around the conference table. They then linked in the banking committee staff on the Polycom, and we waited for Carper to make his entrance.

As the senator settled in at the conference table, I began to regret not talking to him in advance to let him know that this was no ordinary issue meeting; my future with Ashland was hanging in the balance. Carper had everyone introduce themselves before nodding to O'Brien. The big, redheaded Ashland chairman thanked Carper for adjusting his schedule and taking the meeting on short notice.

"Jim," Carper said. "Around here, when John Riley calls, we clear the decks!"

Bingo. The senior senator from Delaware had just saved my job. I knew it, and he knew it. I could tell from the satisfied glance he shot me.

My work on the SLARS issue involved joining with dozens of other Fortune 500 companies to lobby Congress and the Treasury Department to come up with a solution such as creating a government backstop (the loans already had a federal guarantee). The view was that this would allow trading to begin again and companies such as Ashland could gain access to its share of the estimated $80 billion and either pay off debt—the likely course for Ashland—or invest back in their business, thus stimulating the economy with private, as opposed to public, stimulus dollars. When our national coalition decided to commission an economic study to help make the case, we contracted with Jim Butkiewicz and Bill Latham at the University of Delaware, who put together a white paper demonstrating how the program would lead to the creation of tens of thousands of jobs, many in manufacturing. Unfortunately, all our appeals and the best efforts of Tom Carper went for naught. Eventually, though, the market began to free up slightly and desperate to get some of their cash back, companies were simply forced to accept the losses.

As I began to build some credibility with CEO O'Brien and general counsel David Hausrath, my new boss, the company also began to slowly turn back from the brink of disaster. For all of 2009 we were on reduced pay and hours including an unpaid two-week furlough. The continuing focus on cost containment applied to everything from the cost of meals to the use of the Acela train on Amtrak.

Later that year, David Hausrath asked me to join a meeting to discuss a tax issue that he said he needed my help on. We had received notice from the city of Wilmington that as a result of their recent audit of Ashland withholdings for city wage taxes, we owed more than $5 million in back taxes, interest, and penalties for the previous fifteen years. The audit was conducted by an outside firm, and it was essentially the same playbook employed by the state of Delaware with their unclaimed property audit in 2003. The city was facing a deficit and they decided to make it up by going after city businesses.

The wage tax issue was an interesting one. A global company like Hercules had employees who were based in Wilmington but who traveled much of the time—that is, they spent more time away from the city than in it. They would file an expected schedule at the beginning of the year so that only a certain percentage of wage tax would be withheld, and then they were required to confirm through their calendar at the end of the year that the withholding was appropriate. At least in theory, if there was a difference, the employee either paid the city or received a refund. Few took the time to do that, and no one followed up. Furthermore, Hercules had shed hundreds of employees over the previous fifteen years, so it would be extremely difficult and time consuming to find them and have them produce calendars from many years prior.

As with the state's audit for unclaimed property, another major issue was the compounding of penalties and interest. Equally frustrating to the company was that the tax liability should have belonged to the employee—the company was only the vessel that helped Wilmington collect the tax. With Ashland being new to Wilmington, the timing of this exercise was sure to sour Ashland's leadership on the city, so I contacted Mayor Jim Baker's chief of staff, Bill Montgomery to register our objections. Bill referred me to Ron Morris, the finance director. Ron and I had known each other since our high school days and worked together in New Castle County government, but Ron stood by the city's approach. I tried to warn both Bill and Ron that they were risking Ashland's continued presence in the city, but it made no difference.

I did have to give Wilmington credit in the sense that they were not playing favorites. Companies across the city were angry about the audits and as with the state audits they were being referred to as a "shake-down." Another similarity with the state audits was that the initial bill seemed to only be an opening bid. Ashland lawyers indicated that we would fight the $5 million assessment in court, while anticipating that if the demand was reduced to a level less than our expected legal fees, we would probably settle. Soon, Wilmington offered a significantly reduced, settlement number, and the company took it.

While not the top reason Ashland moved out of the city, the episode with the wage tax audit damaged the relationship. No one from the city even bothered to call when we soon announced we were moving nearly three hundred employees to our research center in the county. Ashland/Hercules had been headquartered in Wilmington since its formation in 1912. It would complete its move out of the city in 2012, exactly one hundred years later.

Deep into year two under Ashland, I still felt like I was competing for my job every day. Ashland veteran Mike Toohey and I continued to divide up our coverage, but there were no clear lines of responsibility. Both companies had political action committees (PACs), which we were combining, but Ashland's was much larger than Hercules' and Mike had run it for many years. A typical contribution to a campaign fundraiser averaged $1,000 to $2,500, with occasional major party events costing $5,000 to attend. One day, late in the summer of 2010, I received a call from Congressman Mike Castle's chief fundraiser, Basil Battaglia. He told me that President George H. W. Bush (41) and Barbara Bush had agreed to host an event for Mike at their Kennebunkport, Maine home. The cost for the event would be $15,000. (The amount was above the limit for a single candidate, but the money would go to multiple committees including the national Republican Party.)

Mike Castle had one of the most illustrious careers in the history of Delaware politics, but he was frustrated in his effort to obtain a Senate seat when Bill Roth had decided to seek another term in 2000. Roth, of course lost to Carper, but Joe Biden's seat became an open contest in 2010 because Barack Obama had selected him to become his vice president in 2008. At that time, Governor Minner appointed Biden ally Ted Kaufmann to the Senate seat, but Ted agreed to not seek reelection in 2010. (The conventional wisdom at the time was that Biden's son Beau would run in 2010.) By all accounts, Castle appeared to have a clear path to victory in 2010. He had to get by a primary with an ambitious upstart from the emerging Tea Party wing of the Republican Party, Christine O'Donnell, but no one saw her challenge as a serious threat. The opponent in the general election would be Chris Coons, the county executive, and Mike was heavily favored in that contest as well.

The request from the Castle campaign was a small dilemma, since it was well above the historical limits for contributions. But I felt a strong loyalty to the former Delaware governor, and I wanted to see if I could obtain approval. (I had known Castle for more than thirty years, and he had hired me for executive search work when he was governor and recommended me to governor-elect Carper when he needed recruiting assistance.) I discussed the situation with David Hausrath, and he felt that it needed to go to the company executive committee (EC), which consisted of Hausrath, CFO Lamar Chambers, and CEO Jim O'Brien.

The Ashland executive group gave little indication of any political bias, but I suspected like most business leaders that they leaned Republican. The EC met in the corporate headquarters in Covington, Kentucky, so I called into the meeting by phone from my office in Wilmington. It would be my first presentation to the group. Hausrath introduced the subject I wanted to discuss and then turned it over to me. I hated this arrangement, where I was unable to read body language or have an opportunity for side-bar conversations to tee-up a subject and gauge what the reaction would be. But I went ahead and explained the request from Castle for $15,000 and the opportunity to attend the event at the Bush home. When I finished, Jim O'Brien said, "John, I only have one question, is Mike Castle going to win?"

"Jim," I replied. "I guarantee it!"

I wish I had never said those were three words—and I would be reminded of my bold prediction from time to time going forward.

With the recent passing of our forty-first president, I believe the Kennebunkport story is worth sharing. I arrived in the little town on the Maine coast the afternoon before the reception at the Bush home, Walker's Point, and decided to head over to see it. As I walked along the coastal road, I began to hear a familiar voice singing, but I could not place it. Starting around the bend, I began to see kids holding up signs saying, "I love Taylor Swift." It turned out to be the famous singer herself, practicing for a television concert show she would be filming the following evening.

The next night I connected with CEO O'Brien and his wife, Katie, for the reception. A very gracious Barbara Bush greeted each of us at the door of their home, and we went in to meet the president, listen to remarks by he and Castle, and then have a photo taken with them. President Bush steadied himself on a cane as he spoke. I could see that he had aged greatly from when I first met him at Pine Valley Golf Club in New Jersey back in 1993, but I was immediately reminded of that time because the president was wearing a club blazer. When I stood in for the photo with he and Castle, I reminded him of our previous meeting.. He looked at me as if to say I must be confused, but when I mentioned I was with former PGA Champion Paul Azinger, his face lit up. "I remember that," he said.

The former president's remarks were memorable that night because of how light and unserious they were. After welcoming everyone, telling a little about their home and about how much he liked and respected Mike Castle and his wife, Jane, he announced that he had to leave in a minute and that Barbara would take over. And then he explained why he was leaving.

"Yesterday," he said. "I answered the front door, and this tall young woman stuck out her hand and said, 'Hello, Mr. President, I'm Taylor Swift, and I would like to personally invite you to attend my concert tomorrow night.'"

"My God," he added. "Have you ever seen that woman?" As he spoke, he held his free hand up to indicate how tall Ms. Swift was.

"Well, I promised Ms. Swift that I would bring my granddaughters and join her, so I hope you don't mind if I keep my promise. I can assure you that you will be in good hands with Barbara, and she's more fun than me anyhow."

Of course, this story does not have the ending those in Kennebunkport had hoped for. To the shock of everyone, Christine O'Donnell scored an upset over Mike Castle, proving again that nothing can be taken for granted in a primary. O'Donnell would triumph with 30,561 votes, or about ten percent of the number of votes cast in a general election. Much has been said and written about how this happened, but an even bigger story developed when O'Donnell, in response to a story about her having once dabbled in witchcraft, made her famous "I am not a witch" campaign ad. Polls that had shown Chris Coons losing to Castle by double digits, completely flipped and Coons was elected by a margin of seventeen points. So much for my "guarantee" that Castle would win.

With Mike Castle and President
George H. W. Bush at Kennebunkport
Photo courtesy of Castle for Senate campaign

Chapter 42

The Ashland Years and Retirement, 2009-2016

"I just saw O'Brien's email. Sam must be rolling over in his grave."

On May 31, 2011, I awoke to see an email on my phone from CEO Jim O'Brien to our global leadership team indicating that later that morning, Ashland would be announcing the acquisition of ISP, formerly the crown jewel of Sam Heyman's business empire. The president of our Aqualon business (soon to be renamed Ashland Specialty Ingredients), John Panichella, was known to be a very early riser, so I decided to dial his cell at six o'clock AM to see if he picked up. He answered on the first ring. Before I had a chance to say anything, he said, "John, do you believe it? We just bought ISP!"

"I just saw O'Brien's email. Sam must be rolling over in his grave," I replied. (Heyman had died in 2009.)

We discussed the irony that Heyman had fought so hard to combine the two businesses, but certainly never in the way it eventually turned out.

With my focus turning away from the legacy issues of Hercules, I spent more time on broader policy challenges in Washington. Mike Toohey accepted a position as head of a Washington-based trade association, so I had to grow my relationships in other states, particularly Kentucky and Ohio, where Ashland had its greatest presence. Some of my new best friends would be Mitch McConnell, John Boehner, and the powerful, cigar chomping chairman of the House Appropriations Committee, Kentucky congressman Hal Rogers. Ashland could not have been more geographically and politically well-positioned when the Republicans took over Congress, but I would soon learn that their political clout was no match for the intractable federal bureaucracy—especially at the Food and Drug Administration (FDA).

I enjoyed a great deal of autonomy in the Ashland world, and although strained at first by pressures related to the takeover, I had developed a very positive relationship with David Hausrath, to whom I reported. When he announced his retirement and a search for a successor, I had some concern about adjusting to another boss, but I had been through enough of these things to figure I would adjust and go on. When he called me a few weeks later to tell me that they had settled on a replacement, however, it gave me a jolt. Hausrath said, "John, your new boss's name is Peter Ganz. Perhaps you remember him; he was general counsel to Sam Heyman."

I did not remember Ganz, but I did remember Sam Heyman attacking me at the Hercules shareholder meeting in 2001. Sam took things personally, so I immediately wondered if his lawyer was like-minded.

"Wow, David, should I dust off my resume?"

Peter Ganz did not get where he was in the corporate world by holding grudges, so as it turned out the Heyman connection rarely rated a mention in the years I worked for him. He turned out to be a very supportive boss, and he brought his own insights on politics and government to our deliberations. Thanks to his support, I was finally able to set up a retainer with a Washington government relations firm, Holland & Knight. Their Capitol Hill expertise proved critical in the years ahead as we dealt with a range of issues impacting our business. The most interesting of all of these was legislation to reform the way sunscreen ingredients were considered by the FDA.

An important part of Ashland's personal care product portfolio, we made sunscreen ingredients in Columbus, Ohio, but we could not sell into the U.S. market—all of our products were exported. When I first learned of the problem, I thought a solution would be as easy as a call to the FDA. However, I discovered the FDA had no interest in talking to us—and no interest in allowing more product on the market (several sunscreen filters, including Ashland's, had been through a rigorous European approval process and had been in use for over a decade with no known adverse effects). In addition to sunscreen manufacturers, cancer organizations, dermatologists, and even environmental organizations had argued for years that U.S. sunscreen products were inferior to European products, particularly at blocking the harmful effects of UVA rays. If we were going to change the current system, we would have to mandate a new process through legislation.

Passing a bill in 2014 required a strong coalition (only fourteen bills passed in that year's so-called "do-nothing" Congress), financial resources, and lots of political expertise. Our primary coalition partner was the German chemical giant BASF, but there were also skin care companies such as L'Oréal and healthcare organizations such as the Melanoma Research Foundation and the Skin Cancer Foundation. Our coalition was supported by the public policy team at Holland & Knight.

We needed to recruit lead sponsors from the relevant committees, who would not only put their name on the Sunscreen Innovation Act (SIA) but also commit to champion the cause with all the resources of their office. Our first choice in the Senate was Johnny Isakson of Georgia, one of the most respected and well-liked members on both sides of the aisle. I knew Isakson well from my work in Georgia for Hercules, who at one time had four plants and more than 1,100 employees in the state. He would become the key to our success. Jack Reed of Rhode Island became our Democratic co-sponsor. On the House side, Ed Whitfield of Kentucky, who represented the largest plant in the Ashland system, joined with the dean of the House, Democrat John Dingell of Michigan.

As the bill moved through the process and the legislative calendar, we began to pick up more and more co-sponsors and positive publicity in national publications. In an editorial entitled "Sunstroke at the FDA," the *Wall Street Journal* called the sunscreen ingredients approval delays by the FDA "a government-created public health hazard."

We ultimately knew we would be successful when on the same day, Senate Majority Leader Mitch McConnell, who rarely put his name on bills, and Elizabeth Warren, the liberal from Massachusetts, both joined as co-sponsors. The SIA passed the House and Senate by unanimous consent and was signed into law by President Obama on November 26, 2014. In reviewing the leading innovations in health advances for 2014, *Time* named the Sunscreen Innovation Act as the seventh most important, ahead of two advances in the treatment of Ebola.

The idea that Ashland had led the effort to pass a bill that not only improved our company's business prospects, but according to many health experts would save lives, felt like it could be the crowning achievement of my professional career. Unfortunately, the luster of that shining moment would soon fade away, as the bureaucratic resistance at the FDA ran deeper than the US Congress. The regulators quickly rejected the applications for products that had been awaiting approval for as long as eighteen years and demanded new testing. Their logic was so confusing that, although L'Oréal had gained approval for an earlier product through the process used for prescription drugs, their application for the same product under the new law was rejected.

In 2016, I made the decision to retire at the end of the year. While this decision had more to do with the attraction of spending additional time with family and writing, I also looked forward to leaving the frustrating world of Washington behind. In addition to Congress and the FDA, I had worked with agencies such as the EPA, Treasury, Energy, Defense, and the Federal Trade Commission. I quickly learned that these are not "user-friendly" institutions. To gain an appointment nearly always required congressional intervention or the involvement of one of the major Washington advocacy organizations.

Due to highly publicized lobbying scandals such as the Jack Abramoff affair, the business of lobbying is held in low regard. That is unfortunate because most lobbying in my experience is ethical and vital. Besieged with hundreds of requests regarding complex issues, congressional and senate offices are staffed by young aides with limited knowledge of the issues they work on and little real world experience. They simply would not be able to do their jobs without the help of lobbyists and the organizations behind them. The federal agencies, on the other hand, are staffed by thousands of bureaucrats who are technical experts regarding the policies and regulations they oversee but not necessarily the science. Most meetings I attended involved multiple agency lawyers and congressional liaison staff and rarely resulted in progress.

During the Obama years, compliance with lobbying restrictions reached the level of the absurd. As a member of the East Side Charter School board in Wilmington, I signed up to attend a talk in Wilmington by U.S. Secretary of Education Arnie Duncan. The day before the event, I received a call informing me that I was banned from attendance because I was registered to represent Ashland on chemical industry issues. They did not explain why being in the room with hundreds of others for a speech would be a threat to the integrity of Secretary Duncan. Meanwhile, leading Democrats and labor leaders visited the White House on a regular basis to seek support for their policy priorities.

In our continuing efforts to engage with the FDA to solve the sunscreen issue, we secured a meeting with Vice President Biden's cancer czar, Greg Simon. After one of the country's leading experts on melanoma laid out the sordid history of FDA intransigence, Simon said, "This is one of the worst cases of bureaucratic inaction I have ever heard of." We left the meeting excited about the response, and we became even more encouraged when Biden in a subsequent speech mentioned how the U.S lagged behind on sunscreen technology. Sadly, even the involvement of the White House meant little. The FDA bureaucrats clearly resented our efforts to exert political pressure on them, and they just dug in further. We heard little from Simon after that. As of the summer of 2019, Americans continue to have limited choice on sunscreens and limited protection from the harmful effects of the sun.

On a stormy November 21, 2016 evening, my friends and colleagues at Ashland hosted a retirement dinner for me at the DuPont Environmental Center at the Wilmington Riverfront complex. Organized by my executive assistant, Dianna Maloy, and my daughter Carie, the retirement dinner took on the form of a roast with Senators Carper and Coons, Congressman and Governor-elect John Carney, and Mayor-elect Mike Purzycki all in attendance. Other speakers included Ashland CEO Bill Wulfsohn and my boss, Peter Ganz. Appropriately, I was presented with a classic piece of Beatles' memorabilia—a framed copy of the *Abbey Road* album, which contains the song, "The End."

While I was not as close to Chris Coons as the other leaders present, he may have captured the moment best—and as I look back, it fits a central theme of this Delaware story. Paraphrasing the senator, Coons said, "How remarkable it is that the leadership of this state, all Democrats, came here on this stormy night to honor a Republican. It says something about our little state."

As Coons finished, I thought back to my January 2000 "state retirement party," at Buena Vista, near New Castle, when Governor Carper exclaimed in his remarks, "John, I didn't know you were a Republican!"

Ashland retirement dinner with governor
and mayor-elect, November 2016
Photo courtesy of Dianna Maloy

Epilogue

As I was completing the last chapter of this book, I took a lunch break and headed to Purebread Deli in Greenville. Just after I ordered a sandwich to take out, in came the former vice president of the United States. Joe was with a younger man whom I did not recognize. When he saw me, he came right over, flashing his famous smile and extending his hand. He turned to the other gentleman and said, "I'd like to introduce you to John Riley, a Republican with a brain!"

Vintage Joe Biden, in one short sentence he both giveth and taketh away.

It took me a second to process his combined compliment and insult, but I stammered out a comment about his party and the bevy of progressives running for president. (At that point, Joe was at the top of most polls and was still contemplating a decision to run.)

"John," he said. "You know what my father always said. Don't compare me to the Almighty, compare me to the alternative!"

Such is life in the First State. For over a half century, the proximity created by this little state has generated opportunity and challenges for me, as it has for many others. Some of my friends have expressed that there is a sort of Forrest Gump-like element to my story or at least that there is a certain serendipity to it all. This book has been my attempt to make sense of it.

They say, "What goes around, comes around." Following my retirement from Ashland, I teamed up one more time with old friend Kevin Reilly to help him write his autobiography *Tackling Life*. At that time, I also served on a working group formed by governor-elect John Carney to consider the creation of a new economic development entity for Delaware. This would later lead to my appointment to be the interim CEO of the Delaware Prosperity Partnership. In addition to helping to set a new economic development direction for the state, I worked projects like the Amazon site selection and ran a national search to find a full-time CEO.

Through my Town Square Delaware connection, I have also been able to tell the stories of veterans of different eras, particularly Vietnam POWs who have called Delaware home: Brigadier General Jon Reynolds, Colonel Murphy Neal Jones, and Lt. Commander James J. Connell, the young man honored with the Navy Cross, the highest award for valor of any Delawarean during the Vietnam War. Working with former Adjutant General Frank Vavala, we were able to have the long-forgotten Connell honored posthumously by Delaware on Veterans Day 2018 with the state's highest award, "The Order of the First State."

The adult men and women I grew up around were members of what has been labeled, "The Greatest Generation," but their courage and sacrifice was no greater than the men mentioned above. Through my own story, I have tried to paint the picture of what the draft and Vietnam meant for Delaware. My generation was asked to make enormous sacrifices for a cause that was not clearly defined or understood, yet millions responded in a patriotic and often heroic manner. How many times a day, year after year, did the rescue scene described to me by Marine Jim Dolan in Chapter 17 play out across South Vietnam. Still, some ten years after they returned, these vets had to build their own memorial in Washington to honor their fallen comrades. We will never be able to repay these heroes, but that does not mean we shouldn't try before it is too late; they are dying by the hundreds every day. Our leaders may have failed us more than fifty years ago, but our soldiers did not.

When Ashland acquired Hercules in 2008, they were identified with the state of Kentucky in much the same way as we thought of DuPont and Delaware, but with that acquisition and the subsequent purchase of ISP, the company was trending east. So, when Ashland reorganized after spinning off Kentucky-based subsidiary Valvoline (the last remnant of the old Ashland Oil), it was reincorporated as a Delaware company. Then, in August 2018, the company announced it would be moving its corporate headquarters to Delaware. What goes around, comes around!

As a shareholder of Ashland, in late 2018 I received a notice of the annual meeting and proxy materials. I almost couldn't believe what I was reading. It was "déjà vu all over again" as former Hercules CEO Bill Joyce and my old boss, Allen Spizzo, had initiated a proxy war against the company, much as Sam Heyman had done eighteen years before. To counter the move by Joyce and Spizzo, Ashland had nominated my former boss, Craig Rogerson, to the board. In the days before the meeting on February 8, 2018, Ashland settled the battle by bringing the eighty-three-year-old Joyce into the company as a consultant. When I saw CEO Bill Wulfsohn and my other former boss, Peter Ganz, at the annual meeting, I told them I could save them some money and tell them much of what Joyce was going to tell them. I had heard it many times, late into the night.

I mentioned in my introduction how Delaware landmark businesses had disappeared over the years. About the time I entered the economic development world the changes were accelerating, but I never imagined we would see the disappearance of Hercules and a greatly diminished DuPont. While not "Delaware" companies GM, Chrysler, and Xerox also declined in the face of global competition—or perhaps due to management's failure to react successfully to the challenge. Did these changes occur as a result of structural changes in the economy or a failure of leadership?

In his book *Leading with Honor: Leadership Lessons from the Hanoi Hilton,* leadership consultant and retired Air Force Colonel Lee Ellis writes,

> *In times of tremendous challenges and tumultuous changes, one thing remains constant: the importance of the leader. Think about it. Who's responsible for building the culture of the organization? Who ultimately must attract the talent, communicate the vision, foster the teamwork, and set the standards? Who must provide the inspiration necessary for the organization to overcome obstacles, navigate through uncertainty, and accomplish the mission? The answer of course, is the leader.*[4]

Having known or worked closely with governors, CEOs, members of Congress, and military leaders, and having served in several leadership positions over many years, I have formed my own strong views on leadership. Many leaders I have observed fall prey to the sound of their own voice and fail to listen. They also too quickly reward those who agree with them and isolate or even eliminate those who disagree. As so well described by Colonel Ellis, a good leader is a team builder, whose style engenders—and, in some respects, inspires—the culture of the

---

[4] Lee Ellis, *Leading with Honor: Leadership Lessons from the Hanoi Hilton* (Dawsonville, GA: FreedomStar Media, 2014), xiv.

organization. The culture of Hercules when I joined in 2000 was one dominated by mistrust and paranoia. From what I learned from tenured employees of the company, this was not an environment created by the leaders developed from inside Hercules (former CEOs such as Werner Brown remained beloved by employees during my time there), but rather from the executives brought in from outside the company. While most of those I spoke to on background for this book felt that way, there were a few dissenters who felt that at least Gossage and Joyce were doing what had to be done.

So, who were the best Delaware leaders I encountered over all those years? Although I was vulnerable as the "Republican" under Governor Carper, neither I nor others within the administration felt restricted in speaking our minds. Due to Carper's willingness to listen, he engendered a great deal of trust and loyalty within the organization. Almost to a fault, he would not give up and his persistence would usually pay-off. He had begun his term during troubled economic times but finished his eight years as one of Delaware's most successful chief executives. While I worked with him, Carper often referred to his experience as a naval officer, drawing on those lessons in his role as governor.

In his book, Colonel Ellis adds another important element of leadership. He writes, "Leaders have another equally important responsibility: to develop new leaders. Effective leadership is typically *caught* more than *taught*. That means successful leaders must serve as role models for aspiring leaders."[5]

The development of future leaders may be the strongest element of Carper's legacy. Although they did not have a good personal relationship, Carper's lieutenant governor, Ruth Ann Minner, easily defeated John Burris in the 2000 election. Many in the business community, who backed the charismatic Burris, were shocked that he was not able to gain traction against a candidate they thought would have limited appeal. Carper not only laid the groundwork for Minner's successful run, he reformed the party, pushing out the old party bosses and mentored multiple individuals with ambition and potential: John Carney, Jack Markell, Chris Coons, and Lisa Blunt-Rochester. There were others he encouraged like Mike Purzycki and some with lower profiles who have gone on to successful roles. Delaware Republicans clearly did not keep pace and remain in a deep hole today. I for one am disappointed by this

5   Ellis, xiv–xv

development. I believe it is critical to the long-term success of Delaware to have more balance in our governing principles.

At Hercules, I found Craig Rogerson's leadership style to be lot like Carper's. He was a listener who treated people with respect. As a result, he gained loyalty and trust from employees who had generally looked at previous CEOs with great skepticism. They felt prior CEOs often made poor decisions, such as the BetzDearborn disaster, or that they were driven more by the selfish motive of their own pay package instead of the best interest of the company. In the end, some resented that Hercules was sold on Rogerson's watch, but I believe it is hard to argue that what remained of Hercules could have been sustained for many more years.

In my lifetime, no one has been better prepared to take on the complex job of running Delaware's largest city than Mike Purzycki. I spent primary election day driving around the city with Mike, visiting the many polling places. At one point in the day, he said to me that he felt that he had been preparing for the role most of his life. You could certainly conclude that by reading his resume but the resume is only part of the story. The intangibles of leadership, such as setting a vision, putting the right team together, and ensuring accountability that goals are met, will ultimately determine if our city will continue on a successful path. I am personally optimistic.

One day after a couple bad bounces on the golf course, my friend Tom Ciconte said, "Riley, if it wasn't for bad luck you wouldn't have any luck at all!"

I responded, "Tom, I think I used up all my luck when I was not deployed to Vietnam as an infantry lieutenant!"

Through the exercise of writing this memoir, I can now see that my good fortune actually began when I was born to an extraordinary woman who would be a guiding light for me, my siblings, and many others until she died in 1998. And although in my teen years, I felt embarrassed by our humble home and circumstances on Wilmington's east side, I eventually began to understand its extraordinary value, as well as the support system of our family, parish, school and friends. Even having a cousin with significant disabilities helped me to learn the value of every human being and led to experiences that have had an indelible influence on my life.

I discussed some of my life's inflection points in the early chapters of this book, where I received help at critical moments from caring adults and even hard-nosed drill sergeants. But as my adult life unfolded, the best thing that happened was having a life partner like my wife, Sharon and of course our three children, Amy, Tim and Carie. Also, with Sharon came her family, including her stepfather, James G. "Put" Putman, the man from Calhoun City, Mississippi who became like a second father to me, and her natural father, C. Yancey Tollett, the WWII war hero who became close to us in his later years. As a company commander of the famed 101st Airborne on D-Day, he led hundreds of young men into the fire and flak of the Normandy skies during the hours before the invasion by sea. Learning about his experience in France, Holland, and Bastogne opened a door to a world we should all strive to understand and appreciate. (Over the past ten years, I have intensified my study of the great conflicts and traveled to WWI and WWII battlefields in Europe and Civil and Revolutionary War battlefields in our own country.)

I awoke on the morning of January 1, 2014 with a feeling like no other I had ever had. I could feel myself being drawn to a gravesite I had not visited in thirty-eight years. My father was the first baby born in Wilmington that day, one hundred years before, and I felt an overwhelming need to pay my respects. Although I was at that point six years older than my father was at the time of his death, I felt like a child going to speak to an adult.

Over time, I had learned more about the impact of addiction and the challenges many such as my father faced. I wanted to somehow convey to my father that day that I understood. I searched in my mind to remember the good times. And while I do not recommend my father's style as the best way to raise children, I had come to realize that managing through those difficult years with this complicated and troubled man, had helped me prepare for much of what I would face in later life.

As I stepped away from the grave on that chilly New Year's morning, I was surprised to see a headstone close by bearing the name of Dominick "Dim" Montero, the legendary Salesianum High School football coach. During a study hall, my senior year in high school, to punish me for talking, Montero had hit me hard over the head with a world history book. I laughed to myself as I headed back to the car. I couldn't figure out if my father would have gone after Montero for the offense or if he would have clobbered me for talking in class. After a short reflection, I concluded he would have probably done both. Such was my Delaware world in 1963.

Afterward

The photo below was taken August 3, 2018, soon after I wrapped up my time as interim CEO of the state's new economic development entity, the Delaware Prosperity Partnership. Sorting through photos to include in the book, this one captured my attention. It seemed to touch a range of elements of the story, such as the influence of golf in my life, my partnership with Kevin Reilly, economic development, and experiences with governors and business leaders. My co-chairs, Governor John Carney (to my left) and Rod Ward (next to Kevin), CEO of CSC, had presented me with the golf outing as a departing gift. It was held at Biderman Golf Club, the last place I caddied as a boy. It was a memorable day.

Acknowledgments

There are so many I need to thank for helping me with this project that it may appear to be a "book by committee." My major concern is that I might miss someone since this book has been more than a year and a half in the making. I set out with the purpose of using my personal experience as a way to bring a portion of Delaware contemporary history to life, a period that starts in the late '50s and advances to the present day. While some of the story comes from my personal memories, various documents, and news articles, most is based on interviews with dozens of individuals who were connected to the events that I discuss.

I would like to start by thanking Michael Fleming of Town Square Delaware, who served as both an editor and motivator. He corrected writing errors and provided guidance on what to include and what to discard—which is often difficult for a writer to judge. Michael's rich knowledge of Delaware and superb writing skills helped to make this book possible.

Early in the process I shared drafts with Verna Hensley and Ariel Gruswitz. Both excellent writers, their edits and suggestions were extremely helpful.

Don Kirtley was the first person to read the entire manuscript, and his insights and recommendations have been influential throughout. Like me, Don felt it was important to tell the Hercules' story. He was a mentor to me while I was at the company and continued in that capacity during my book project. Kevin Reilly also read the entire manuscript and offered ideas and encouragement. Both Kevin and Don urged me to work harder at painting a picture of what Wilmington looked like in the 1950s and '60s.

Cheryl Corn, Tom Ogden, Buck Simpers, Skip Pennella, Bill Moeckel, Raga Elim, Lou Romanoli, cousin Phillip Quinn and daughter-in-law Ashley Riley read early drafts and provided ideas and encouragement. My brother Curt and Fred Dingle helped me recall early golf experiences, while Bill Wheeler, Dennis LaFazia and Wilmington mayor Mike Purzycki weighed in with reflections on our University of Delaware days. My sisters, Bernadette, Rebecca and Phyllis read the early chapters and provided family insights.

Jim Burke, Larry Windley, Bob Coy, John Pastor, and David Weir were particularly helpful with details on the economic development years, while Mike Parkowski and Tony Felicia helped recall and clarify elements of the AstraZeneca negotiations. Bill Wheeler and OCS classmate Al Hecker added insights on the Army experiences I discuss. Henry Milligan and Murray Sawyer helped provide details on the Henry Milligan/PMI year with Murray weighing in further on the *News Journal* lawsuit. Bob Berman, Jim Dolan, and Kevin Reilly added to the Xerox chapter, while Mike Harkins and Mike Ratchford helped recall various political campaigns and county government experiences. Joe Purzycki assisted with confirmation of certain details on the MBNA/Dover Downs story.

The Hercules story required the most research, and it could not have been told without the help of several individuals, including Tom Strang, Michael Rettig, Linda Rudnick, Mike Hassman, Tom Ciconte, John Montgomery and Don Kirtley.

While most of the photos came from personal sources or old News Journal clippings, I would like to acknowledge Frank Shanhan and Howdy Giles for photos that appear in the chapters on the Leukemia Golf Classic, the Vietnam Memorial dedication and the Oliver Golf Club chapter. Army basic training photos are courtesy of Ft. Dix.

Working with Kevin Reilly on "Tackling Life" provided publishing experience and an introduction to Michael Fontecchio and Michael Flickinger. Fontecchio designed the cover and the book content and finalized printing and publishing. Michael Flickinger served as copyeditor, proofreader, and advisor.

Finally, I would like to thank my wife Sharon, the redheaded cheerleader who read the entire manuscript, helped to recall or confirm events from long ago and provided the moral support to bring this to the finish line.

The conclusions reached and opinions stated in this book are mine alone. Every effort was made through multiple sources to confirm exactly what happened and what was said, but memories can fade or differ over time. In some cases, individuals who were present for certain events and conversations saw things somewhat differently. Typically, if there was a strong variance in our recollections, I left out the conversation or event.

Names Index

About the Author

John Riley retired in 2016 after leading government relations for two global corporations. He has also served in various economic development roles including interim CEO of the Delaware Prosperity Partnership. He has been a contributor to Town Square Delaware and other publications since 2012 and in 2017 joined former Philadelphia Eagle Kevin Reilly as co-author of his book, *Tackling Life*. John is an Army veteran and continues to be active in veterans' affairs. As a board member and past chairman of Easterseals Delmarva, he has been a leader on disability issues for two decades. John and his wife, Sharon, live in Wilmington. They have three children and seven grandchildren.